Mister
Broadcasting

To Madame Jeanne Sauve

From An old renegade of Broadcasting

Hope you enjoy some parts
of it -

Ernie B

Mister Broadcasting

The Ernie Bushnell Story

Peter Stursberg

PETER MARTIN ASSOCIATES LIMITED

© 1971 Peter Stursberg

ALL RIGHTS RESERVED

No part of this book may be reproduced or utilized in any form or by any means, electronic or mechanical, including photocopying, electrostatic copying, recording or by any information storage and retrieval systems without permission in writing from the publisher, except for the quotation of passages by a reviewer in print or through the electronic mass media.

Library of Congress Catalog Card Number 72-174573
ISBN 0-88778-061-X

printed in Canada by Web Offset Limited

Peter Martin Associates Limited
17 Inkerman Street, Toronto 5, Ontario

Contents

Introduction

I have known Ernie Bushnell since the war, and I have a letter from him dated 10 October, 1942, assuring me that I would not be overlooked when it came to making changes in the CBC Overseas Unit; I was a news editor and roving reporter in Vancouver then and had written him saying that I wanted to become a war correspondent. As always, Bush was as good as his word: I had signed up in the Navy, and he had warned me in that letter that it might be difficult to get me out. But after a formidable struggle with wartime red tape lasting fully four weeks, he was able to spring me loose and send me on my way that winter. I missed the first boat but I caught a passenger-freighter that was loaded with high explosives; we were part of a convoy of forty ships, and it was an uneventful if rather jittery crossing for me.

Although he was the general program supervisor, the Overseas Unit came directly under him, so that it could be said that Bushnell was my boss. Even when I was under contract as the CBC's United Nations correspondent, he had the over-all responsibility. I was in the Railway Committee Room that June day during the parliamentary hearing into the "Preview Commentary" affair when he was really on trial, and I recall his cross-examination on the innocent comment he had made during a telephone conversation that "heads will roll". Later, when he quit the CBC and hung out his own shingle, I joined with him in forming the company that was awarded the "second" television licence in the Ottawa area.

So I have worked for Ernie Bushnell (he always said "with")

both within and without the CBC. That could mean that I was not far enough removed to be objective, and I plead guilty to sharing many of his views. Although we have had our falling-out with the corporation—and who could love such a soulless agency, although Bush did, calling it "my second best love (in broadcasting)"—we both felt that there had to be a Canadian Broadcasting Corporation in order to combat the cultural invasion of Canada's unguarded and unguardable air waves by the rich and powerful American networks. Yet, the corporation, as a government organization, was bound to develop a bureaucracy, and "housekeeping" (to use the term made infamous by the second Fowler Report) would become the main concern of any bureaucratic broadcasting body.

When I became the United Nations correspondent, I found that our bureau included a CBC producer who was technically over me since I was under contract and he was on staff. As might be expected, the other correspondents couldn't make out what he was supposed to do and put him down as the sort of boondoggle that might be expected with "government broadcasting". Not even the BBC had such a person at the UN headquarters, although there was a BBC representative who had his office somewhere in Gotham, well away from the Glass Tower. That was in the days before Canadian television—and I should point out that no producers had dogged our paths as war correspondents, which might have been due to the fact that the CBC was much smaller in those days and the army on active service would not put up with such camp followers. The over-staffing of the CBC was to become a scandal, and, of course, the main job of the producer at the UN bureau was "housekeeping".

Then, there was the inherent timidity of a bureaucracy, and the corporation was especially scared of reporters—so much so that it pretended not to have any, which was a reason why I was under contract, so that the CBC could disclaim responsibility for what I said on the air. (In the fifties, the only CBC reporters were foreign correspondents; the management eschewed Ottawa like the plague.) I argued that this attitude was fraudulent, that no one, aside possibly from the corporation's brass, believed that I was anyone else but the CBC correspondent. In writing this book, I came across an item in the minutes of a 1952 administrative control conference:

CBC Correspondents—Identification with the CBC
It was *agreed* that not only should correspondents such as Halton and Stursberg identify themselves on their broadcasts as being "of the CBC", but staff members such as Herbert and Beattie should also identify themselves in a similar manner on programmes such as News Roundup, Actualities, etc.

It is a wonder that Ernie Bushnell could have lasted as long as he did in the sort of stultifying bureaucracy that developed in the CBC during the postwar years, and yet it was a pity that he had to leave. Someone like himself who had trod the boards of the chautauqua circuit and had grown up in the hard school of commercial radio was needed to counter the organization men who were taking over most of the top positions. Ernie was essentially an entertainer, and he was the last of the programmers to have any position of power in the CBC. He was no intellectual, as he himself would admit, but he was no anti-intellectual, as one of his longer-haired colleagues was to assert. He sang on the first commercial radio stations in the early twenties, and inaugurated the first television stations in the early fifties. His career covered a half-century of broadcasting, and his story is really the history of broadcasting, both in the private and public sectors that make up the peculiar Canadian system.

Hence, the title of the book, "Mr. Broadcasting", which Bush did not like and considered pretentious.

1 The Homestead and Omemee

An unseasonably early blizzard had swept the rolling country-side above Lake Ontario, covering the dirt concession roads with a white blanket and leaving such drifts that Dr. Brerton couldn't get through to the homestead in his cutter. The date was November 19, 1900. The twentieth century had just begun but in Bethany, Ontario, it might just as well have been the nineteenth. Though the automobile had been invented, none had been seen this far from Toronto and, if the natives of rural Ontario gave it any thought, they would have said that it would never replace the horse. As for broadcasting, the word was unknown except in the biblical sense of scattering seed.

Ernest Leslie Bushnell was the name given to the child born that day; two months premature, his survival was due to the pioneer resourcefulness of an aunt and the wood-burning kitchen stove that became his incubator.

Both his maternal and paternal grandparents had immigrated to Canada from Ireland during the potato famine of the eighteen-seventies. His father's family took up a homestead in the eleventh concession of the township of Manvers in the county of Durham—not the best farming land, being stony and sandy, but they were pleased because they had been told it was good ground to grow potatoes.

They set to with a will at the back-breaking task of clearing the stones and boulders from the land; they subdivided the 150-acre homestead into fields of ten to twenty acres in size, and the rough stone walls which they piled by hand or with the help of a horse can be seen to this day. They used the stones to build their house. And they did grow Irish Cobbler potatoes.

The identity of the Bushnell forebears is lost in the mists of the Irish bogs: it is assumed that they came from Ulster as they were all God-fearing Methodists; even their name, or the spelling of their name, was uncertain. Ernie remembers his father being addressed by friends and relatives as "James Bushell".

James married a childhood sweetheart, Adeline Stinson, whose family had a neighboring farm. The Stinsons were also devout Methodists, and one of Adeline's brothers, Leslie, felt he had to escape from the rather repressive religious atmosphere of their home by sailing to Australia. He was never heard from again and was regarded as the black sheep of the family, but he must have been a favorite with Adeline because she named her only son after him—Ernest Leslie Bushnell.

After his birth, his mother's health failed; such was the agricultural economy of those days that James could not carry on without the labour of his wife. In 1902 he sold the homestead for $7,000 to Charlie Armstrong, a flaming Pentecostal (one of Ernie's earliest memories was of the violent religious arguments which developed when Charlie came to make the mortgage payments to his father), and the Bushnells moved to Peterborough, then a marketing town on the Trent Canal with a population of some 20,000.

James joined a local businessman, Andrew Brown, in a real estate firm, and prospered. With the money from the homestead he bought twenty acres of land south of the Bushnell home on Charlotte Street, and by 1906, when industry began moving into Peterborough, he sold the property at a handsome profit.

"My father," Ernie recalls, "was a great man for wheeling and dealing, and later became known as a superb horse trader, always insisting on 'something to boot' which, of course, meant a few dollars in cash as well as the exchange of land or horses or whatever commodity was being traded."

A countryman at heart, James Bushnell longed to get back to the land; with the money he had made in the real estate deal he could afford to buy a farm with much better soil than the stony acres of the original homestead. His professed reason for leaving the comfortable house on Charlotte Street was that the city was "no place to bring up a boy", a good enough excuse since it was still commonly held that a city, any and every city, was a wicked place, a veritable Sodom or Gomorrah.

Even though Ernie had spent only his early childhood in Peterborough, the city left its mark. Ernie remembers seeing his first movie in a tent in Jackson's Park, but more important he recalls a friendship that taught him as a small boy about the bigotry and racial antagonism that divided Canada. The Brioux, a French Canadian family, lived next door on Charlotte Street, and it seemed natural to speak French when playing with them. Ernie also had a collie named "Carlo" which his father had given him as a pup. He spoke to the dog in both English and French, but mostly in French because that was "kids' language", and the dog would respond to either. One day, some three months after the Bushnells had left Peterborough to settle in Omemee, the dog was found dead beside the railroad track; Carlo had been killed by local farmers who were furious at "Jim Bushnell's boy" speaking French and had taken it out on the dog because he seemed to understand what they could not.

Omemee lies on the edge of the Kawartha Lakes, the magnificent hunting ground of the Mississauga Indians, and Omemee, which means "pigeon" in Algonquin, was the totemic name of the Mississauga clan which had a campsite where the present village is situated. The Pigeon River and Pigeon Lake, into which the river flows, were both named after the same clan.

Except for its name, there is nothing remarkable about Omemee, nothing to distinguish it from any other small Ontario town. It is situated on Highway 7 between Peterborough and Lindsay, seventy miles from Toronto. Just east of the village, on a hilltop overlooking the rolling countryside, is the Emily (for Emily Township) Cemetery, where James and Adeline Bushnell are buried.

There are really only two streets in Omemee, the main street which is Highway 7 and called King Street, and Sturgeon Street which crosses it and is a secondary road to the north. It is the Pigeon River that makes Omemee more than just a crossroad like Fowlers Corners further back on the highway, but much of the community lies beyond the waters that provided the power for the early grist mill and sawmill. The combined high school and public school was on the banks of the millpond, and Ernie remembers looking through the school window and often seeing a fisherman land a twenty-five- to thirty-pound muskie.

According to the road sign, the present population of Omemee is 850. When James Bushnell bought his farm, half of which was in Omemee and half in the township of Emily, the population was 600; it hasn't grown much in sixty years.

Ernie did all the things that a boy usually did on a farm; he hoed the potatoes and the turnips and the corn; he stooked the hay and went berry picking and tended the livestock. However, he was not enthusiastic about farming and his father became reconciled to the idea that Ernie would never spend his life at it.

So the farm was sold, and the Bushnells moved into a three-storey red brick house with a white glassed-in porch on Sturgeon Street in Omemee. It is still standing, next to the grey brick Presbyterian Church near the main intersection of the town, and a lofty television aerial is a suitable marker for the house where the boy who was to become known as "Mr. Broadcasting" lived.

Despite the move, James Bushnell maintained his love of the life of a countryman by buying two ranches just three miles from Omemee; even in town, life was still fairly bucolic. Ernie remembers one of the characters of Omemee, Ira Toole, as a kindly man who could be persuaded to teach any youngster to bait a fish hook, snare a rabbit or skin a muskrat, whose hide Ira would then buy for fifty cents. However, Ira Toole's main source of income came from catching bullfrogs, the legs of which were packed in small wooden boxes and shipped to restaurants and hotels in New York City. It was said that during the few "bullfrogging" weeks he made between $250 and $300 which was enough to meet his simple needs and assuage his considerable thirst for a year. Ernie and the other kids long believed that Ira Toole had some sort of spooky appeal for the bullfrogs; that was why, they supposed, the frogs sat on their lily pads and stumps night after night, crying out in gutteral tones "Ira Toole, Ira Toole, Ira Toole", as if they were calling him to come and get them.

In winter, after the first hard frost, there was skating on Pigeon Pond. Ernie recalls the fun they had: "We built a fire at the edge of the pond, and sat on a log in front of it to put on our skates. On a moonlit night, we'd form a long line of boys and girls and play 'snap the whip'."

Another colourful character was Edward "Teddy" English, the boozing barber of Omemee. He must have been a sore trial for his father, who was an elder of the Methodist Church and a staunch teetotaller. One night Teddy sneaked into the back pew during a service. The barber was quite obviously somewhat the worse for drink but, since he didn't disturb anyone, he was allowed to stay. "Suddenly, he rose from his seat and launched himself down the aisle toward the altar, crying out: 'I repent, I repent. God shave me. God shave me'." He was duly saved, "but the next day he had no recollection of what had happened the night before" and, so far as Ernie knew, "never darkened the sacred portal of the Methodist Church or any other church again."

Ernie's sister Lulu (later Lulu McCaffrey) became a school teacher, and taught at the one-room schoolhouse three miles east of Omemee. Her salary was three hundred dollars a year, out of which she paid two dollars a week for room and board, as well as providing fifty cents a week for piano lessons for her brother. Thus, reluctantly, Ernie took the first step towards a career in entertainment and broadcasting. Later, he was asked to join the choir of the Methodist Church and invited to sing at "fowl suppers" throughout the area.

Both his parents were devout Methodists and deeply religious. Until he left for university in Toronto at nearly eighteen years of age, he had to attend church three times on Sunday and three times during the week; with another two hours of choir practice on Friday night, he spent some ten to fourteen hours of his spare time in the gloomy interior of the Methodist Church.

In retrospect, Ernie felt that "one could get too much of a good thing. I know as a child I did, and I'm afraid that it produced a negative rather than a positive effect on me. It's possible, though, that some of the fundamentals drummed into me at the time may have been instrumental in what is called 'character building'."

He was fourteen years old when he joined the choir as a boy soprano, but within a year or two his voice changed and, unknowingly, he took the second big step toward an entertainment and broadcasting career.

The organist of the Methodist Church (now Trinity United Church) was Mrs. R. J. Mulligan, the elder sister of Mrs. J. C. Eaton. It was the regular habit of Sir John and Lady Eaton to visit her parents, Mr. and Mrs. John McCrea, whose home on King Street near the intersection with Sturgeon Street, is one of the sights of the village. On one of the Eatons' visits to Omemee, Mrs. Mulligan asked young Ernest Bushnell to sing a solo at the coming Sunday service which Sir John and Lady Eaton would be attending. That was in the spring of 1918.

A short time later Mr. Mulligan died and, during the summer holiday period, Ernie volunteered to help Mrs. Mulligan in her husband's drug store, cleaning up, doing odd jobs and selling sundries and patent medicines. High school days were over for him that spring, and it was generally understood that Ernie would be taking up law. He was to article for a law firm in Lindsay of which his mother's first cousin, T. H. Stinson, was a partner; Mr. Stinson was prominent politically and was the member of Parliament for Victoria-Haliburton from 1925 to 1935. The plan was for Ernie to go to Victoria College at the University of Toronto that fall to take an arts course which would lead to further studies at Osgoode Hall.

Shortly after his arrival in Toronto, Ernie received a telephone call from Lady Eaton; she thanked him for helping her sister and went on to say that, in her opinion, he had a definite future as a tenor soloist. She offered to help him in such a career if he were so inclined. At first he wondered if he should accept—after all, his plans were to become a lawyer—but then, after a moment's consideration, he decided to take advantage of the offer. Lady Eaton told him to report to Arthur Blight, a teacher at the Royal Conservatory of Music who had taught her at one time, for lessons three times a week at her expense. The lessons continued for almost four years.

A half century later, Ernie said of Lady Eaton's generosity, "It is to Lady Eaton who, I know, has assisted many other artists in a like manner, that I owe a debt of gratitude. It was she who changed the direction of my life, and any small success I have had in the intervening fifty years can be attributed to her generosity."

2 *The Adanacs and KDKA*

Shortly after the war ended, Lady Eaton invited Edward Johnston, then a celebrated Metropolitan Opera star, to give a charity recital at Massey Hall in aid of wounded veterans. While in Toronto, Mr. Johnston held auditions for some of the more advanced pupils of Arthur Blight's class, among them Ernie Bushnell. It turned out that Mr. Blight was going to study under one of the greatest singing teachers in the world, Lombardi of Italy, and four students selected by Mr. Johnston would accompany him abroad, all expenses to be paid by Lady Eaton. Ernie was one of the four selected. This was a great opportunity, but he turned the offer down.

Why, he didn't know. If he had accepted, he might have ended up as a great tenor soloist, but more likely as a teacher of singing in some small conservatory of music somewhere.

Ernie Bushnell is a fatalist, and he feels that this decision, which reversed the one he had taken only a short time before, must have been the result of an external guiding force. This approach to life is probably responsible for his ability to accept the ups and downs of broadcasting with such equanimity. He was fortune's favoured son—destiny was leading him. So, he was able to sit out the "Mr. Sage" turmoil, fully expecting to be fired from public broadcasting but convinced that if this happened, it would be for the best, only to find himself promoted to program supervisor of the new Canadian Broadcasting Corporation. He went down in the "Preview Commentary" uproar, but within a year was up again with his own company, Bushnell Television, which was to become the biggest

8

private broadcasting company in Canada.

It may well have been the nineteenth of the month that he decided not to go to Europe, but Ernie doesn't remember, because the number nineteen has kept coming up in his life, and this was a turning point—many of his friends figured that he was out of his mind to give up such an opportunity. His fixation about nineteen is part of his fatalist philosophy.

"You know, you label yourself as a bit of a 'kook' when you admit this," he says, "but the fact is that the number nineteen has kept recurring. I was born on November 19, 1900. I was married on August 19, 1926. My father died on February 19, 1934. My oldest grandchild was born on July 19. It was announced that we had been awarded the licence for CJOH on August 19, 1960. The figures of my private office telephone number add up to nineteen; the figures of my automobile licence for last year and this year add up to nineteen—and they're just by chance, I didn't do anything to bring this about."

Meanwhile, he continued his studies at the University of Toronto, and resumed his singing lessons after Arthur Blight returned from Italy. At the age of eighteen, he was hired as tenor soloist at the Elm Street United Church and paid $250 a year, so he was never short of pocket money.

At Victoria College he was chosen head boy in his freshman year. He also played hockey for the college; he was the goalkeeper, not because he had any special aptitude for this position but because he had inherited a full set of goalie equipment from one of Lady Eaton's nephews. One of his teammates at Victoria College was a dashing young veteran who had returned from overseas to complete his studies, Lester B. "Mike" Pearson. Ernie used to say of the former prime minister that he was a good left winger, to which Mike's reply was that he played defence and had been doing the same thing ever since.

In 1921 Ernest Bushnell was asked to join the new Adanac male quartet; its founder, Ruthven Macdonald, one of Canada's great bass singers, had formed the group during the war to carry out such patriotic duties as promoting the sale of Victory Bonds, but he had found it difficult to keep the group together in the immediate postwar years as its members were busy earning a living. Macdonald decided to reorganize the quartet on a full-time professional basis, so that its members could devote all their time and talents to practice and performance. One of the members of the original Adanacs was Arthur Blight, and Ernie assumes that it was because he was one of Mr. Blight's pupils and also because he could play the piano that he was chosen. He became accompanist and second tenor; Riley Hallman, who had a lyric tenor voice much like that of the great John McCormack, was the first tenor; Joseph O'Meara was baritone, and Mr. Macdonald bass.

That spring, the Adanacs got their first contract to perform on a midwestern chautauqua circuit for a period of six weeks. After this engagement, the quartet took on odd jobs and was performing at an independent chautauqua in Texas when it received an offer from the Redpath Chautauqua and Lyceum Bureau of Chicago for a forty-week contract beginning in March 1922. It was like an up-and-coming actor in a provincial repertory company getting a bid from Hollywood, and Ernie said: "We felt that we were on our way to fame and fortune." Although not yet twenty-one, he was earning one hundred dollars a week—a fortune in those days.

Chautauqua Lake in northern New York state is a beautiful summer resort, a long shimmering stretch of water surrounded by verdant countryside, a place of cool respite from the hot and dusty days; great trees shade the quiet town with its white clapboard houses, red brick hotels, woodsy outdoor theatres and meeting places. This was an earlier, more serious if less sophisticated America, non-conformist, non-drinking; and it was here in 1874 that the first experiment in using the summer vacation for adult education was held. The Chautauqua Assembly, which became the Chautauqua Institution, provided an eight-week program of lectures, music, opera and plays, all of "high uplift"; the success of this venture led to the name being borrowed by a multitude of circuits or travelling "chautauquas". The greatest of these was organized by a Scottish immigrant, James Redpath, who was a brilliant journalist, a superb war correspondent during the American Civil War and an ardent abolitionist and reformer. He began by booking lecturers (and then added musicians, magicians and other entertainers) through the Boston Lyceum Bureau which was soon renamed the Redpath Chautauqua and Lyceum Bureau.

It was radio that killed chautauqua, by "slow strangulation stretched over the twenties, and the arrival of the talking pictures finished the job", as the *Saturday Review* was to say in a nostalgic article forty years after. But in the early twenties it was still at its zenith.

The entertainment took place in tents, some of which were as big as circus tents, holding two thousand or more people. The leap-frogging of three tents was necessary to maintain a touring company and, as there was always one in reserve, there were four tents to each circuit—for example, while the Adanacs were performing in city B, the tent in city A was being torn down and moved to city D, while another tent was being erected in city C. A crew of six to eight was assigned to each tent, including not only the student roustabouts but the publicity agents and the "chautauqua girl", whose job was to get the young people enthusiastic about the approaching show and spreading the word that "chautauqua is coming to town".

On the Redpath circuit, there were three performances a day: a children's show in the morning, a lecture preceded by a short program of entertainment in the afternoon, and the same at night, or a full program of entertainment in the afternoon and a lecture at night—the arrangement depended largely on the calibre of the lecturer. Chautauqua could boast such stars as William Jennings Bryan, Mark Twain and Horace Greeley. For one season, the lecturer with the Adanacs was a Polynesian medical missionary from Samoa, Dr. Wherahiko Rawei, who was over seventy years old and had been a close friend of Robert Louis Stevenson; Ernie was to write years later that "to listen to dear old Dr. Rawei tell of his work as a doctor and healer of souls was an entrancing experience".

Actually, the first lecturer with the Adanacs was something of a charlatan: Stephen Haubusch claimed to have begun life as a shepherd boy in Palestine and wore the flowing robes of a Bedouin when he lectured—the Adanacs were sure that he had been no closer to the Holy Land than his home in Brooklyn and that he had cribbed history books for the experiences that he so eloquently recited. That wasn't to say that they didn't like Stephen Haubusch, whom they found to be a charming and amusing companion.

The Redpath company guaranteed a minimum of forty weeks a year on tour, and usually it worked out at more than that. The chautauqua tent circuit started in late March in Florida and moved through the South to the midwestern states, up to the Canadian prairies, and ended, for the Adanacs, in Ontario about the middle of August. Shortly after Labour Day the quartet began rehearsals for the fall and winter season, and they had to go to Chicago for auditions as the Redpath Bureau insisted on vetting their repertoire. The Lyceum circuit was divided in two, with the fall tour from mid-October to mid-December, and the winter tour covering most of January and February. The cycle repeated itself with a period of rehearsal before the chautauqua circuit began in late March.

On the Lyceum circuit there were no tents and the Adanacs performed indoors, in concert halls and in high school auditoriums; they travelled by train whereas on the chautauqua circuit their means of transportation was a car—all five of them (the lecturer went along with them) and their ten pieces of luggage were stuffed into one Buick touring car. They had remarkably few accidents considering the amount of driving they did.

In the more than five years that Ernie Bushnell was with the Adanacs, he visited every Canadian province except Prince Edward Island and British Columbia, and every state in the union but four. There was the thrill of having a little old lady, after one of their first performances on the prairies, put her arm around him and say, "Boy, you sure done good." It was the sort of encouragement that Ernie needed.

He remembered the frontier hotels in the West, many of them without indoor plumbing, and the inevitable Chinese restaurant in every Canadian cowtown. The Americans with them on the chautauqua circuit were afraid to eat in Chinese restaurants; they weren't used to them in the American midwest and apparently believed all the stories about sinister Orientals.

12

Ernie had happy memories of the Adanacs, and there were very few quarrels considering how closely they lived for such a long time. However, there was one row that he did remember and it was over a game of chess. Riley Hallman had bought a chess set to while away the time on the train, but neither Riley nor Ernie knew anything about the game. The first time they took it out, they fell to squabbling about the rules. When Ruthven Macdonald, who was the manager of the quartet, heard them arguing, he picked up the chess set and threw it out the train window. And that put a stop to that.

But the constant travelling began to pall, especially since Ernie wanted to get married. He had met Edna Alberta Wood in the winter of 1920, before he had joined the Adanacs; they had both sung in the choir of Trinity United Church on Bloor Street West in Toronto, but it was not till 1924 that they became engaged. His engagement was one of the reasons for his leaving the Adanacs, reinforced by the realization that, though the group was rated as the second-best quartet in North America, its style was a bit old-fashioned. This was made clear to him one day in 1925 when they visited a music store in Atlanta to listen to a recording of a new male quartet, the Revellers, who were becoming the rage.

"The piece they sang on one side of that recording, I recall very clearly, was 'Blue Room', specially arranged. We looked at one another," Ernie said. "We had been singing from what were called stock arrangements. But the style of quartet singing had changed, and we knew our day had passed."

It was an experience that same year at KDKA in Pittsburgh that made him decide to go into the newly burgeoning broadcasting business. The Adanacs were booked to sing on the Westinghouse radio station and, as was their practice, they demanded their cheque before going on the air. They were told that they would not be receiving a fee. The program was between 6:30 and seven o'clock on Sunday evenings. KDKA (the first broadcasting service on the continent) was powerful enough to be heard clearly in Canada; the Adanacs had wired all their friends and relatives to listen to their broadcast and felt that they were obliged to fulfill this engagement even if they were not being paid.

Afterwards, Ernie asked the manager why they had not been paid, and was told that they were on a "sustaining program". This was the first time he had ever heard that term used. And what was a sustaining program? The manager's reply was: "It's not a commercial program. On a commercial program, the sponsors pay and you get paid. But if a station puts on a program, that's a sustaining program, and you don't get paid—it's as simple as that."

The experience made a deep impression on Ernest Bushnell, and it was not long after, in the autumn of 1925 in a little town in Nevada, that Ernie made up his mind to leave the quartet and get into the radio advertising business back in Canada. He and Edna intended to get married the following year. Settling down, it turned out, was easier to decide than to do: he had to get a replacement for himself in the Adanacs, and it took a full year before he found a very good tenor, Lawrence DeFoe, who had also been a pupil of Arthur Blight's. He did not leave the quartet till December 1926, some four months after his marriage.

3 The First Singing Commercial

On November 2, 1920, KDKA began regular broadcasting with the results of that year's presidential election, won by the Harding-Cox Republican ticket. It was followed a month later by the Canadian Marconi Company's station in Montreal, XWA, which became CFCF and still broadcasts under those call letters. Progress was faltering and slow, and when Ernie Bushnell decided that the new medium might prove to be a lucrative career for a young fellow, there were no radio advertising agencies as such in existence . . . in spite of the fact that there was nothing but commercial radio!

Conditions were chaotic with "phantom" stations which didn't have any equipment of their own broadcasting through the facilities of others. Some of these were licensed to religious sects, and one used the airways to carry on a holy war against opposing sects. Broadcasting was comparatively free of any rules or regulations, although no station was allowed to refer to the price of an advertised item.

Under the circumstances, it is small wonder that Ernie's Broadcasting Services was an instant success, and Ernie made more money than he ever had before. From the day he decided to give up the chautauqua circuit and leave the Adanacs, he made good use of his time. He persuaded a friend, Charles Shearer, who had also been a pupil of Arthur Blight's, to join him in this uncertain undertaking, recounting time and again his experiences at KDKA. His friend was impressed and was fed up with school teaching, so he sought leave of absence from the Toronto Board of Education to enter into the partnership to be

15

called Broadcasting Services. They rented a room in a bailiff's office in the Federal Building on Adelaide Street.

While Ernie was still singing for his living, Charles Shearer went to work. He made arrangements with CJYC, a 500-watt station owned and operated by Universal Radio of Canada, to sell programs for the time slots not already occupied by the Word of God, as understood by the International Bible Students. (Universal Radio was a cover organization for the Bible students, the sect that was to arouse a storm of controversy in Ottawa and throughout the country for using the air waves to attack other religious groups.) Broadcasting Services, as its name implied, would do everything for the would-be sponsor—it would write the advertising message, pay for the station time, announce the program (Shearer was a good announcer), direct and produce it and, in fact, do the work of what became known as the radio representative or time broker.

On leaving the Adanacs in December 1926, Ernie threw himself into the new endeavour and came up with four sponsors, all under contract for thirteen weeks: Maple Leaf Milling Company, Toronto Wet Wash Laundry, Underwood Typewriter Company and Leyland Trucks. For the Maple Leaf Milling Company, the new agency engaged a sixteen-piece orchestra conducted by Reginald Stewart, an up-and-coming young maestro who was to become conductor of some of the best symphony orchestras in North America. Broadcasting Services brought in vocalists and instrumental soloists from the United States, especially those who had started in Canada, and one of its star performers was Ernest Seitz, then a great concert pianist.

Mr. Seitz will be remembered as the man who wrote the popular song, "The Whole World Is Waiting for the Sunrise", which he composed for a minstrel show produced by the employees of Underwood Typewriter Company. His appearance on the Maple Leaf Milling program brought forth so much favourable comment that his Father, J. J. Seitz, who was then president of Underwood, was easily persuaded to have his son appear in another twelve-week series with the Underwood string trio: violinist, Geoffrey Waddington; cellist, John Adaskin;

pianist, Miss Mildred "Billy" Baker, who shortly after became Mrs. Waddington.

It was for the Toronto Wet Wash Laundry that Ernie Bushnell invented the singing commercial. No one has ever challenged this claim, made repeatedly in a variety of articles and commentaries about the development of broadcasting in Canada. Ernie explains it this way: he and his partner, Charles Shearer, had sung together in the Aeolian male quartet before he joined the Adanacs. Since the laundry wanted a lighter type of music-hall program, they decided to revive the Aeolian and in that way to get paid for singing, as well as producing and directing the show. Like his father, Ernie knew the value of money.

Something akin to Freudian forgetfulness has destroyed his memory of the lyrics of that first singing commercial, as well as the reason why they put the sponsor's message to music except that it seemed like a "good idea". At any rate, Ernie wrote a ditty about the benefits of the Toronto Wet Wash Laundry which was sung to the tune of "Three Blind Mice". "God forgive us for our sins," he was to say, for it wasn't long after that that the singing commercial became the vogue.

Sponsors were ready to accept the singing commercial, but not the spoofing commercial which made fun of the sponsor's product: that was another innovation of Broadcasting Services, a brilliant idea which almost brought about disaster. Ernie decided to hire a relatively unknown English comedian, Fred Emney, to do the commercials for the Maple Leaf Milling program. The comedian had recently immigrated to Canada and had opened a studio at the corner of Bay and College streets where he hoped to teach piano playing and the art of mimicry. Broadcasting Services signed a thirteen-week contract with Mr. Emney who was to be paid fifty dollars a show; he was to write and perform the commercials. The idea had the approval of the advertising manager of the Maple Leaf Milling Company, J. W. "Johnny" Moore, but not that of the general manager, A.R. Macdonald.

Everything was done to make the first Maple Leaf Milling show an artistic triumph. Madame Jeanne Dusseau, one of

Canada's outstanding sopranos, was brought up from New York City at great expense; Reginald Stewart and his orchestra had prepared a program of classical but lively works; full page advertisements had been taken in all the Toronto newspapers and the radio columnists showered words of praise on all who were to be involved. At nine o'clock on a night early in 1927, the show began, and by ten, when it was all over, there were congratulations all around—the participants felt that "a new day had dawned for commercial radio in Canada".

In the midst of the celebrations, a telephone rang and Ernie answered it, expecting praise but getting instead an earful of invective. The general manager of Maple Leaf Milling Company, Mr. Macdonald, was at the end of the line and he was furious. Who the blankety-blank was responsible for that blankety-blank idiot, Fred Emney, who had the blankety-blank nerve to make fun of Red Rose flour and the company's other fine baking products? Contract or no blankety-blank contract, that was the last Maple Leaf program that would ever be broadcast. Poor Ernie was speechless and almost in tears. But, but, but, he stammered. To hell with the buts, the general manager said, that was that, and they could sue the company or go jump in the lake. . . .

All that Fred Emney had done was to mix a bag of flour in a pail of cold water, stir it (with sound effects by Ernie Bushnell) and, in a most delightful English accent accompanied by a thumping crescendo of chords and scales on the piano, put the whole mess in the oven where in a second or two it was baked brown into a majestic, wholesome, tasty loaf of the finest bread anyone had ever seen. Obviously, it was satire and it had most people chuckling. But not the humourless Mr. Macdonald.

Gloom settled on the departing company. However, a telephone call to Ernie's home shortly after midnight relieved him of a sleepless night. It was from Johnny Moore, the advertising manager of the Maple Leaf Milling Company, who said not to worry; he had felt the lash of the general manager's tongue, but he had told him that he personally had approved the advertising copy to be used by Fred Emney and thought that it was hilarious. The contract would be honoured in full; he assured Bush (as Ernie Bushnell was known to his friends) of that but he had had to give in to one condition—no more Fred Emney.

Broadcasting Services Limited was stuck with an agreement, which had been duly signed and attested, for a further twelve performances by the comedian, a matter of six hundred dollars. The next day, Ernest Bushnell and Charles Shearer called on Mr. Emney. They told him the whole sad story and offered to pay him in full. He walked over to his desk, reached in a drawer, took out the contract, lit a match to it and with the flame lit his pipe. His only comment was: "Well, old chappies, I guess that's that."

Shortly after this disappointment, Fred Emney, who had been only a few months in Canada, returned to his native land to become one of England's most renowned comedians. At the beginning of the Second World War, Bushnell visited London and saw Emney perform; he went backstage, and the two of them had a hearty laugh about the one and only appearance Emney had made before a microphone during his stay "in the colonies".

Thirteen weeks passed quickly. No one was supposed to be listening in the summer, and advertising budgets for radio were practically nonexistent. By May 1, Broadcasting Services had no clients, although the prospects seemed good for the following season. The partnership had received a letter from Mr. Moore at the end of February, saying how "highly pleased" Maple Leaf Milling Company was with the results of the broadcasts.

For three months, Bushnell and Shearer had made a lot of money, about five hundred dollars a week, but, try as they might, they could not drum up any summer business, even though they slashed their rates. The two young men were footsore and frustrated, but they had been pioneers in the burgeoning business of broadcasting; they had made a success of a new venture, and, they were the talk of the town.

Early in June 1927, Edward Rogers, the inventor of the Rogers batteryless radio, asked them to come to his home on Russell Hill Road. No reason for the invitation was given, although they guessed that it had something to do with the fact that Mr. Rogers had opened a new radio station in February of that year, CFRB, with a 500-watt transmitter at Aurora and studios in Tommy Ryan's art gallery on Jarvis Street. It wasn't long after they had been ushered into the library of Rogers' palatial residence that Harry Moore, the secretary-treasurer of the Rogers Company, offered them jobs as joint general managers of the new station. The terms were fifty dollars a week in salary between the two of them, and fifteen per cent commission on all sales of time. They accepted, fully realizing that they were the ninth general managers to be hired in a matter of four months (all their predecessors having been fired or resigned), and started work immediately.

One reason they took the job was that they had just been "stabbed in the back" by the International Bible Students, who had approached all their former clients and offered to supply the facilities of CJYC free of charge if they would continue their programs in the fall; the Bible students were desperately anxious to have these shows because they felt that such quality programming would offset the rising storm of protest over the way they were using their radio licence to promote their own sect and to attack other churches. Only one of the clients, the Maple Leaf Milling Company, accepted their offer; the other three did not resume broadcasting.

When Bushnell and Shearer took over as joint managers of CFRB, the station had no commercial revenue. By the time they left, they had rounded up some three hundred dollars a week of advertising, which meant that each of them was earning nearly fifty dollars a week. Charles was the announcer, and Ernie acted as producer-technician, lugging batteries, microphones and other essential equipment to remote pick-ups at the Prince George Hotel, the Tivoli Theatre and various churches. There were fringe benefits to be had: every time they put on Gilbert Watson and his trio from the dining room of the Prince George Hotel, they were treated to dinner; when they were asked to broadcast Gilbert Watson and his dance band on Saturday nights, they could bring their wives and two guests each to the dinner dance and have a fine time, with a bottle of gin hidden under the table. One of their most popular programs was Clifford McCormick playing the giant Wurlitzer organ at the Tivoli Theatre from eleven till midnight, and when he let go with "All Alone at the Telephone", the studio telephones would ring and there would be invitations from lonely women to "come over and have a nightcap". They had a budget of fifty dollars a week for live sustaining shows, forty-five of which was spent on George Wade and his Corn Huskers, an old-time band that became nationally famous a few years later.

They had lasted longer than all the previous general managers put together, but they still hadn't sold enough time and, in March of 1928, Mr. Moore told them that their services were no longer required. Charles Shearer was later rehired as an announcer and once again became manager of CFRB . . . but Ernest Bushnell was out of a job.

His only steady income was the weekly ten dollars that he received as the tenor soloist at Trinity United Church. And there he was, married to Edna for two years. Fortunately they had no house and mortgage to worry about; in fact, they were living at his mother-in-law's. In June, a friend found him work in the construction business; his job was to count the number of strokes that a pile driver took to sink a thirty-foot wooden pile into the silt of Hamilton Bay and, if it went down too easily, to tell the operator to sink another pile right beside it.

Then he had an accident and had to give the job up. He was driving home one night with a friend in his tin lizzie when they were hit by a heavily loaded Dodge panel delivery truck. Ernie went through the roof and landed up against the corner of a brick house thirty feet away—or so he was told when he woke up in the hospital forty-eight hours later. There were no broken bones but he did have a slight concussion: "A good concommitant," Ernie was to say, "for continuing my career in broadcasting." But that opportunity didn't come for several months, and he did what so many unemployed did: he tried selling insurance, without much success.

In December 1928 he received a telephone call from the manager of CKNC, the Canadian National Carbon Company (manufacturer of the Eveready battery) station, who asked him to audition for an announcer's job. Although he had sworn to give up broadcasting after his experience with CFRB, he agreed to go to Toronto to try out. On his way in he had grave misgivings—he knew he was not a very good announcer. But he tried out and was accepted, largely because—or so he assumed—the manager of the station, Hartley Currie, had been his scout master in Omemee.

He started in January 1929 with a salary of $125 a month, and he was to do three fifteen-minute vocal recitals a week for which he was to be paid fifteen dollars each—a total of more than three hundred dollars a month. However, shortly after Bushnell joined CKNC, he had a severe attack of laryngitis and could neither sing nor speak for the next two weeks. As a result, he lost his singing engagements, and had to make do on $125 a month.

Geoffrey Waddington was the musical director of CKNC, and he and Ernie became fast friends. Six months after Ernie started to work for the station, his scout-master friend left, and Ernie might have taken his place as manager except, he was told, for his "red-headed temper". Instead, Waddington and he were made joint managers. As Waddington had no interest in administration and Bushnell had made an attempt to restrain his temper, he was eventually appointed sole manager of the station at a salary of three thousand dollars a year. That, by his reckoning, was before the end of 1929.

The next four years were among the happiest of his life. The station had the cream of the sponsored programs: the Neilson Hour, the Buckingham Hour, the Wrigley Hour, Shirriff's Breakfast Hour and the Coo-coo-noodle Club; under his management, CKNC grew in stature and prospered. He had a feeling of achievement and satisfaction, and he was grateful to the "kindly guidance" of his bosses, the men who ran the carbon company. He stayed with CKNC until the Union Carbide Company of the United States ordered its Canadian subsidiary to stop broadcasting and surrender its radio licence.

4 The Making of Roy Thomson

One summer afternoon in 1930, Ernest Bushnell sat sweltering in the hot box that was his office in the sprawl of the Canadian National Carbon Company's plant on Davenport Road, when his secretary announced that a Mr. Thomson wanted to see him about buying a radio transmitter. Ernie heaved himself out of his chair and lumbered over to the CKNC waiting room to meet two men, the larger of whom had glasses with the thickest lenses he had ever seen.

"Mr. Bushnell," the larger man said, "I'm Roy Thomson," and he introduced the other man as his brother-in-law. Both of them looked sweaty, hot and down-at-heel in their dusty, threadbare clothes. The larger man came straight to the point.

"You have a transmitter for sale," he said.

"Not that I'm aware of, Mr. Thomson," Bushnell said, eyeing the seedy pair rather suspiciously. "The only transmitter the carbon company has is on the air right now and I certainly haven't been told that it's for sale."

"Oh, no, not that one. I understand that you have a fifty watter, the original experimental transmitter installed in 1923, a small one built by the Northern Electric Company."

Bushnell had never heard of this but he went to the control room to inquire of the engineer, Jack Barnaby, whether there was an old 50-watt transmitter kicking around.

"That old thing," Barnaby said. "Yeah, I guess we still have it somewhere—maybe in the back of the shop, in the storage

23

room. But it's no good. It won't work. It hasn't any tubes and the wiring is probably shot. What would anyone want with that antique."

"Jiggered if I know," Bush replied, but there was this chap who wanted to buy it—so how much was it worth?

The engineer didn't think that it was worth anything unless it could be made to work, and he very much doubted that, although he admitted that with new tubes it just might be possible to rebuild it. Shaking his head and muttering to himself that everyone was crazy with the heat, Barnaby went to look for the old transmitter. Bushnell returned to the waiting room where he reported that a search was being made for the equipment. But what did Thomson propose to do with it, if they were able to locate it? Did he have the permission of the radio branch of the Department of Marine and Fisheries to install it, and where? Did he have a licence, or had he applied for one?

No, not exactly, Thomson said, but he had a promise from the department that if he were able to obtain a transmitter, the department would recommend that he be given a licence to operate in North Bay.

"North Bay! Good Lord, man, that's a frontier town," Bushnell exclaimed; he had the narrow outlook of a typical Torontonian and did not know that North Bay was an up-and-coming trading centre for the whole north country. It didn't take long for Roy Thomson to tell him, in that soft-selling voice of his. Thomson's eyes glittered behind his monstrous spectacles as he predicted a fantastic future up there and said that he intended "to get in on the ground floor".

Jack Barnaby came to the waiting room and announced that he had found the "box", as he called it; it was dirty and not in a very good state of repair. Again Bushnell warned that the transmitter did not have any tubes, but Thomson was anxious to clinch the deal and asked for the price. As the son of an astute horse trader, Bushnell stalled, but in the end he was forced to name a figure; he suggested, rather timidly, five hundred dollars as a good round sum. This was more than Thomson wanted to pay, but he was in no position to bargain as he admitted that he had no cash, that he had gone through bankruptcy in Ottawa and was broke.

"All I can do is to give you a three-month promissory note."

What gall, Bushnell thought, trying to buy something without a red cent to his name—to hell with him. He was ready to call off the deal but agreed to talk to his superiors about it. With some trepidation he told his boss, Ewart Greig, about the whole weird proposition, and was relieved to see him lean back in his executive chair and hoot with laughter.

"Ernie," Greig said, "that's one of the craziest stories I've ever heard. Come in to A. Mac's office and tell it to him."

A. Mac was the nickname for Alexander Mackenzie, the general manager of the Canadian National Carbon Company. His reaction was that of a hard-bitten Scottish businessman: the 50-watt transmitter was not worth a thing to the company, and the promissory note might not be worth any more, but it was a fair trade. Bush could go ahead, which he did. After signing the note, Roy Thomson and his brother-in-law, Fred Irvine, went to the back to pick up the "box", humped it down two steep flights of stairs, put it in the trunk of their beat-up old car and drove away.

But that was not the end of the story. A couple of days later, Bushnell received a long-distance telephone call (collect) from North Bay. Roy Thomson was on the line; he apologized for being a nuisance but he had a problem: the Northern Electric Company, to whom he owed "quite a lot of money" already, would not give him two tubes on credit. Would the carbon company order the tubes for him and add the cost, which was $160, to his promissory note?

Ernie almost exploded and so did A. Mac. Of all the screwball deals—but the general manager's business instincts got the better of him and he argued that if they didn't get the tubes for Thomson, the transmitter wouldn't work and they wouldn't get paid. So Bush telephoned North Bay to say that the tubes would be ordered and shipped there the following day.

It turned out to be a good risk, and Thomson paid the promissory note for $660 on time. In the meantime, however, he had "stolen" Bush's engineer. The agreement had been that

Jack Barnaby should go to North Bay to try to make the "box" work; as A. Mac had said, if it didn't work there would be no chance of getting paid. Still, it spoke much for Roy Thomson's persuasive powers that he could inveigle Barnaby, once he'd arrived, into leaving a forty-five-dollar-a-week job with a great national organization to join a fly-by-night outfit like Thomson's in North Bay for twenty-five dollars a week. Thomson had frankly acknowledged that, at the moment, he couldn't afford to pay more, but he said: "Jack, why don't you stay with me; you stay with me and you'll do alright." And Barnaby believed him.

A year and a half later, in the midst of the great depression, Bushnell met Roy Thomson at the entrance to the Royal York Hotel in Toronto, and Thomson proudly produced his first audited statement; it showed that the North Bay station's gross income, which was derived entirely from the broken-down "box", was well over eighty thousand dollars.

Bushnell was tremendously impressed with this, and he remembered it years later; he asked himself whether he would have had the courage or the foresight to seize the opportunity as Roy Thomson had done. On reflection, he doubted if he would have succeeded, admitting that he didn't have the extraordinary desire or the dogged persistence that Thomson had. Ernie has always respected Thomson and has found him to be "a genial, honest, fearless rogue, astute and far sighted, who made no bones about the fact that he loved to make money".

Years later, when he himself had been successful in business, he wondered how Roy had spent his enormous fortune, and suspected that many had benefitted from his generosity.

5 Big Bill Campbell and All

Big Bill Campbell was "a most unlikely prospect", as Bush's secretary said; a huge rambling wreck of a man, six-foot three inches tall and weighing more than 250 pounds; his hair uncombed, his clothes dishevelled and his shoes unshined, he held out a great grimy hand with what Ernie described as a "pound of dirt" under his fingernails, and announced himself as "Big Bill Campbell, salesman, announcer, compère extraordinaire", and fished out of his soiled suit a wad of press clippings to support his claims. His appearance never concerned him but, on this occasion, as he was looking for a job, he did explain that he and his wife and two children had just driven all the way from Texas; he didn't say that a sheriff was hot on his heels for a large number of unpaid debts he had left behind. He had served in the First World War, as his veteran's pin showed, and said that he was a Canadian born in Ottawa, the son of an aide-de-camp to the Governor-General.

Although Campbell looked unwashed and unreliable, he was such an engaging fellow that Bushnell told him to report to CKNC the next day as a salesman. Ernie wasn't really taking any chance with him, as he put him on commission—fifteen per cent of time sales—with no salary and no drawing account. Big Bill went to work selling spot announcements for which the station charge was ten dollars per minute in prime time.

Within a few days he had sold ten of these commercials, and on Friday he came to collect his commission. It amounted to around fifteen dollars and was not enough to provide food and lodging for a family of four—so he asked for a "small advance".

Bushnell, who had been astonished at his sales prowess, felt that he deserved a twenty-five-dollar advance, but when he went for the cheque the company's cashier, a Miss Kelly, said, "You'll be sorry, Mr. B. I've seen him and he's a no-good bum."

However, Campbell turned out to be a super-salesman no one could resist. After two weeks of selling one-minute commercials, which he insisted on writing himself, he came to Bush and asked which was the toughest account in town, a company that the CKNC staff had tried to sell but had failed. He was told that that was Shirriff Marmalade. After finding out where the head office of the company was, he set out to see them that morning. Before noon, Ernie got a telephone call from Bill asking him if he could give Shirriffs one hour of time at eight o'clock each morning, starting the following Monday.

"But we're not on the air at eight o'clock in the morning," Bush said. "We don't come on until nine."

"That's fine," Bill said. "You get an engineer to turn on the transmitter at 7:45 and I'll do the rest."

Ernie gave his consent, although his boss thought he was out of his mind. The program, which consisted of semi-classical recorded music with Big Bill as the announcer, went on as planned. Shortly after nine o'clock that day there was a telephone call from J. D. Neill, the sales manager of Shirriff Marmalade. Neill had been away on a business trip when Bill had made the deal with two of the Shirriff brothers, and he was beside himself with rage.

"Who," he screamed, "who in hell has given CKNC or this fellow Campbell the right to broadcast on behalf of the Shirriff Company . . .?"

There was no reasoning with him and finally, in a fury, Neill banged down the receiver. Bush called in Big Bill and told him what had just happened.

"Oh, that's all right," Bill said. "I'll just drop around to Shirriff's and sell him [Neill] on the idea."

And that was what he did. The following Monday, Shirriff's Breakfast Hour went on the air with Roland Todd, organist; Gordon Calder, tenor, and Big Bill Campbell as announcer, poetry reader, commentator and story teller. The Breakfast

Hour stayed on the air fifty-two weeks a year for five years, and during the latter two years was extended by network to London, Ottawa and Montreal. It was one of the great success stories of broadcasting. Shirriff's products became a household word and the company found it difficult to keep up with demand. One morning when Bill was describing the virtues of Shirriff's marmalade, he referred to it as "that jar of golden sunshine". The phrase was picked up by the company and even in 1971 could be found on every jar of Shirriff's marmalade, although the company had by then been absorbed by a large international competitor.

For the Shirriff program, Bill was paid not only as a salesman but as a copywriter and master-of-ceremonies. He got other programs for the station, and he insisted on playing a major role in these too. His success was such that CKNC was paying him eighteen thousand dollars a year, ninety per cent of which it collected from his sponsors. But if Bill made eighteen thousand a year, he spent at least twenty-five, and he was always being pursued by creditors. How he parted with his money, no one ever knew for certain. Ernie's guess was that what he didn't spend on entertainment (that is, on drinking) he gave away to his cronies.

Bill started the Coo-coo-noodle Club; he sold the idea for the program to the Wentworth Dry Ginger Ale Company, a small soft-drink manufacturer located in Hamilton whose owner-manager delivered his bottled products in the trunk of his automobile. Bill had assured Wentworth that his business would grow by leaps and bounds if he sponsored the program. The first show of the Coo-coo-noodle Club was on the Saturday night after Bush had left for a summer vacation at his cottage on the Kawartha Lakes; Stan Long's six-piece orchestra was on it, and so were Gordon Calder and Big Bill Campbell.

On the following Monday morning, a messenger hunted Bushnell up at the lake and delivered a telegram to him which ordered him to return to 805 Davenport Road at once—there was hell to pay over the Coo-coo-noodle Club. What had happened was that Bill and everyone else on the program had agreed that Wentworth dry ginger ale should make a good mixer and had proved this to be so by mixing it with rye whiskey from a bottle generously provided by Bill. The result of these libations became more and more apparent as the show progressed. The sponsor was indignant at "such an outrageously drunken performance", and not only refused to pay but threatened to take CKNC to court although, even as he protested, he could hardly keep up with the orders for his "mixer".

At any rate, Bush was sent to smooth things over. He apologized profusely and said that if the sponsor would consider continuing with the show for the next twelve weeks, he would not only act as script writer and director but, to ensure that there would be no more hanky-panky, he would take part in the show. Wentworth finally accepted his offer, and the comedy team of Bill and Swifty, Big Bill Campbell and Ernie Bushnell, was born and flourished for four years. Bushnell admitted that he stole most of the jokes for the show from *College Humour* and *Chase's Almanac*. A woman in Hamilton sent him three volumes of jokes and conundrums, bound in red leather, that her late husband had collected and, while he has long since lost them, he says they are still turning up on the front pages of the daily papers.

Another great show that CKNC produced during Bush's regime as station manager was the Nielson Hour. George Metcalfe, the energetic assistant sales manager of the William Nielson Company who was to end a distinguished business career by becoming president of the huge Loblaws chain of supermarkets, was really the father of the Nielson Hour; he sold the idea to the company and promoted the program by visiting the Toronto newspapers every week and handing out boxes of chocolates. He would have been called the executive producer nowadays, as he attended every rehearsal and sat in the control room during the broadcast. After the show he would plan the next week's program with Geoff Waddington, often working till three o'clock in the morning, going over the numbers used in past Nielson Hours and deciding whether this one or that could be repeated. Metcalfe, who has been a championship lightweight boxer in Toronto, fighting for the West End YMCA, did not like slow music,

The scene changed. It was early 1934, and Bushnell was now program director of the Canadian Radio Broadcasting Commission in Ottawa. His secretary was Miss Georgie Appleby, who was to remain with him through thick and thin, whether he was up or down, and was to become an officer of the expanding Bushnell TV Company (renamed Bushnell Communications Limited). On that day in 1934, Miss Appleby announced that a Mr. Campbell, "Big Bill, he calls himself," wanted to see him.

And there he was, the same derelict figure, his hair rumpled and enough dirt under his fingernails to start a garden, a wide grin on his face which did not hide his bloodshot eyes, the telltale result of a hard night's drinking.

"Bush, my dear old friend," Bill said, "I'm on my way to England. With this outfit that you're with now, there'll be little opportunity for me in this country."

How had he got enough money to go to England? Campbell explained that he had been wounded in the war but hadn't bothered to have the shrapnel removed from his leg or to ask for a pension. However, the wound had begun to act up and he had gone to Christie Street Veterans' Hospital in Toronto to have the shrapnel removed, at the same time applying for a disability pension retroactive to 1919. His claim was approved, and he pulled out of his wallet three thousand dollars which, he said, would keep him until he got started again over there.

Six weeks later, Bushnell was listening to the radio receiver in his office in the National Research Building on Sussex Drive in Ottawa—there were the ringing tones of Big Ben, and then, a voice that was extraordinarily familiar came booming out of the loudspeaker: "This is the B.B.C.—Big Bill Campbell and his Rocky Mountaineers."

"Good God," Ernie said to himself, "he's done it again." No one, to his certain knowledge, and Bushnell came to know the BBC well in later years, was able to reach the inner offices of Broadcasting House in such a short time, let alone get on the air. But Big Bill had done it, and in Britain he became famous, wealthy and respectable. Not only did he broadcast, but he and his troupe played the music halls. When Bushnell was in London in 1938, he met him once more. By then, Campbell had become president of the Actors' Guild, the British equivalent of Actors' Equity. He lived in Hampstead; his name was a household word; he was affluent and happy and sober. But tragedy was to close his life; his son was killed in the Second World War and Big Bill Campbell died of a heart attack shortly after.

6 Graham Spry and the CRBC

Shortly after he formed the Canadian Radio League, Graham Spry visited CKNC to make a broadcast and met Ernest L. Bushnell. Spry remembers well that the bulky young station manager was "very kind and helpful"; Bushnell does not recall the meeting at all but has remarked rather dryly that his courtesy would have been due to the fact that he had been warned to be careful about "this guy who was out to nationalize us". It must have been in the spring of 1931, for Spry remembers that it was a warm day and that he didn't have an overcoat when he was shown out into a yard after the broadcast by a slim young man who was probably Geoffrey Waddington.

Although Bush fought the CRL and all it wanted, on the air and in Parliament's smoke-filled committee rooms, he never had any doubts about the sincerity or integrity of both Graham Spry and Alan Plaunt. In retrospect, he is willing to admit that "their foresight did in the long run provide Canada with at least a foundation stone on which, and around which, the present system can and does operate reasonably well". However, he does point out that the Canadian compromise of private and public broadcasting was "a far cry from what Messrs. Spry and Plaunt envisaged or indeed the kind of system recommended by the royal commission headed by Sir John Aird".

It was inevitable that the government should step into broadcasting, which was in a chaotic condition, and even an ardent free-enterpriser like Ernie Bushnell agreed that there had to be some new rules and reorganization. CKNC and the other radio stations were licensed under the 1913 Radio-Telegraph Act which, as its title implied, was meant to govern communication rather than commercial broadcasting, and let the stations do what they liked in programming. Yet it was not political broadcasting but religious broadcasting that forced the government to consider the whole question of a Canadian broadcasting policy.

By the end of the twenties, several radio stations were operated by various religious denominations and sects: some of them were "phantom stations" broadcasting only once a week, usually on Sundays, but a majority of these stations were in the hands of the International Bible Students, a Jehovah's Witness organization, and they were on the air more than other phantom stations. Furthermore, CJYC, the station which gave Bush his start in broadcasting, was operated by Universal Radio of Canada, a Bible students' front, as a regular commercial station. The Jehovah's Witnesses seemed to consider their radio licences as licences to vilify other churches, and they were not beyond calling the regular gentlemen-of-the-cloth "Judases and polecats".

As a result of increasing complaints that these stations were broadcasting programs that were "unpatriotic and abusive of all churches", the government screwed up its courage and decided to close four of them. The resulting controversy led to a debate in Parliament and the appointment of a royal commission chaired by Sir John Aird, retired president of the Canadian Bank of Commerce; its job was "to inquire into the radio broadcasting situation throughout Canada, and to advise as to the future administration, management, control and finance thereof". At the time, not much attention was paid to the tendency of most Canadians to listen to American stations, or to the way that the biggest Canadian stations were joining the US networks.

On September 11, 1929, the Aird Commission handed in its report which was a model of conciseness, being only nine pages long. The report had been written largely by the commission's secretary, Donald Manson, who was chief of radio inspection, Department of Marine, but represented the views of the chairman and the opinions of the other commissioners, Charles Bowman, editor of the *Ottawa Citizen,* and Dr. Augustin Frigon, a distinguished engineer and educator from Montreal. The commission believed that Canadian radio stations should be owned and operated by a publicly owned company, to be called the Canadian Broadcasting Corporation or Company. There would be no room for any private stations in this system. The report said that the objective of Canadian broadcasting should be "good reception" throughout the country and, in order to achieve that, proposed the construction of seven 50,000-watt stations from coast to coast at a cost of three million dollars. It suggested that the system should be financed by a three-dollar licence fee and government subsidies.

That was it, and the Aird Commission's report got a surprisingly good press at first. *La Presse*, which owned CKAC, was against it from the beginning, and other papers such as the *Toronto Globe,* as they became associated with radio stations, came out against "civil-service broadcasting". However, the real stumbling block to implementation of the report was the summer election of 1930 when the Liberals were overthrown and the Conservatives came to power. It was that which prompted Graham Spry (who had a political sixth sense and realized that a commission's report was often shelved in a change of government) to consider forming a body that would act as a public broadcasting lobby—Bushnell paid the CRL the compliment of saying that it had done "one of the best lobbying jobs" ever on Parliament Hill; he also called its work "the greatest snow job ever".

As the national secretary of the Association of Canadian Clubs, Spry travelled extensively and kept in touch with Canadian opinion makers from coast to coast; he found that his alarm at the encroachment of canned American culture by means of the air waves was shared by others, including many prominent citizens. There were signs that eighty per cent of the Canadian people were listening to American broadcasts and, by the end of 1929, CFRB had joined the Columbia Broadcasting Service, while CKGW had become a member of the National Broadcasting Company's Red Network.

Graham Spry was a Rhodes scholar from the University of Manitoba in the early twenties. After serving for a while on the League of Nations staff in Geneva, he returned to Canada to become the first paid secretary of the Association of Canadian Clubs. As a project for the diamond jubilee of Confederation, to be celebrated on July 1, 1927, Spry proposed a national radio "hook-up", as it was called in those days—which showed his early obsession with broadcasting and its importance to national life. A hook-up was provided by the Canadian National Railway, which had not only the land lines necessary but also a number of its own radio stations and was the only "national broadcaster" at the time, as E. A. Weir was to tell the Aird Commission.

Alan Plaunt, the scion of a wealthy lumber family, had independent means and could subsidize his social conscience; he became the unpaid secretary of the Canadian Radio League. He had also been at Oxford, several years later than Graham. Between the two of them, they knew most of the bright young men and women of Canada and were able to recruit them to the cause of public broadcasting, as against commercial radio with its smack of huckstering, and American huckstering at that. They belonged to the best fraternities when fraternities counted: Spry was a Zeta Psi, and one of his fraternity brothers, R. K. Finlayson, was to become Prime Minister Bennett's secretary; Plaunt was a member of Kappa Alpha and so was Brooke Claxton, a leading light in the Liberal party and later Canada's Defence minister.

In September 1930, the Bennett government met the new Parliament elected at the July 28 election. In October of that year, the Canadian Radio League was formed at a meeting in the Ottawa home of Alan Plaunt, according to the official account in the March 1965 issue of the Canadian Historical Review. Ernie Bushnell suggests a much more dramatic setting for the birth of the CRL; he says that the initial discussions on the "sad state of radio broadcasting" took place under the portrait of Sir John A. Macdonald in the lounge of the Rideau Club in Ottawa to which both dashing young men belonged. Bushnell adds that if his assumption is correct, "it would not have been the first time nor the last that such conspiracies were hatched there."

Plaunt and Spry went to work with a will; they papered the country with pamphlets and sought out new members. Aside from Finlayson and Claxton, another notable working member was E. A. "Ned" Corbett, then a professor at the University of Alberta. Bushnell maintains that it was a "nebulous, will-o-the-wisp organization", which it was—there were never very many individual members, and "the big shots on the letterhead didn't know what its aims were." But the league could claim the support of a number of national organizations. In fact, early in 1931 the CRL was boasting that it spoke for fifty newspapers with a daily circulation of one million, for women's organizations with a membership of over 600,000, and for other national associations and labour and farm organizations numbering 327,000. It had the support of twelve university presidents, six provincial superintendents of education, the heads of the Anglican, Roman Catholic and United Churches, and had been endorsed by prominent businessmen across the country, many of whom were Conservatives.

However, it was on the "old-boy network" that Spry and Plaunt proved to be most effective—so many of the top civil servants in Ottawa, and even the political movers and shakers in the country, had been to Oxford or Cambridge or were fraternity brothers. There was a meeting of minds at the conferences that the Canadian Radio League arranged; the participants spoke the same language and had the same national objectives.

One of Graham Spry's first acts was to enlist the support of W. D. Herridge with whom he had been associated in the work of the old Canadian League, an organization that had promoted the study of national topics in various Canadian cities. Thus, the CRL had the ear of the new prime minister, for Herridge was not only a close friend and advisor of R. B. Bennett's but was to become his brother-in-law when he married Mildred Bennett in 1931. The prime minister and the Conservative cabinet were greatly impressed by the growing evidence of widespread public support for the idea of a nationally owned radio system, and

Bennett encouraged the CRL to carry on its good work. The prime minister even used Spry as an agent: Bennett phoned him one evening to say that the government didn't know how the prairies felt on the radio issue, and could he do anything? Spry left immediately for the West and, in a remarkably short time, talked up a storm of letters to MPs. He even got the provincial governments to wire Ottawa their support of the public ownership of broadcasting.

It was really the "establishment" that Spry and Plaunt had rallied to the cause of Canadian nationalism and against the threatened American dominance of the air waves: there were the academics and opinion makers across the country, the power élites in various areas, the heads of national farm and labour organizations and women's institutes, and of such patriotic bodies as the Canadian Legion. They were a formidable force but a minority. The vast majority (which must have included the eighty per cent of Canadians who were said to be listening to American stations) was silent and content with the way things were. Most Canadians listened avidly to Amos 'n Andy, Eddie Cantor, Jack Benny and other American shows and showmen, and were so thoroughly conditioned by American commercial programming that they resented the radio licence fee, small though it was, or any attempt to foster Canadian programming. (The licence fee that every set owner had to pay was raised from one to two dollars a year in 1932.)

Against the establishment led by the Canadian Radio League, the proponents of private broadcasting floundered around hopelessly. It was an unequal match. The Canadian Broadcasters Association, then rather loosely knit and poorly organized tried to counter what Bushnell called "the propaganda campaign" of the CRL, which was aided and abetted by the press. Publishers "could envisage huge cuts in newspaper and magazine advertising if this young snob called radio was permitted even a teeny weeny bit of the advertising dollar." Bush charges that "politicians, at that time, believed in the power of the press" and "swallowed holus-bolus the widespread editorial approval with which the league was encouraged and blessed." On the other hand, he admits that broadcasters "were afraid to open their mouths in front of their microphones just in case they lost their licences".

However, Bush was the exception to his own rule and went on the air with editorials attacking the campaign to nationalize broadcasting. One of the letters submitted by the private stations in Toronto to the 1932 parliamentary radio committee was addressed to CKNC and said: "After listening to the remarks of your Mr. Bushnell, the writer wishes to go on record as being absolutely opposed to government control of radio broadcasting in Canada. . . . I take pleasure in opposing this and wishing you the best of luck in having the bill defeated good and proper." Alex Mackenzie, the general manager of the Canadian National Carbon Company, was a strident defender of private enterprise. He attacked the Aird Commission's report publicly again, in a speech to the Canadian Manufacturers' Association:

> Remember that private ownership persists in the United States. Will Canadian manufacturers be able to compete on equal terms with those to the south of us, if they can still use the air for advertising and our manufacturers cannot? This is an important point the commission has not considered.

CKNC was in the forefront of the private broadcasters' stand against nationalization, and Ernie Bushnell became a familiar figure at the 1932 radio committee's hearings, the first of an endless series of parliamentary committee meetings that he was to attend. He wrote the Canadian Broadcasters Association brief and eventually found himself acting as Graham Spry's opposite. Ernie said that he opposed the CRL for two reasons: First, he was the loyal employee of a privately owned and operated station, CKNC, and felt that they were doing a "pretty darn good job of informing and entertaining an ever-growing radio audience"—almost forty years later, he said that he had no reason to change his mind about that assessment. Second, he was convinced then as later that there was a danger that any publicly owned system of broadcasting would eventually become a pawn of the federal government; his opposition to such a system was reinforced by the bland arrogance of Sir John Reith, who was quoted as saying that he, and not the people, knew what was good for them on the "wireless".

Bushnell drew attention to the likelihood that academics or government officials would be deciding what Canadians might listen to on the radio if there were public ownership of broadcasting. Spry asserted that, under the present system of private enterprise, advertisers were already doing just that.

Most of 1931 was taken up with legal proceedings before the Supreme Court of Canada and the British Privy Council. Premier Taschereau of Quebec insisted on referring the issue to the Privy Council after the Supreme Court had found, by a split 3-2 decision, that broadcasting was within the federal jurisdiction. When the Privy Council confirmed this ruling, Prime Minister Bennett moved quickly to have a special committee of the House of Commons set up which would "advise and recommend a complete technical scheme of broadcasting for Canada".

The battle lines were drawn. The Canadian Broadcasters Association wanted to continue the existing system of private ownership with government subsidies for national network programming and the extension of services to distant and sparsely settled areas. The Canadian Radio League presented a brief which was much longer and more comprehensive than the Aird Commission's report: Spry proposed the formation of a Canadian Broadcasting Corporation, to be set up on a basis similar to that of the BBC, which would take over the whole of broadcasting in stages and eliminate the private radio stations; he even provided a financial forecast of the operation of such a corporation, but this was based on raising the licence fee to three dollars a year.

In a unanimous report, the special Commons Committee came up with the usual sort of Canadian compromise: a commission instead of a corporation to nationalize broadcasting. Public ownership was to be achieved simply and solely through the licence fee, and there were to be no government subsidies as the Aird Commission had proposed. The Canadian Radio League and its supporters welcomed the report, largely because it embodied the principle of public ownership, although Spry was critical of the establishment of a commission rather than a corporation. Legislation was passed setting up the Canadian Radio Broadcasting Commission, and Prime Minister Bennett appointed Hector Charlesworth as chairman, Thomas Maher, vice-chairman, and Lieutenant Colonel Arthur Steel as the third commissioner.

At the beginning of December 1932, E. A. Weir, who had run the Canadian National Railway's radio service, joined the CRBC as program director. Spry and Plaunt in their paper, the *Farmer's Sun,* hailed his appointment and predicted that he would be the "mainstay of the Commission". Weir made the arrangements for the first Empire Christmas broadcast to be carried in Canada, which proved to be a great success.

In the beginning, the commission drew most of its staff from the CNR radio stations which it was taking over and which alone constituted the public sector of broadcasting at the time. But in its haste to get going, mistakes were made; the commission ran into staffing problems and began reaching into the private sector for management personnel. The first to be taken on was J. Arthur Dupont, manager of CKAC, the *La Presse* station in Montreal which had been a most bitter opponent of nationalization. The services of Ernest L. Bushnell, the manager of CKNC, were sought to make a survey of the potential for network programming in western Canada.

There is a memorandum, written three years later, wherein Bush tried to justify his expense account for that three-month trip; in retrospect, it is rather amusing as it would appear that his bosses had persuaded him that he was expected to travel like a minor potentate when he was on a government mission. He explained in this memo that he was "loaned to the commission by the Canadian National Carbon Co. Ltd." and added, "I might tell you that the Canadian National Carbon Company is a national concern, distributing its products from coast to coast. The executives of this company demand that its travelling representatives conduct themselves in accordance with the high standards maintained by the company as whole. In plain words, the best is none too good." Unfortunately for Bush, the best was too much for the government, and the auditor general cut his claims to the point where, he says, his first experience with

41

the commission "cost me personally between two and three hundred dollars".

Bushnell was offered the post of program supervisor for Ontario and western Canada shortly after he returned from the western trip. Dupont, who had fought as hard against the concept of public ownership of radio as Bushnell, had become program supervisor for Quebec and eastern Canada. Years later, long after he had left the CBC, successor to the CRBC, Bush was still puzzled over why the commission should have wanted them. Joining the commission was another turning point in his life, but he could not understand how it came about. Why did the CRBC hire two of its most vocal opponents?

With more than thirty-five years of hindsight, Graham Spry suggested that this was a case of hiring "know-how". Certainly, the commissioners knew little or nothing about broadcasting: Charlesworth was best known as a music and drama critic, although he had been editor of *Saturday Night* when he was named chairman; Maher was a forestry engineer and business-man; Colonel Steel could be said to have had some knowledge of radio but from the technical side; he was with the National Research Council before becoming commissioner. The only persons who knew anything, according to Spry, were running private radio stations and were on record as being opposed to public ownership.

Austin Weir had been the exception. But he had fallen foul of the commissioners, which was partly the fault of the broad-casting act as there was no clear distinction drawn between those responsible for policy and those responsible for operation. Weir had had experience administering a national program system for the Canadian National Railway and he expected to be the chief executive of the new broadcasting body, but the commissioners saw themselves in that role. At any rate, Bushnell thought that he was going to be offered a job under Weir when he was summoned to report to Colonel Arthur Steel in Ottawa. "Summoned" was an accurate description of the telephone call that Bushnell's boss at CKNC, Ewart Greig, had received on October 22, 1933; the colonel, who was a bit of a martinet, demanded that Bush come to see him, and Greig

42

advised him to go.

Bushnell took the night train to Ottawa, and early next morning was making his way through the concourse of Union Station to have breakfast in the Chateau Laurier when he decided to phone Austin Weir to find out what the summons was all about. He reached him at his residence, but Weir rather turned the tables on him by asking him what he was doing in Ottawa. Bush told him of the call that Mr. Greig had received and then added in an off-hand manner that he supposed they were still pressing him to join the commission. (There had been suggestions made earlier that he should come on staff.)

"That's right, Bush," Weir said. "I presume they are offering you my job. They fired me yesterday."

Bush was shocked and, after expressing incredulity, said angrily:

"To hell with them. I'm not a bit interested."

Weir came to the Chateau to have breakfast with Bushnell. During the course of the meal he urged Bush to see the commissioners; although he admitted that he had "lost all confidence" in them personally, they still represented the concept of public ownership of broadcasting in which he believed. What was the reason for E. A. Weir's dismissal? He had already been demoted, early in the spring of 1932, from program director to supervisor of programs for Ontario and western Canada; Dupont had been given the other half of his job as supervisor for Quebec and eastern Canada. Bushnell figured that his gradual fall from grace was due to the fact that J. Arthur Dupont had organized such a large number of programs in Montreal, and many of them had been fed, with French and English announcements, to Ontario and western Canada. It was true that during the 1934 Parliamentary committee's hearings on radio, there had been numerous complaints about French-language announcements. In fact, there were westerners who said that the use of French outside Quebec was unconstitutional, and that this was a "concerted effort by people of French origin to make Canada a bilingual country", while others maintained that all this was doing was "building a wall of hostility" in Canada. (There was another aspect of the story that Weir did not mention—that his work for the commission was affected by personal tragedy, the death of his first wife in childbirth.) At any rate, Weir made it quite clear during breakfast that he intended to take legal action against the commissioners for wrongful dismissal.

Sure enough, Bushnell was offered Weir's job when he kept his appointment with Colonel Steel in his office in the National Research Council building on Sussex Drive. Bush was suitably noncommittal and told the commissioner that he would go back to Toronto "to think it over". Before leaving Ottawa, Bush called Weir and told him of the proposition; he said that he had no intention of accepting.

The next day in Toronto, he told his boss what had happened and declared that he did not want to leave the carbon company and CKNC. Ewart Greig nodded his head, then replied rather somberly that there was something he should know and take into consideration. Union Carbide of New York had ordered its subsidiary in Canada to shut down its radio station on December 31, 1933; he said how much he and Alex Mackenzie regretted this decision, but the simple fact was that the carbon company did not wish to continue to operate such a tiny piece of its overall industrial empire under any kind of bureaucratic control. If Bush wanted to remain with them, then Greig and A. Mac would be very pleased to place him in their advertising or sales departments. But if he wished to stay in the radio business, then it was Greig's opinion that Bush should give serious thought to the CRBC offer—better talk it over with his wife.

Ernie did, and "rather reluctantly" came to the conclusion that he should accept. He wired his decision to Colonel Steel on October 24; he was told to report to the Toronto office on November 1, and to be in Ottawa on November 2. In his own words, "That was the beginning of a twenty-six-year, mostly happy association with Canada's national broadcasting system."

7 "Sentenced to Siberia"

On October 23, 1933, when Ernie Bushnell came to Ottawa for his interview with Colonel Arthur Steel, the capital city's streets were covered with an inch of snow. On the night before November 2, there had been a fall of six inches of snow, so that he had to "mush" along Sussex Drive to the commission's office in the palatial, neo-Greek, National Research Council building. "Good God," Bush recalls, "I thought I'd been sentenced to Siberia."

The winter of 1933-34 was among the worst that Ottawa had ever had: Ernie claims that during January and February, the temperature was seldom above twenty below and usually much lower. The Ottawa City Council, which has always had a tendency to play low comedy to the high drama on Parliament Hill, had fallen flat on its collective face over snow removal. It had let the contract for clearing the streets to the old Ottawa Electric Railway Company but, since the previous winter had been one of the mildest on record and almost bereft of snow, the worthy city fathers figures the company had cleaned up in more ways than one and took the contract back. Then, the heavens opened up and the blizzards swirled. The city didn't have enough equipment and, even after hiring everything the streetcar company had, it could not cope with the heavy falls. There were two-foot-deep ruts; there were cars abandoned in the middle of the streets; there were pedestrians floundering waist-deep on the sidewalks—and Ernie and Edna longed for the relative warmth and order of Toronto. Even on May 8, 1934, when the Bushnells went looking for a cottage in the Gatineau, the snowbanks were higher than the roof of their car.

When he was summoned to Ottawa, Ernie's principals at the Canadian National Carbon Company had advised him to demand five thousand dollars a year, which was a good salary in the depression days and more than he was making at CKNC. Although Colonel Steel did not demur outright, he said that there was nothing in "the establishment" which paid that much for one with his qualifications. However, he had a place for a "chief engineer" at $4,500 a year, and if Bushnell would accept that, Colonel Steel assured him that another post paying the amount he wanted would open up within three months' time. So Bushnell officially began at the CRBC as a chief engineer, although his job was supervisor of programs for Ontario and western Canada. All of which made him more scornful than ever of the "whole crazy civil-service set-up of the commission". Bush continued as chief engineer on the records of the CRBC not for three months but for twelve before the five-thousand-dollar-a-year position became vacant—and this, he discovered, was more or less the average government disparity between promise and fulfilment.

Although the winter weather was abominable, Ernie would have preferred to have spent longer in Ottawa with his wife and baby daughter—they had taken a furnished flat in the capital—but found he had to spend almost half of his time in Toronto. There, it was like returning to the old days of CKNC, because the CRBC had rented the old studios and facilities in the carbon company's plant at 805 Davenport Road. The commission had expropriated CKGW, the Gooderham and Worts station in Toronto, but had closed down its studios in the King Edward Hotel as they were not big enough. (As a result of this, Charles Jennings, a young announcer at CKGW, had joined CKNC for the last year of that station's life before it folded by order of the Union Carbide Company in New York.)

Not only were there the old familiar studios and offices of CKNC—down below were his old bosses, Ewart Greig and A. Mac, always ready to josh him about working for the government and being a "civil servant"—but he had seen to it that the staff was the same. After he had been appointed

46

supervisor for Ontario and the West, Bushnell hired almost everyone who had worked for him at CKNC—and "why the hell not? They were the only ones who knew a damn thing about radio." He also felt that he owed it to them, as the station was being closed down because of the radio commission that had given him a plushy job.

So Rupert Lucas joined the CRBC: he had been an announcer and producer at CKNC and was to be best known as director of drama in the CBC. Stanley Maxted joined too: he had sung with Rex Battle's orchestra in the Royal York Hotel but was to gain enduring fame as the war correspondent for the BBC who, at over fifty years of age, landed with the airborne troops at Arnhem and escaped to tell that heroic story. There was Charles Jennings, who was to become the voice of the new national radio, the man who broadcast the news and the weather report. Jack Radford, who had also been with CKNC for only a short time as a salesman and artist, was absorbed in the commission staff. George Taggart, from Vancouver, had belonged to the Bushnell "gang" since he had been hired by Bush during the western tour he made for the CRBC in the summer of 1933; Taggart became manager of CRCT, the commission's station in Toronto, and he was the man responsible for starting "The Happy Gang", one of the most successful of Canadian radio shows.

Bushnell's first and foremost task was to increase production; E. A. Weir had been accused by the commissioners of not providing enough programming from Ontario and western Canada, with the result that there had been too many shows from Montreal and too many bilingual announcements drawing angry denunciations from English Canada. From the beginning, the commission had accepted advertising and sponsorship and, with the closing of CKNC, Ernie was able to take over most of its commercial shows—the Nielson Hour, the Wrigley Hour, the Buckingham Hour, Shirriff's breakfast program, the Coo-coo-noodle Club and others, many of which he and his colleagues had developed. He revived George Wade and his Corn Huskers (from his CFRB days) and this oldtime country-dance group became one of the most popular programs.

Then there was the news, and the commission signed an agreement with Canadian Press to provide a news bulletin service "without charge"—the only benefit the agency received was the acknowledgment that the program was "by courtesy of the Canadian Press". No commercials were permitted and it was written into the agreement that the CRBC was to be the sole sponsor. This was the beginning of a Canadian tradition, that there should be no advertising with the news.

A survey conducted by the *Western Producer* early in 1936 showed the news bulletins to be the second most popular show, after Farmer Fiddlers, a group that took the place of the Corn Huskers in the West. Hockey broadcasts already had a big following, and a new band, Mart Kenney and his Western Gentlemen, was beginning to catch on—in fact, H. N. Stovin, who was the western regional program director, noted that he would have put this band at the top of his list but "it bumped against Eddie Cantor" for a time.

Much of the CRBC programming, which amounted to four hours a night, was on some sort of a limited network, such as a regional network, and while a coast-to-coast "hook-up" was not unknown, it was uncommon enough still to be a thrill to hear people talking to each other across the continent—as Bush recalls, "listeners in the earlier days were not quite as blasé as some of them seem to be now." He himself was excited about the fascinating possibilities that the vast stretch of land lines leased from the Canadian National and Canadian Pacific railways presented, and wanted to try them out. Why not have what he called "a choral hopscotch" across the country, which would be "a stunt, but a fantastic stunt?" A choir in Halifax would sing the first line of "O Canada"; a choir in the next city would sing the next line and so on, across the Great Lakes, the prairies, the Rockies, until Vancouver was reached, and all the choirs would join in the final chorus. The engineers, who were just as anxious to test the network, said that it should be possible with some rehearsal and a little luck to make the pick-up of these choirs from east to west.

It was first tried on the broadcast celebrating the silver jubilee of King George V on May 6, 1935. During the first rehearsal, Ernie Bushnell happened to be on a western tour and heard it in the Edmonton studios; his account of it, which appeared in the press, showed how elated everyone was over this technical triumph.

> Came the cue: "All right Halifax"—a moment of breathless suspense—and we heard the first few bars of "O Canada". Thus it went right across Canada, our national anthem played by nine bands but sounding like one. It could be done, had been done and will be done again. It was then that even I, toughened to this game as I am, got the thrill of my life.

It was done again during that year's Christmas broadcast, but this time the choirs played "choral hopscotch" with "Good King Wenceslas", varying it slightly after the first verse so that the first solo was sung in Vancouver and the second in Halifax. All of which amazed experienced newspapermen like I. Norman Smith of the *Ottawa Journal*, who asked in an editorial page article: "How did it work? How were the choirs presented in succession with flawless harmony and perfect beat?" The technicians and officials of the Canadian Radio Broadcasting Commission preened themselves.

One of the "actualities" in the Christmas broadcast, which was meant to present a cross-section of the way Canadians were spending the day, was the arrival of the transcontinental railway train at Banff, and Bushnell learned some time later that this hadn't been exactly what it seemed. Frank "Tiny" Elphicke, the manager of the local station, was a great showman and had everything "laid on", but the weather spoiled his plans. Snow and ice held up the arrival of the train for some two hours. However, Tiny was not one to be easily defeated; he gathered together some members of his staff and about fifty citizens of Banff and got the railway to have a yard engine pull up at the appointed time—it must be remembered that everything was done "live" in those days. The phoney passengers disentrained to be greeted by shouts of welcome and the interviews took place as though nothing untoward had happened. Tiny Elphick played a dual role, acting the part of the interviewer and also that of a coloured dining-car chef. No one spotted the hoax or the fact that the chef's negro accent had a slight cockney ring—Elphicke had come from England and was to become a leading executive of the Taylor-Pearson-Carson radio chain.

It was during his CRBC days that Bushnell ran into the sort of labour troubles that were to plague the national broadcasting system. The best musical shows originated in Montreal, and that was where the first rumblings of revolt among the musicians were heard. There were complaints about working conditions, charges that there were in-groups and cliques and that conductors had "pets", some of whom were on every program. Bushnell has admitted that "in all fairness, the fees paid were not overly generous", but went on to say, "You've got to remember that when I officially joined the CRBC in November of 1933, our total annual budget for programs amounted to three hundred thousand dollars, out of which Arthur Dupont and I had to provide a minimum of fourteen hours of radio programs a week."

There were several abortive visits to Ottawa by the leaders of the Montreal musicians' union who warned that the men would down their instruments and strike. Neither Dupont nor Bushnell really believed that they would do so; when they did, there was a great "scurrying around" to replace the Montreal originations with similar programs from Toronto, Winnipeg and elsewhere. The Montreal chapter appealed to headquarters in New York to put a stop to what it called "this scabbing", and Walter Murdoch, then head of the Toronto local, ordered the musicians outside of Montreal to show solidarity with their striking brothers. Such eminent conductors as Percy Faith, Geoff Waddington and Mart Kenney were furious that a group of "malcontents" in Quebec should have made them lose their fees. Some band leaders refused to obey the order and recruited non-union players.

Finally, Joseph Webber, the international president of the American Federation of Musicians, appealed to CRBC Chairman Hector Charlesworth to settle the dispute—Charlesworth knew Webber and had been an admirer of his as the union leader was a celebrated flautist. They met privately in the chairman's office and, over a bottle of whiskey, they settled the strike. Bushnell said that he and Dupont were "brokenhearted" at this because they felt that they had won; they saw to it that those conductors and musicians who were fined as much as one thousand dollars for disobeying union orders to walk off their jobs were recompensed so that they didn't lose anything.

One of Bush's compensations for working for the government-owned broadcasting system was his office, a spacious room fully thirty by forty feet in the southeast corner of the monumental NRC building, with a magnificent view of the Rideau Falls and, across the Ottawa River, the Gatineau Hills. It was an office worthy of the highest panjandrum of bureaucracy, a minister or deputy minister at the least, and Ernie Bushnell was never to have a better office, not even when he was running the Canadian Broadcasting Corporation or head of his own broadcasting empire.

8 "Mr. Sage" and the 1936 Committee

In a short time, the Canadian Radio Broadcasting Commission had performed wonders; even Austin Weir, who had no reason to look at its achievements through rose-coloured glasses, said that its regime was a "notable one in radio history". Ernie Bushnell felt that, "from a program standpoint, the CRBC had done an exceptionally fine job, considering the miserably small budget" that the depression-ridden Bennett government allowed and the fact that it began from scratch with inadequate studios and little equipment. The commission was to end as it had begun, in controversy; nevertheless, the "Mr. Sage" scandal resulted in the adoption of rules and regulations for political broadcasting. And during April 1936, almost with its last gasp, the commission made history; its harrowing half-hourly account of the efforts to rescue men trapped in the Moose River goldmine in Nova Scotia was the first on-the-spot broadcast and "radio at its greatest".

The reporting of that event, which was a minor disaster although a great human drama, was a breakthrough for radio. No longer would people be dependent on the presses rolling out "extras" for the news; they could hear it as it happened. In a sense, society was returning to the earliest form of communication, the human voice. Just as a nation sat listening to the old-fashioned wall telephone at the pit-head of the Moose River mine, so people would recoil in shock and horror a year later, on May 6, 1937, when they were told, while listening to a description of the docking of the dirigible Hindenburg at Lakehurst, New Jersey, that it had caught fire and that the bodies of passengers were falling from the blazing airship. Actuality broadcasting on radio was to reach its zenith during the Second World War, when the Canadian home reverberated to the sound of battle in Europe.

J. Frank Willis had to battle a horde of newspaper reporters for the use of that single telephone line from the Moose River mine. The story of his exploit has been told many times and would not be repeated here if it did not need to be corrected: in most accounts, it is said that he broadcast his half-hourly bulletin (five minutes long) for sixty-eight hours. But among Bushnell's papers is a copy of a special news release put out by the CRBC which said that he had broadcast continuously for forty-eight hours—the figure 48 had been exised and an arrow pointed to the following, printed in the margin: EXACTLY 111 HRS. JFW. The correction had been made by Frank Willis himself.

So he broadcast every half hour for more than four and a half days—this was the age of endurance tests, of walkathons and danceathons and six-day bicycle races, and Frank Willis set a reporting record that has never been beaten. His graphic descriptions of the frantic struggle of the draegermen and other rescue crews to reach the three men (one of them dead) who were trapped by a rock fall for ten days kept many of his millions of listeners up all night. "So great was the tension," Austin Weir wrote, "that all fifty-eight stations in Canada and some 650 stations in the United States carried these broadcasts." Of the 650 American stations, most were affiliates of the National Broadcasting Company, the Columbia Broadcasting System or the Mutual Broadcasting System. Of the fifty-eight stations in Canada, thirty-nine were linked together in the national network of the CRBC, according to a wire-line contract which was dated July 17, 1935, and was to last for five years.

As supervisor of programs, Bushnell was largely responsible for the notorious "Mr. Sage" broadcasts. He admits as much and regrets the fact that this series spoiled the record of the CRBC—"two years of reasonably good program service"—and led to the commission's demise. He blames himself for not being "wise to the wiles of politicians or organizers of political parties at election time." At any rate, it all seemed innocent enough when a representative of the J. J. Gibbon Advertising Agency approached George Taggart, the head of the Toronto studios, and wanted to buy fifteen minutes of time each week on the CRBC network during the election campaign—Prime Minister Bennett had called for a general election in the early fall of 1935. Since the commission did accept some advertising, Bush couldn't see why such a request should be refused. "We were told that the fifteen-minute period would be occupied by some narrative and some dialogue of entirely fictitious persons who, at one time or another, had cause to comment on the role of Parliament, that it would be quite innocuous and, indeed, it was hoped that it would be entertaining as well as informative."

Such was the political naïveté of Bushnell and his colleagues that they thought there was nothing wrong with the script, although it referred to the strange absence of the Liberal leader (Mackenzie King) from Canada during the First World War. If anything, they probably chortled at this barb. But the allusion to Mr. King taking refuge with the Rockefellers during the war, which was in the second episode, so infuriated Liberal adherents that the switchboards of the stations carrying the broadcast "lit up". In the first episode, there was a reference to the way that the Liberals were using a war scare (the Ethiopian war) to arouse anti-conscription feeling in the province of Quebec. This occurred in the script after an opening discussion about the reason why the election was called for October 14 instead of sooner; "Mr. Sage" receives a telephone call which he says is from his niece, Mary, whose husband "got so crocked up in the war":

SAGE: I guess Mary takes things too seriously, Bill. She's been hearing about Mackenzie King's war speech.
BILL: War—what war?
SAGE: I mean his speech about the Ethiopian trouble with Italy.
BILL: What did he say about it?
SAGE: (slowly) Why, he said that if Italy went to war, Canada would be drawn in.

54

BILL: What's he know about it?

SAGE: Perhaps not as much as he wants us to think he does. But where war's concerned, it's always serious—too serious to be made an off-hand argument in an election speech.

BILL: But Mr. Sage, we don't want war days back again in Canada.

SAGE: We do not, my boy. That's why I hate this attempt to stir up old war wounds.

BILL: I see what you mean. Too serious a thing to serve a party purpose.

SAGE: Exactly. It looks like a deliberate attempt to frighten people—women and the younger . . .

BILL: (interrupting) Surely King wouldn't stoop to that.

SAGE: No? He did it before—in 1930—and there was no world crisis like there is today. I happened to be staying with my brother-in-law in Quebec at the time. Mr. King's henchmen used to call up the farmers and their wives in the early hours of the morning and tell them their sons would be conscripted for the war if they voted against King. . . .

Three of the six "Mr. Sage" broadcasts were produced in the commission's Toronto studios, the former CKNC studios, and the remainder in the studios of CKCL (which became CKEY). Bush recalled that Rupert Lucas, Stanley Maxted and others on staff were chosen to play the dramatic roles in the script written by R. L. Wright, the head of the research department of the J. J. Gibbons agency; the producer of the series was Don Henshaw, a radio executive who had come to Canada from the United States to assist in the Toronto centennial. Rupert Lucas played the part of Mr. Sage in the first two broadcasts and quit because he "did not think it was the sort of thing that I wanted to do", as he told the parliamentary committee; Maurice Boddington, a veteran actor, had the principal role in the third episode, and Vaughan Glaser, another accomplished performer, took over for the rest of the series.

What was considered "good clean fun" by Bushnell and his fellow broadcasters was regarded as "scurrilous and libelous misrepresentation" by Mackenzie King and his Liberals. The series became a cause célèbre, and broadcasters of that era, who were admittedly politically ignorant, found out that politicians, exemplified by the Liberals in this instance, did not mind being accused of past sins on the hustings but considered it a heinous crime if these same sins were put in a dramatic context. This was the way the first "Mr. Sage" broadcast dealt with the Beauharnois scandal, which had not been hushed up by the passage of time but was being shouted from every Tory platform:

SAGE: . . . he led his party down into a valley not so long ago—he himself called it the Valley of Humiliation.
BILL: I remember that—but I guess most people have forgotten by now.
SAGE: That's exactly what Mr. King is hoping for. He doesn't want this brought up. It wasn't such a creditable matter for his party.
BILL: Slush fund from Beauharnois, wasn't it?
SAGE: Yes, Bill—over seven hundred thousand dollars—and that's the man who wants to be prime minister of Canada. Can you beat it?
BILL: Yet, they say he's got a good chance.
SAGE: I don't know, Bill, I don't know. In the old country, Beauharnois would have finished him. In Canada—well, I guess that people here don't like that sort of thing any more than they do over there. Canadians are pretty honest folks, Bill.

At first, there was no indication of the program's sponsor, and Hector Charlesworth, who regarded the whole "Mr. Sage" business as a "piffling affair" over which there had been an "absurd clamour", did describe this as a "rather shabby trick"; he intervened to the extent of telephoning the president of the J. J. Gibbons agency, demanding that future broadcasts be identified as presentations of the Conservative party. There was an understanding between the two of them that the name of the agency might be substituted for that of the party, since it was well known as the advertising representative of the Tories. However, this was not done and the sponsor named for the rest of the broadcasts was "R. L. Wright [the agency script writer] and a group of Conservatives", never the Conservative party.

The "Mr. Sage" broadcasts were not the only indication that Tory leaders and organizers were much more sophisticated in their use of the electronic medium than their opponents. During this same campaign, the Liberals neglected to consider the effects of the time zones on a coast-to-coast broadcast. The Grits wanted to have the last word on the Saturday night before the Monday polling date, but they ignored the three-hour time difference on a live network broadcast between Toronto and Vancouver—so what might have been the last word in the East left hours of free time in the West, and the Conservatives quickly booked the balance of the time up to midnight for their candidates. However, this display of imagination didn't do the Conservatives any good, and the Liberals under W. L. Mackenzie King won an overwhelming victory which was to keep them in power for the next twenty-two years.

It was time for retribution, and Bushnell, Lucas, Maxted and all were hauled into court before a House of Commons committee which met in the spring and summer of 1936. So were Hector Charlesworth and the commissioners who were regarded by the Liberals as their real political enemies. Since Arthur Roebuck, the former attorney-general of Ontario, was sick, the mantle of "chief prosecutor" fell on the round shoulders of a newcomer, Paul Martin, a pudgy, pop-eyed young lawyer from Windsor, Ontario, who had been elected in the Liberal sweep of 1935 and was beginning an extraordinary parliamentary career; the main "defence counsel" was the veteran Conservative member, Denton Massey.

Altogether, it was a gruelling experience. Bushnell recalls, for example, the "plaintive voice" of Rupert Lucas when he was testifying. "Mr. Lucas, is it correct to say that the theme song of this scurrilous broadcast was a popular song entitled 'Blue Skies'?" To which Lucas replied: "Yessir, but the skies weren't very blue the morning after the broadcasts."

However, while those who took part in the series came in for a buffeting, the real wrath of the Liberals was visited on the bearded but unbowed head of Hector Charlesworth and, to a lesser extent, on the other commissioners, who were finally responsible for broadcasting the program. They were all dismissed. Of Mr. Charlesworth, Bushnell has said that one could not speak too kindly; "Probably he was not the greatest executive in the world, but he had so many fine qualities that he had endeared himself to a hard-working lot of employees, small in number but large in their desires to provide a truly distinctive Canadian national radio broadcasting service." Ernie himself emerged almost unscathed from this political retribution, although he had fully expected the axe to fall on him.

As one result of the "Mr. Sage" series, a whole set of new rules for political broadcasting was adopted, including a black out for forty-eight hours prior to the polls opening. (Some of these restrictions are still in effect; Bushnell describes them as "a farce" and feels they are "in dire need of overhauling".

During the course of the committee hearings, Ernie was asked to give his expert advice on how the CRBC might be reconstructed; even then he was regarded as the man with the most practical experience in broadcasting and he was soon to be called by the *Saint John Evening Times Globe* "one of Canada's pioneers in the promotion of radio communication". However, the situation was so tense at the time, with everything in flux and nobody knowing what was going to happen next, that Bushnell wanted to keep quiet the fact that the committee had been in touch with him. So he took the precaution of not having Miss Appleby type out his comments; he insisted that they be entirely confidential and that they be returned to him immediately after they had been read. They were filed among his private papers and only came to light in the course of the preparation of this book; Bush had forgotten about them and could not recall who among the members of the committee had asked him to submit the memorandum.

The comments are on fourteen pages of ruled paper and appear to have been hastily scrawled, although they are quite legible; they summarize his views on national broadcasting, which have not changed much in all the years since and are remarkable for their maturity and perspicacity; he was only thirty-five at the time he wrote these notes and had had only three years in the new realm of national broadcasting.

His proposal for a Canadian Broadcasting Corporation to succeed the radio commission was similar to the one adopted. Only he saw its primary purpose as the development of "good, wholesome entertainment"; there was no mention of the objective of "national unity" which the Canadian Radio League liked to talk about. Bush would have regarded this as impractical dreaming ,and, at the end of the handwritten memorandum, he warned the committee against "idealists and pure theorists". The memorandum expressed his philosophy of broadcasting, a philosophy that was derived from the days when he was a singer and entertainer on the chautauqua circuit; information and education were worthwhile objectives but they could become propaganda—witness the "Mr. Sage" broadcasts. During the war, Bush was to help in the promotion of broadcasting as a propaganda instrument, and he came to regard the motto of the BBC, "And Nation Shall Speak unto Nation" as a pompous bit of empty rhetoric. In the end, what better objective could there be for broadcasting than that it should provide "good wholesome entertainment?"

It took almost a quarter of a century for one of his recommendations to be carried out, the transferral of regulatory functions from the CBC to the newly formed Board of Broadcast Governors. Bush suggested, in his memo, that both control of the private stations and technical supervision be returned to the radio branch of the Department of Marine. Later, as assistant general manager of the Canadian Broadcasting Corporation, he wished that the government had taken his advice as he listened to the constant clamour from the private operators about the "CBC being judge and prosecutor as well as competitor".

Most of the fourteen pages of his submission were devoted to finance, and it was apparent that, as a practical businessman, his advice had been sought on the costs. Furthermore, Ernie Bushnell had known how hard it was to put on a national service with the meagre budget that the CRBC had been allowed. "One thing," he wrote, "is apparent to me. Unless Canada intends to permit broadcasting to become relegated to a very obscure background, someone has to spend considerably more money than is being spent on its development at the present time." He estimated that seven million dollars were needed to provide "a sixteen-hour-a-day service of radio entertainment"; this amount could be obtained by raising the annual radio licence fee from two dollars to seven dollars, as there were a million sets in the country then, but such an increase "would appear to be quite out of the question". So, as a former private broadcaster who never saw anything wrong with commercials and believed that the majority of listeners did not object to a limited amount of advertising, Bushnell proposed that the new organization "be empowered definitely and aggressively to enter the advertising field in order to supplement revenue".

At the beginning of the handwritten memorandum, Bushnell admitted that he had been opposed to the "nationalization of radio" and had fought against it at the time of the 1932 parliamentary committee, but he had changed his mind and saw this now as a "thoroughly sound principle" which he was prepared to defend. The commission, however, which was the first expression of nationalization, had been part of the government's bureaucracy and was enmeshed in the government's red tape. He wanted the CBC to be a crown corporation quite separate from the civil service. He also proposed that the divided authority of the three commissioners be replaced by a single general manager with "an honorary and advisory board of directors".

The qualifications he listed for this post of general manager suggest that Bush had his eye on the job at the time, and would go a long way to explain his secretiveness about the memorandum. He wrote: "If one thing is needed more than another in the days to come, it is the necessity of having at the helm [of the CBC] a man with practical radio experience, a man who knows how and is capable of gauging for the future the requirements of the average radio listener; a man who understands the problems of the private station owner and who is willing at all times to lend a sympathetic ear; a man who is fearless of criticism (of which there will always be plenty); a man who is young enough in years, and has the necessary energy and health, yet old enough in wisdom to guide radio broadcasting through its many and varied vicissitudes."

9 The CBC and the News

On November 2, 1936, with the proclamation of the new Broadcasting Act, the Canadian Broadcasting Corporation officially came into being and the Canadian Radio Broadcasting Commission ceased to exist. The change at first was barely perceptible; the new corporation occupied the old commission offices in the National Research Council building on Sussex Drive; CBC signs replaced the former CRBC signs; quires of new letterheads were on order but meanwhile the secretaries x-ed out the old letterhead and typed in Canadian Broadcasting Corporation (and sometimes Canadian Broadcasting Company).

It was a happy enough transition after all the anxieties and anguish of the committee hearings that spring. Bushnell had seen W. E. Gladstone Murray, the newly appointed general manager, a few days before and had been assured by him that the Liberal government's wrath over the "Mr. Sage" broadcasts would not be visited on the CRBC's second level of management. The commissioners were summarily dismissed despite the fact that Hector Charlesworth and Colonel Steel had four years to go in their seven-year order-in-council appointments; their "shabby" treatment did not increase Bush's regard for politicians or make him very sanguine about his chances of survival in Ottawa. Once again, it was a case of hiring "know-how", and Bush remarked rather wryly that the powers-that-be were "not prepared to take a chance on the possibility of a complete collapse of the system at a time when to say the least, its framework was a bit shaky"; any axing of the real broadcasters would have brought about that collapse.

Alan Plaunt and a revived Canadian Radio League concentrated on getting their man appointed general manager and didn't worry about the lesser officials. Their man was Gladstone Murray, a senior BBC executive who had acted as an advisor to the Canadian government on broadcasting. The only other man in the running for the top job was Reginald Brophy, then station relations manager with the NBC and an executive of proven ability; he had run CFCF in Montreal, but it was as a salesman with the Canadian Marconi Company that had come to know every radio man in Canada. Brophy and Bushnell had travelled together through the west on more than one occasion, talking shop in the smoker of the pullman car while drinking rye from paper cups. Murray and Brophy represented the opposites in broadcasting, the anglicised Canadian with his elegant appreciation of the arts, and the hustling salesman with his knowledge of American commercial broadcasting.

From the beginning, Bushnell never figured Brophy had a chance, but Plaunt was concerned with the way that CFRB Toronto, CKAC Montreal and other private stations were lobbying for him, and by the fact that C. D. Howe and other ministers seem to be wavering in the support that he had wrung from them for Murray. Plaunt's best ploy was to harp on Brophy's commercial background, that he was working for the NBC, and this he did assiduously. He got the *Winnipeg Free Press* and the *Ottawa Citizen* to warn that if Brophy became general manager, broadcasting would "certainly pass into the US orbit". At the same time, the *Financial Post* was suggesting that Gladstone Murray was "too close to the BBC to realize all Canadian requirements".

When Plaunt heard that Mackenzie King had doubts about Gladstone Murray's reliability, he got Brooke Claxton to write to Norman Rogers, the minister of Labour and close confidant of the prime minister. Claxton did not attempt to defend Murray; instead, he spent most of the letter attacking Brophy, whom he described as a "Marconi production" who had always opposed national radio in Canada. The same sort of thing might have been said of Bushnell, and actually Brophy had not played as prominent a role as Bushnell in the struggle against

63

nationalized radio before the 1932 committee. Claxton asserted, in his letter to Norman Rogers, that Brophy "could not help unconsciously representing and taking the part of the private interests", and that his appointment would be a sell-out "to the private and predominantly American interests". However, the real condemnation of Brophy was contained in Claxton's declaration that a plain businessman, no matter how brilliant, unlike the socially conscious Murray, would not see the CBC as an instrument to strengthen national unity and "heal the rapidly widening gap between the races and sections of Canada".

Then Plaunt learned from John Dafoe, the editor of the *Winnipeg Free Press*, that the prime minister had been persuaded to support Murray but that most of the other ministers were leery—there were rumours about his drinking. In order to answer them, Plaunt insisted that Gladstone Murray write him a letter saying that he had not had a drink or a smoke for two years.

In the end, the opposition dissipated; William Ewart Gladstone Murray was named general manager, and Dr. Augustin Frigon, a distinguished Quebec educator and former member of the Aird Commission, became assistant general manager. It would have been difficult to imagine a board of which Alan Plaunt was a member appointing anyone else, but Plaunt knew that such appointments had to be approved by the government and that the real decision was the cabinet's. The first CBC Board of Governors set a high standard; in fact, Bushnell called it "probably the best board the CBC ever had". The chairman was Leonard W. Brockington and the vice-chairman, René Morin; among the members, besides Plaunt, were Nellie McClung, the author and feminist, and N. L. Nathanson of the Famous Players Corporation. While the members of the board were a remarkably distinguished group, they were, if not outright supporters of the Liberal party, well disposed towards it, or as Bush observed, there was not even by inference one who could have been said to be close to the Conservatives. They would have agreed to whomever the government wanted, even Reginald Brophy, although that might have led to Alan Plaunt's resignation.

Politics had played its part in the formation of the CBC, and some of the less reconstructed Liberal MPs might be forgiven for having regarded it as a new and promising area of political patronage. One of Bushnell's first jobs with the corporation was to put paid to this gravy train. By then, he had come to regard Gladstone Murray as a "pretty good guy" and "certainly not likely to become a carbon copy of Reith of the BBC", who represented, to Bushnell's mind, all that was harsh and magisterial about public broadcasting. Early in their association, Murray called Bushnell into his office to discuss a request from a group of Toronto Liberal members for some CBC jobs for their friends—they were demanding to see him.

"Ernie," the general manager said, rubbing his hands together, "you should know these monkeys rather well—why don't you go and talk to them?"

"Mind you," he went on, and with a twinkle in his eye which made Bush feel that he was up to some deviltry, "I don't want to give into them if you think their demands are unreasonable—but at least, listen to what they have to say."

So, Bushnell set off for Parliament Hill where he met with half a dozen Liberal MPs, among whom were Arthur Roebuck and Sam Factor. There were various complaints, expressed in general terms, of CBC employees taking part in politics, but the only specific charge laid was against one woman whose husband, it was claimed, "headed up the Tory publicity campaign in the last election". This was true enough, but the lady in question had been separated from her husband for five years and furthermore, as Bush pointed out, the husband was a freelance journalist who worked for both political parties and had been actively engaged in propagandizing for the provincial Liberal party headed by Mitch Hepburn. When he said that he looked quizzically at Roebuck who had recently broken with Hepburn. There were no more suggestions that anyone should be fired but the members did want jobs for their friends, and Sam Factor mentioned the name of Wishart Campbell, a leading baritone who had sung at some of the Liberal election rallies. Bushnell said that they would like to have him work for the

CBC, but what sort of salary did he expect?

"Not less than ten thousand dollars a year," said Sam Factor firmly.

"Good," Bush answered, "then you'd better give him my job, and at the same time increase the salary for the job by three thousand a year."

Another singer's name was mentioned, Branston Hall, a popular Caribbean tenor who had sung at some of Roebuck's meetings. When it turned out that he had been paid one hundred dollars a night, Bush chortled and told the members, "You were taken for sure—I've hired him many times in the past to do a broadcast recital for twenty-five." In any case, he said that he had on file a strong recommendation on behalf of this same singer from a former Conservative minister, and that seemed to end their interest in him. But Sam, who belonged to the old political school, was insistent.

"By God," he said, "we must have some appointments."

"I'll tell you what I'll do," Bush said. "If any of you have some really first-class stenographers in your constituencies, I'll hire them—provided, of course, they're as good as any others who may apply."

On that conciliatory gesture, the meeting ended. Sam Factor did forward applications from two young ladies living in his constituency. They were given the usual tests, proved to be capable secretaries and were hired.

Aside from this half-hearted and ineffectual attempt at patronage, the transition from the CRBC to the CBC took place in "orderly, well planned and well-organized" stages. The political heads of the commission had been axed, but no one else that Bushnell could recall was fired, the corporation inherited the whole staff of 160 persons; "scarcity of money" still restricted the staff to "skeleton dimensions". As might be expected, the first task was reorganization. Five production centres—Halifax, Montreal, Toronto, Winnipeg and Vancouver —were delineated in an internal memorandum from Gladstone Murray; the fact that Ottawa was left out was to inhibit the CBC's programming, especially in the important public affairs field, in the years to come. According to the memorandum, Dr.

Frigon was to assume "special responsibility for the organization and the work of the corporation in French-speaking Canada"; Bushnell was named head of the program department, although "Western Division" was still in parenthesis after his title. For all practical purposes, it meant that he was in charge of English-language programming while all the French-language programming would be left to Dr. Frigon. Donald Manson, who had been secretary to the Aird Commission and was secretary to the CBC Board of Governors, was made executive assistant to the general manager.

The newly formed CBC spent much of its early energy in a struggle with C. D. Howe, the minister through whom it reported to Parliament, on the fundamental issue of whether it was to have its own chain of high-powered transmitters. Mr. Howe was old-fashioned enough to regard the CBC as a production agency rather than a broadcasting corporation. But Brockington and the board, who were a formidable team, won. Two 50,000-watt stations were erected in the main population centres of Montreal and Toronto and were opened before Christmas 1937; two 15,000-watt stations which were capable of being boosted to 50,000 watts were planned for the Maritimes and the prairies. First things had to come first, and obviously domestic transmission and the urgent need to provide reception for the far corners of a vast country had to take precedence over foreign transmissions; in any case, the government had neither the inclination nor the funds to build a short-wave station, although this situation was hurriedly rectified during the war.

Then, there was the lack of news. Except for a pedestrian broadcast prepared entirely by the Canadian Press and bicycled around to the CBC where it was read over the air at eleven o'clock eastern time, there was no news. That might seem astonishing for a national system that was designed as a unifying force, but it was typical of the liberal idealists of the day who were afraid of a government agency, even one that they had created themselves, turning news into propaganda. In the end, it was Bushnell who urged the CBC to increase the number of newscasts and to set up its own news service; after a three-month visit to Europe in 1938, he wrote a separate report on the news in which he said: "In none of the countries that I have visited have the press or the daily newspapers the control of the broadcasting of news as is the case in Canada."

He had been sent overseas on a "fact-finding mission, the purpose of which was to investigate radio studios, their size and their accoustical qualities", as the corporation was planning to build new studio facilities for its high-powered stations. It was the first trip abroad for Ernie and Edna accompanied him as they intended to take their holidays over there. They arrived in England just in time for the Munich crisis.

As soon as he got to London, Bush called at Broadcasting House and met J. B. Clark, the director of foreign services, and a score of the BBC "top brass". He visited the BBC regional offices in Edinburgh, Glasgow, Belfast and Birmingham, as well as the Irish radio studios in Dublin. Edna went with him on this tour, and by the time they arrived in Birmingham they had begun to realize that they were sightseeing on the brink of war. They had been invited to a performance of *Victoria Regina*, and Bush recalls that the atmosphere was tense and expectant—in the next few hours, the world could be plunged "into a frightful holocaust", or so it was said or whispered. When they left the theatre, they saw a "long line of lorries loading gas masks". Early next morning, they took the train to London and, with hundreds of other frightened travellers, tried to arrange for passage home. The sight of men digging trenches in Green Park only increased their alarm, but they were so relieved by Prime Minister Chamberlain's "peace in our time" speech over the wireless, which they heard in the lobby of the Park Lane Hotel, that they cancelled their passage back and went on their grand tour of Europe, to Belgium, France, Italy, Switzerland, Germany and Holland.

While in Berlin, they were driven around the city in cars painted in camouflage colours which were said to have returned from service with the Wehrmacht in the Sudetenland. They were royally treated by Dr. Goebbels's officials but they breathed more easily when they boarded the overnight ferry at the Hook of Holland and returned to Britain, despite the suspicious, unfriendly looks they got from customs and immigration officers who "must have wondered what two Canadians were doing wandering around Europe at a time like that".

In his special report, Bushnell said that in the totalitarian states, the broadcasting of news was controlled by the governments. That came as a surprise to no one, but more interesting was the fact that in the democracies as well—Great Britain, Belgium, France and Switzerland—"this is perhaps the most important function of the state-controlled broadcasting systems". He went on to describe the way in which the Belgians broadcast the news in two languages—French and Flemish—each on its respective transmitter. Besides subscribing to two news services, Reuters and Havas, "the Belgians also have their own staff of reporters taken from the field of journalism".

Bushnell noted that "in London, the BBC has equal rights with the newspapers" to any government announcement, and that such an announcement was given simultaneously to the press and the broadcasters. This report was written late in 1938, but it took almost quarter of a century for the CBC to achieve such equality in Ottawa; it was not till 1959 that electronic reporters were admitted to the parliamentary press gallery on the same basis as newspaper reporters. Why should Canadians, of all people, show such servility to the press that they would allow it to control the broadcasting of news when, as Bush pointed out, this didn't happen in any other country he visited on his European tour?

The answer probably lies in the origins of the corporation. The CBC, unlike any other national system, was largely the creation of a group of intellectuals and idealists banded together in the Canadian Radio League. To begin with, Graham Spry and Alan Plaunt were beholden to the press in a very real manner; they were always seeking newspaper support for their campaigns and endeavours and may have felt that if the CBC were to broadcast its own news, the papers would regard this as a challenge and would oppose their concept of nationalized radio. Then, there was the fact that the CRBC and the CBC came into being during the rise of Hitler's Reich; there was a genuine fear among liberals of the day that behind every state broadcasting system lurked a Dr. Goebbels. The broadcasters themselves suffered from an inferiority complex as far as the newspapers were concerned; Bushnell touched upon it when he spoke of the "young upstart radio" seeking to challenge the press giant for advertising revenue. It was to disappear with the advent of television, when the newspapers tended to be treated rather contemptuously by broadcasters.

In the report, Bushnell gave an example of BBC reporting that he had witnessed: it happened on the morning that Prime Minister Chamberlain flew to Munich—

> He was not only met at the flying field by newspaper reporters but by the BBC with its microphones and recording equipment. That night in the news broadcasts, when referring to the departure of the prime minister, the technique used was something like this. "This morning the prime minister left for Munich. Before getting into the special aeroplane which was to take him to the important conference, he said"—and here a record of the prime minister's statement in his own voice was cut in.

Of course, the same statement had been carried in the newspapers, but Bushnell felt that the voice of the man who had made the statement had a much greater impact. He wanted the CBC to have the right to record such events:

> That is a concession that I feel the CBC must obtain without delay from the Canadian Press. In order to do this we may have to lengthen the period of the news broadcast. We may also have to establish in Montreal, Toronto and Vancouver a small news staff of former journalists—men qualified to judge proper news values. We will undoubtedly have to have more and better equipment and additional mobile pick-up facilities. Nevertheless I strongly recommend that steps be taken at once to see this is done.

Such a development would mean that the CBC would have to have more than one newscast a day, and Bushnell felt that the corporation owed it to the Canadian listeners who paid the annual two-dollar licence fee for their radio sets to provide them with a more complete news service. He said that the news should be "by far the most important function of a nationally operated broadcasting system such as ours".

The fact is that the BBC news has become an institution of national importance and justifies the existence of the BBC if for no other reason. I strongly urge that a definite plan of action be discussed as soon as possible and preparatory steps taken to strengthen what I consider one of the weakest links in our structure. I realize only too well that this may precipitate trouble between the CBC and the press but I am absolutely convinced that the time has come for us to give those who pay a licence more than we have been giving them in the past.

10 Royal Tour: For King and Empire

In the early summer of 1938, the Canadian Broadcasting Corporation went through an organizational convulsion, as a result of which it split amoeba-like into three parts: French-language broadcasting, English-language broadcasting and the headquarters staff. The division along linguistic lines had always been apparent but now it had been widened to an unbridgable chasm, for all those concerned with French-language broadcasting moved to Montreal, while the program and operations department of the English network moved to Toronto. Dr. Frigon, who had been given "special responsibility for the organization and the work of the corporation in French-speaking Canada", accompanied the broadcasters to Montreal; as he was also in charge of engineering, the engineering headquarters of the CBC was established in the Quebec metropolis. Ernie Bushnell, as supervisor of programs, became the senior officer of the corporation in Toronto and was, to all intents and purposes, the head of English-language broadcasting. The headquarters remained in Ottawa but left the National Research Council building on Sussex Drive for the Victoria building on Wellington Street. Gladstone Murray had a spacious office on the third-floor-front from which he could look out over the hill at the Peace Tower and "his masters" in the Parliament buildings; as assistant general manager, Dr. Frigon was part of the headquarters establishment and had an office next to the general manager's, but he seldom occupied it.

The move to Toronto added to the complexities of the Bushnells' first trip abroad and, when Ernie got back, he hardly had time to get used to his new office in the Monetary Times building on Church Street before he had to return to Ottawa to work on plans for the radio coverage of the royal tour. In a press release dated January 5, 1929, Prime Minister Mackenzie King outlined "certain guiding principles which are being followed by the Canadian authorities who are in charge of the arrangements for the visit to Canada of Their Majesties . . .". The principles were many, but they indicated a single patriotic purpose for this ceremonious junket, so heavily larded with pomp and circumstance: to rally support for King and Empire now that the threat of war was so clear.

A directive on "Royal Visit Broadcasting Policies" was issued by the station relations department of the CBC (another department that had accompanied programming and operations to Toronto) on March 10, but some time before that Bushnell had already assumed responsibility for the broadcasts and had begun work in a hotel bedroom in the Chateau Laurier. He had been asked to take the job by Walter S. Thompson, who was in charge of all press and publicity for the royal tour and who, in Bush's view, deserved most of the credit for the great success of this super-patriotic endeavour—after all, the first objective of the visit, according to the January 5 press release, came within Thompson's terms of reference, as it was "to enable as many Canadians as possible to see the King and Queen", and to make all Canadians aware of their presence.

Walter Scott Thompson was by any measure Canada's biggest public relations man: he was the publicity director of the Canadian National Railway, and he weighed a good three hundred pounds. He was a legendary figure—in fact, many claimed that he had invented public relations—and while he was alive, no one quite knew his age: there was a story that Hannen Swaffer, the great British journalist of the first part of the century, had shared a hansom cab with Walter Thompson when they were both drama critics on Fleet Street. According to his biography, he was born in Newcastle-on-Tyne; he worked for such forgotten papers as the *St. James Gazette* in London, and the *Montreal Witness* and the *Montreal Herald* after he came to Canada in 1911. In 1914, he was appointed press representative

73

of Grand Trunk and Grand Trunk Pacific Railways, and in 1922 became publicity director of the CNR. To succeeding generations of newspapermen he was an avuncular figure, old Uncle Canada, always singing the praises of the vast land that he had adopted, always telling them of the opportunities they had. He knew everyone from the prime minister to the lowliest cub reporter, and his advice was sought by everyone.

It was a rare education to see Walter Thompson at work: there he would sit beside the president of the CNR at a press conference, immaculate in his dark suit and white shirt with a starched white handkerchief sticking out of his breast pocket, a massive but elegantly dressed figure overflowing his easy chair like some benevolent monarch watching over a favorite satrap. Now and then he would shift his bulk to interrupt a reporter with the kindly and soft-spoken admonition that "you can't expect the president of the Canadian National Railway to answer that kind of a question". Thompson was a big man and public relations to him was a big job. He is credited with preventing the union of the Canadian National and the Canadian Pacific railways; he would have regarded such an achievement as being well within the realm and responsibility of public relations. Similarly, the royal tour, although there was no mention of it when he was awarded the CBE after the war. A great trencherman, which accounted for his girth, he liked to eat and drink and talk; his conversation, which he carried on in a mellifluous voice while chain-smoking Craven A cigarettes, was witty and amusing and, according to Bush and so many others, he was the best of companions. He retired from the CNR in 1950 but his advice on public relations was sought long after that, and he was to be in charge of a second royal tour, that of Princess Elizabeth and the Duke of Edinburgh, in 1951. It was only after his death in 1966 that his friends learned he was nearly 81.

The directive of March 10 made it clear that the CBC had control of all broadcasting of the royal visit; the man exercising that control was Ernie Bushnell, who had to look after not only Canadian broadcasters but the representatives of the BBC and the American networks as well. It was the first time that the CBC had exerted its authority on the whole national broadcasting system. The directive said that the private stations would not be allowed to "fade into or withdraw from Royal Visit broadcasts while the program is in progress"—in other words, the broadcasts had to be carried in their entirety or not at all. No commercials would be permitted, and "the fifteen-minute periods preceding and following the broadcasts during which either of Their Majesties speak before the microphone shall be free from commercial or other sponsorship".

There were to be two reporting teams covering the royal visit, according to this CBC directive, one to be headed by R. T. Bowman and the other by T. O. Wiklund. The idea was that these two teams would leapfrog each other; one would be broadcasting while the other was on the move or making preparations to broadcast. However, Bob Bowman and Wiklund were to be more than commentators—they were to be the corporation's liaison officers with the private stations, which had been told to make contact with them.

Actually, most of the commentators for the visit had to be specially recruited and trained, as the corporation in its short history had had no experience in broadcasting an occasion like this one. Bushnell recalls that they combed the private stations and other sources in Canada for commentators who would measure up to the standards required and, "after we had assembled such a staff, we brought the party to Ottawa for instruction". The men were taken to Government House where they were schooled in the proper terminology to be used in describing the progress of the King and Queen from place to place, and were acquainted with state dress and the intricacies of royal etiquette and tradition. As an "exam", they had to prove themselves in trial broadcasts. In addition to this instruction, the commentators had to be made familiar with the special equipment which would be used on the tour.

In a CBC bulletin on the broadcasting of the royal visit, dated May 6, 1939, Gladstone Murray said: "Probably no other problem of quite the same dimension has been faced before in broadcasting," and added that, previous to this, "the biggest actuality broadcasts were the coronation [1937], which lasted

75

only one day, and the Berlin Olympics, which lasted one week",
whereas the royal tour was to go on for a month. A great deal
of special equipment was required—remote amplifiers and
special microphones were designed by CBC engineers and were
purchased in wholesale lots—and Bushnell is proud of the fact
that some of this equipment was still in service thirty years
later. He told a service club luncheon in Saint John, NB, just
after the royal visit was over, that forty microphones had been
used to cover the arrival of the royal couple in Quebec City:
there was a double service for broadcasting in French and
English, and there were "stand-by mikes" for emergencies.

As the supervisor in charge of broadcasting, Ernie Bushnell
was assigned a place on the pilot train which preceded the royal
train by twenty minutes and was nicknamed the Bomber, as it
had the precautionary role of uncovering or exploding any
bombs that might have been placed on the track. The only
other CBC person on the train besides himself was Charles
Jennings; even Bush's faithful secretary, Georgie Appleby, was
with the first reporting team under Bob Bowman. In fact, most
of the corporation's staff, which numbered some four hundred
at the time, was engaged either directly or indirectly in
broadcasting the royal tour.

It was a great release for Bush to be on the train after all the
weeks of planning, of working in his hotel bedroom office on
endless memos, of sitting up nights in stuffy committee rooms
threshing out the details of this truly formidable operation.
Now there was nothing more for him to do, and he could relax
in the comforting knowledge that the reporting teams had the
best possible facilities that could be provided for their task; he
could relax and take delight in the imperial pageant moving
majestically across the vast dominion of Canada, from Quebec
City to Vancouver and Victoria and back, with departure from
Halifax. All of Bush's true-blue loyalty to the monarchy came
out in the reminiscences of the royal tour that he jotted down a
quarter of a century later.

He described the King and Queen "as two of the world's
most gracious people" and compared "one day, a high level
reception with pomp and ceremony, jewels, robed officialdom

76

and mink", with the next, a whistle-stop welcome that "erupted spontaneously from hundreds of young and old alike, many of whom had driven for hours and stood for many more in the shade of a lonely prairie grain elevator". He said "Scenes like these beggar description but many were among the most moving it has been my privilege to watch and many were beyond the literary ability of any save a poet laureate to describe." He added "Only a few times in the history of man have such scenes taken place as those it was my privilege to witness on the royal tour."

Since the government refused to provide any special subsidy, the CBC was short of funds, and Bushnell claims that he spent five hundred dollars of his own money in buying formal clothes so that he could properly represent the corporation. He was glad that he had done so, because a morning coat or white tie and tails became as necessary as an accreditation card if one didn't wish to risk being manhandled by the police as a gate crasher. Apparently the police, including the RCMP, were even more forceful in guarding royal personages before the war, and Bush recounted that on the night they left Quebec City, some of the photographers on the train "nursed open wounds caused by blows from the truncheons of an over-zealous constabulary". The supervisor in charge of photographers, he said, came to his bedroom on the Bomber that night and swore that he was through, that he would resign, that he wouldn't go through that kind of thing again—"those bloody cops, who in the hell do they think they are"—and, having delivered himself of this, rolled over and went to sleep in Bush's bed.

Most of Bushnell's memories have to do with broadcasting. For instance, when the King and Queen landed at Quebec City at the beginning of their tour, a veteran radio reporter was so overcome with emotion that he froze. Not a sound, not even a splutter came from his lips; it was as if he had been turned to stone. However, none of the listening audience knew that this had happened because Bush, who was acting as director for this broadcast, seeing the reporter's plight, signalled Bob Bowman who gave a "lucid and heart-warming" description of the landing. After the official greetings the royal entourage started slowly up the hill, and Frank Willis took over. He was perched high in a church steeple, the home of hundreds of pigeons, and the commotion they made and their angry cries blended with the rich, vibrant tones of Frank's voice.

Next day, in Ottawa, "a red-breasted robin in a nearby maple tree provided a joyous welcome to Their Majesties as the Queen laid the cornerstone of the new Justice building". Bushnell heard the re-broadcast of this program late that night and angrily ordered the producer to put a stop to "any more such nonsense as the insertion of recorded sound effects"; to his astonishment, he learned that the robin was for real. However, it was in the country that the most memorable scenes occurred. Bush recalls the arrival of the King and Queen at the town of Melville, Saskatchewan, which had a population of 4,000: "But there were six to eight times that number lining the streets, and most of the people were from Central Europe, with not a drop of British blood in their veins."

There was the odd ugly incident and Bushnell was as indignant as any loyal monarchist would be when a woman reporter from a mass-circulation American paper wrote intimate details about life aboard the royal train—she claimed to have eluded the guards and visited the train while it was at a siding in Montreal. No one really believed her description of the Queen's "undies", and such below-the-belt reporting was not appreciated. On another occasion, Bushnell threatened a second American who was going to report a private conversation with the King and Queen. Ernie said that he would put on a broadcast to expose the drunken and insulting behaviour of this columnist, who had embarrassed everyone with the questions that he put to the royal couple at a press party in the Banff Springs Hotel. At this, Walter Thompson intervened, and said that the freedom of the press to print anything it liked must be upheld—but somehow that story never came out; the copy was lost or, as Bush says with a grin, "the telegraph key refused to work that night".

The next day was Sunday, and most of the reporters missed the train because they didn't go to church. According to the printed instructions, the King and Queen were to return to the hotel after the church service, which would have left plenty of time for the correspondents to board the Bomber. However, "some idiot" didn't follow the schedule, and the royal couple proceeded directly from the church to their train, leaving more than a hundred stranded at the Banff Springs Hotel.

It was the only time, Bush said, that he saw the urbane Walter Thompson really angry. He and his aides rounded up three charabancs, piled the newsmen and their luggage into these open-topped buses and took off in hot pursuit of the Bomber and the royal train. It was a magnificent scenic drive, but a rather terrifying experience for those unused to the mountain road with its rocky curves and sheer drops of hundreds of feet to the chasms below. Some of them didn't dare look over the sides of the buses. They expected to catch up with the trains at Lake Louise but didn't quite make it; they drove on, swallowing dust from the gravel road and getting drenched with rain even when the canvas tops were up. As the buses swung around one curve on the edge of a precipice, the *Toronto Star*'s Fred Griffin muttered under his breath: "Jesus, Jesus, oh Jesus." He paused, and then turned to Bush. "You know, Ernie," he explained, "I'm not swearing, I'm praying." Finally, after what was the worst trip of the tour, they caught up with the royal train at Field, British Columbia.

Once aboard the Bomber there was comfort and well-being and entertainment. A floating crap game moved between the dining car and the observation car. However, Bushnell had his own peculiar problems. Although he was in charge of all broadcasting and had to look after some twenty radio correspondents across the country, the fact was that "radio those days didn't seem to be very important to the correspondents of the *Times* of London, or the *New York Herald Tribune*, or the *Los Angeles Examiner*." It was the contempt of the well-established for the newcomer, and Bush had a hard time getting his fair share of press passes. "However," he wrote, "by fair means or foul, by placations and promises, sometimes by pooling and sometimes by swapping, we managed to get in to see the show and most of my boys on the train went to bed reasonably happy."

At the end of this historic royal visit, Bushnell recorded his impressions of the departure from Halifax. It was sunny and warm. All the passengers of the Bomber were invited aboard ship to say farewell. Crowds lined the harbour, and "a thousand-voice choir sang prayerfully 'Will ye no come back again', the strains of which echoed and re-echoed from every loyal heart throughout the nation." Although his heart was full, Bushnell does recall a gaffe by a CBC announcer which was almost as good as "the fleet's all lit up" but never got the same publicity. Bob Anderson was on one of the reporting teams and he described the way the royal ship set sail. "There she goes," he said. "The Queen is standing on the deck, and you should see the sun shining on her stern."

11 War Reporting as Never Before

During the war, the task of "welding together the diverse elements of the population" which had been given to the CBC by Parliament took on a much greater sense of urgency; the CBC was to become the main instrument for keeping the home fires burning and maintaining the nation's confidence and morale. As such, it was to be drawn tighter into the open arms of government; war-time restrictions, including censorship, made such a shift inevitable. It was a time when Ernie Bushnell could say that the corporation "with honour and distinction fulfilled the role envisaged of it by those who founded and launched it". Not only was he in charge of programming from coast to coast, but he organized the CBC war reporting, a unique contribution in that it brought the sound of battle to the Canadian hearth and was acknowledged to be a much more comprehensive coverage than that provided by the vaunted American network. This was due to Bush's insistence that "each war correspondent or newsman had to have adequate recording facilities which required the personal attention of a first-class engineer".

On the evening of Monday, December 4, 1939, Bushnell rang Bob Bowman at his apartment in Toronto: He wanted to know where the portable recording equipment was and how soon Bob could get to Halifax with it. There was a mysterious urgency about his call, and he could only answer Bob's questions by saying: "Don't ask me why because I don't know. How soon can you start?" Bush had been phoned a few minutes before by the general manager, W. E. Gladstone Murray, who had told him that the CBC had been allotted a place with the first Canadian troops to sail overseas. Bowman, intrigued by Bushnell's secretiveness, was eager to go but all he had on him was twenty-five cents; Bush told him not to worry, that he would scrape together a few bucks somehow.

There was a train leaving for Halifax within the hour, and Bushnell was at Union Station with twenty-five dollars he had borrowed from Edna; he gave Bowman the money together with the further instruction that, on reaching Halifax, he should report to the local military commander, Major General C. F. Constantine. After giving the password, "Constantinople", he would be told what his mission was all about.

When Bowman reached Halifax two days later, he had no need to ask why he had been sent there. Five great liners, the *Aquitania,* the *Empress of Britain* the *Empress of Australia,* the *Duchess of Bedford* and the *Monarch of Bermuda* were at dockside, while at anchor in the stream was the British battleship, *Resolution.* Obviously, Canadian troops were going overseas. However, while General Constantine informed him that the First Canadian Division would be sailing in a few days' time, which was something he had already surmised, the military commander didn't tell Bowman that he was to accompany the troops overseas. This was the first recorded SNAFU (Situation Normal All Fouled Up).

Bowman had figured out on his own that he should sail with the First Division, not just cover its departure, and did not know this had been authorised. After pondering the situation, he telephoned Bushnell. While war-time security forbade any mention of troops or ships, "I explained things as best I could," Bowman said later, "without actually being able to tell him what it was all about." At any rate, Bush twigged on to what had happened, and got on to the Department of National Defence immediately. For once, the mills of bureaucracy moved quickly. Authorization was received in the form of a telegram from the director of Military Operations and Intelligence: ALL ARRANGEMENTS MADE STOP PARTY SHOULD REPORT TO OC COMMA MD6.

Art Holmes was the engineer selected to accompany Bowman. Again, he didn't know what the assignment was, but followed instructions and took the train to St. John, NB; there, he was told to take the ferry across the Bay of Fundy. On the other side, at Digby, NS, he was met by a CBC car which drove him to the Halifax pier where the *Aquitania* was berthed. He joined Bob Bowman aboard the great liner packed with Canadian troops on the night before the convoy sailed.

Shortly after the First Division reached Britain, a special program about the crossing put together by Bob Bowman was broadcast by "trans-Atlantic beam"; the CBC described it as "a unique departure in war-time news coverage". It was certainly the first time that the actual sounds of troop movement—of the entertainment aboard ship, of the men marching ashore—had been broadcast, all of which was due to recordings cut by Art Holmes. (The American networks had a rule that forebade the use of recordings in news programs, which was to hamper their coverage of the Second World War.) The broadcast was so well received that it was decided "to leave the Overseas Unit, as it became known, in England for a period of four to six weeks to see what would develop". However, it didn't take that long to persuade the corporation that it had started something which would not only have to be continued for the duration of the war, but would have to be expanded. So, the general supervisor of programs was ordered to go overseas to survey the situation and make a report as to what future plans should be.

Ernie Bushnell set sail from New York on the *Britannic* at the end of February 1940, and arrived in London on March 8. First of all, he wanted to find out whether there was enough program material available—this was, after all, the period of the Phoney War when nothing was happening—and he was given immediate reassurance. Then he discussed with Bob Bowman and Art Holmes his main concern, which was to have a CBC unit accompany the First Canadian Division into action. "At that time [March 10th]," he wrote in the report he made on his return, "it was presumed that this move on the part of the forces would take place about May 1st and their destination was to be France." Bushnell, Bowman and Holmes decided that they would have to see the Canadian commander, General A. G. L. McNaughton, about this.

An appointment was made, but before going to Aldershot Bushnell talked to the BBC about the use of their short-wave service for transmitting CBC programs to Canada. This was a necessary bit of housekeeping. Until then, the output of the Overseas Unit had been relayed to Canada "by means of the radio/telephone-beam circuit which, while somewhat more convenient, more reliable and less subject to atmospheric disturbances, was also very costly". The plain fact was that the CBC could not afford the heavy telephone-beam charges if it were to have the planned regular service of an hour or more of programming a week; Bush proposed that the BBC should carry this programming on its short-wave services directed at Canada and North America. He took up the matter first with J. B. Clark, the assistant controller of overseas programming, and also explained his proposition to F. W. Ogilvie, the director general.

While he did not get any committment, he felt that their reaction was sufficiently encouraging to allow him to go ahead with his interview with General McNaughton. Bushnell and Bowman spent an hour and a half with the Canadian commander discussing the possibility of CBC personnel with a mobile recording truck accompanying the First Division to France. The general agreed and said that "he would help us in every way he could in obtaining for our staff of two observers [Bowman was to be joined by Gerrard Arthur, who was to be the French-language commentator] and one technician [Holmes] the full and accredited status of war correspondents". Bushnell wrote in his report: "Up to this point in our discussions everything appeared to be moving along the exact channel we had hoped it would."

However, "the picture changed somewhat when General McNaughton went on to outline the plan he envisaged for broadcasting in co-operation with a motion-picture unit," with both groups to be put under the command of an army officer. Bushnell bristled at this attempt to gain military control of the Overseas Unit but kept his own counsel. It was perhaps because of his experience in private broadcasting that he was ever mindful of threats to the independence of the CBC and its freedom of action. Before going to Aldershot, he had wondered

84

whether the close association with the Overseas Unit with the First Division would not inhibit its coverage of the air force. He had heard that "there was a certain amount of jealousy existing between the CASF [Canadian Active Service Force] and the RCAF". His misgivings were even greater now that he knew what the general wanted to do with this newfangled radio reporting unit.

On the way back to London, Bushnell discussed the matter with Captain (later Colonel) Bill Abel, the public relations officer for the CASF. Abel served as a liaison officer between the broadcasters and the brass; Bush had a high regard for this former advertising executive and remembers that, after each of the many times he got the broadcasters out of a scrape, Bill would hitch up his uniform and deliver himself of a short lecture in his gruff boardroom voice on how to avoid running foul of the military. Abel advised Bush to "seek the advice of the High Commissioner, Mr. Vincent Massey, and his assistant, Mr. [Lester B.] Pearson". The following day found Bush at Canada House explaining the problem to Mr. Massey and Mr. Pearson.

"The High Commissioner advised us to attach our Overseas Unit to the GHQ of the British Expeditionary Force and not to the HQ of the Canadian Active Service Force," he wrote in his report. When Bush wondered aloud whether General McNaughton would not feel slighted, Mr. Massey offered to explain the CBC position to him, that the Overseas Unit had to cover the activities of all services and might be inhibited in this task if it were attached to the First Division. The High Commissioner added that he "would make applicaton on our behalf to the War Office".

This proved to be fortuitous, for Bushnell learned immediately after his visit to Canada House that Bill Abel had been in touch with the War Office, and that his request (made presumably at General McNaughton's behest) for permission for a Canadian broadcasting unit and a motion-picture unit to accompany the First Division to France had been flatly refused. Bush told Abel of the discussions he had had at Canada House and said that he "felt confident that with Mr. Massey's endorsation of our plans we could not fail".

Since Canada House did not expect any reply from the War Office for some days, Bushnell decided that this would be a good time to go to Paris. If the Overseas Unit were allowed to go to France with the Canadian troops, there would have to be arrangements made with the French broadcasting agency (Paris Mondial), similar to those they were trying to make with the BBC, for the transmission of the unit's material. So Ernie and Bob Bowman set off, after spending "two days getting our passports, visas and permits to export money". They enjoyed themselves greatly, and saw little to indicate that there was a war on. In any case, "what fighting there had been had almost come to a standstill behind the Maginot Line". It was a fool's paradise, the last Easter before the fall of France The weather was balmy, the boulevard cafés full. They called on Pierre Dupuy, who was then second secretary of the Canadian Legation, and met the minister, Colonel Georges P. Vanier, both of whom were interested and helped them to meet the right people. The French radio officials were friendly and co-operative and quickly agreed to put "their facilities at the CBC's disposal for two thirty-minute periods every week".

When Bushnell and Bowman returned to London on Friday, March 22, they were chagrined to find only a skeleton staff at Broadcasting House—most of the BBC executives had taken off for the long Easter weekend, and "we were able to accomplish very little until the following Tuesday". It is apparent from his report that Bushnell was becoming increasingly impatient with the slow, deliberate ways of the British, and with what seemed to him to be "delaying tactics". They had come back early from Paris because they were anxious to get the question of the transmissions to Canada settled, only to find everyone on holiday—didn't they know there was a war on? It was not till the end of the next week that Bush was able to report: "The BBC agreed to provide the CBC with one thirty-minute period and two fifteen-minute periods weekly on Daventry for programming especially designed for Canadian listeners."

Another irritation was the "cubby-hole of an office" provided for the Overseas Unit, scarcely big enough for Bob

Bowman, Art Holmes and the recording equipment, let alone a visitor or someone to be interviewed. More serious was the evident desire of top BBC officials to have the unit become part of their war-reporting team. "You know, the British were still treating us as colonials," Bush says. He soon disabused the BBC of this imperialist scheme; he did tell them that he was willing to let certain CBC personnel come over and join the war-reporting team (among the first to do so was Stanley Maxted, who was to gain lasting fame for his broadcasts of the ill-fated Arnhem jump), but they would be joining as individuals. The Overseas Unit, he said firmly, was part of the CBC and quite separate from the BBC.

Before returning to Canada, Bushnell had another row with the BBC. It was over his request for additional CBC periods on the forces program. When BBC officials became "sticky" about this, Bush expressed surprise at their attitude, and said that "Canada would soon have one hundred thousand soldiers within range of their transmitters, and unlike the main body of the forces of the United Kingdom, these men had left their homes and families for the duration of the war". It was only when he warned that he was "quite prepared to make an issue of this" that they capitulated.

It took some three weeks for the War Office finally to give its consent to the dispatch of the CBC Overseas Unit to France, but Bushnell had never been concerned about this; he had been "completely confident" that a request made by the Canadian High Commissioner would not be turned down. The members of the Overseas Unit would be accredited as war correspondents, which meant that they had to fill out forms, be inoculated and vaccinated, and be suitably uniformed. Bush arranged for the CBC correspondents to be outfitted at Burberry's in the Haymarket.

Early in April, he got a cable from Gladstone Murray saying that the rest of the staff he had requested (Gerrard Arthur, the French-language broadcaster; Gerald Wilmot, who was to take Bob Bowman's place in London when the Overseas Unit moved to France; and Albert Altherr, another engineer) would leave Canada on April 10 but that the earliest date for the shipment of the recording van would be May 1. As Bushnell noted in his report, "the former was welcome news but the latter was disturbing". The date of the departure of the First Division for France had been set at May 15, and Bushnell was particularly anxious that the van should be in England ready to move with the Canadian forces. However, before he returned he learned that the movement had been postponed till June 1, and the Nazi sweep through the Low Countries and the catastrophic Battle of France meant that the recording van was to arrive in plenty of time. At the end of his report, Bushnell wrote: "I think it is also important that we should begin looking about for replacements for the men of our staff already in the field. The danger element cannot be overlooked entirely— neither can the stress and strain upon the minds and thoughts of these men be entirely disregarded. Their youthful ardour may stand them in good stead for a while but it is almost a foregone conclusion that eventually, because of the hardships they are almost certain to have to endure, they will begin to lose their grip. When that time comes others must be ready to replace them if the CBC is to maintain and raise the standard which, I am fully confident, our present staff will set." These were prescient words, for Bowman and Arthur had gone and an entirely new generation of CBC correspondents was to cover the Canadian forces in action; only the veteran engineer, Art Holmes, remained.

12 British Propaganda Chief

It was the middle of May 1940 when Ernie Bushnell returned to Canada, and there was never a more fateful time during the war. The Battle of France was raging and Nazi panzer forces had smashed their way to the English Channel; although there was at first hopeful talk of the new and extraordinary "elastic defence" containing the invaders, soon there was no hiding the magnitude of the disaster in slick commentaries or censored news reports. Europe was gone; it was Hitler's. Never before had so much territory been conquered in such a short time, and there were not many Canadians who would have given much for Britain's chances of survival. Yet, by the middle of August, just three months later, Bushnell was back in the old country; he reached London at the beginning of the Blitz.

The BBC had asked him to help them, the same BBC with whom he had fought only a short time before. Bush was astonished. "I thought I'd be a most unlikely person," he admits, but there was the letter requesting his secondment to the BBC to direct the reorganization of their North American short-wave service, lying on the CBC general manager's desk with Gladstone Murray rubbing his hands in that gleeful manner he had when there was good news to impart. "We're very proud that they should have asked you," the general manager said, "and I think I would have to say that you should accept."

Aside from his run-in with the BBC when he was organizing the CBC's war reporting, Bushnell had written a report after his first 1938 visit to the United Kingdom that was hardly complimentary. While admitting that the majority of Britons might like the BBC service, he charged that the corporation "cares very little about the wishes of the listeners". He compared the BBC to a young and healthy tree "which in its very early youth began to bear good fruit" until its owner said: "What a perfect thing I have produced—now I can sit back and reap the benefits of my labour" and forgot to use the pruning knife and the spray, "the one to lop off excess limbs and leaves and the other to kill the parasites". Bush was writing as an unregenerate private enterpriser who had been conscripted into the public service and had come to regard the BBC as all that was bad about nationalization; he was afraid that the CBC when it had reached maturity would go the way of the BBC. Bushnell could make no greater condemnation of British broadcasting than to say that it had "lost sight of its primary function—to entertain and instruct its listeners". However, he did recognize that there was enthusiasm, even in a blighted socialist state, for any new development, and said: "There is one branch of the BBC that I feel can be rightfully exempt from criticism, that is the new department of television." There was an entirely different atmosphere there, despite the fact that in 1938 the TV directors were recruited mainly from BBC pioneers. "They seem to have a new lease on life and a new joy in again being able to cut fresh sod. It is a spirit kindred to that which I believe exists in the CBC today." Later in his report, he wondered if he hadn't been unfair and left the impression that everything was wrong with the BBC, which was not true. It had "excellent personnel" and "first-class facilities and studios" but, he added, "What it seems to lack is either a soul or a purpose or both."

Then, there were personal relations: Ernie Bushnell, brought up in the fast-talking, wise-cracking, North American entertainment circuit, found most of the BBC executives, who were almost all products of the British ruling-class, public-school system, to be languid dilettantes; Bushnell and the "old boys" brushed each other the wrong way, and there was little understanding or communication. However, Bush did mention one exception in the report that he wrote on his visit to the United Kingdom to organize the CBC's war reporting: R. A. "Tony" Rendall. He had been the first assistant to Gerald Cock, the head of the first BBC-TV studio at Alexandra Palace, which discontinued production with the war. Rendall "seemed to have a greater realization of the needs of the Dominions than anyone with whom I had come into contact up to that time," Bushnell reported. "We had many long and interesting discussions," and Bush was delighted when Rendall was appointed first assistant to J. B. Clark, the acting chief of the overseas service, and became "the liaison between members of our Overseas Unit and the Overseas Programme Division of the BBC".

It was because he would be serving under Tony Rendall that Bushnell accepted the invitation to become North American program organizer, and he said years later that he suspected Rendall was largely responsible for the BBC asking him in the first place. "I suppose," Bush said, "they wanted someone with a firm hand who knew the broadcasting scene in North America. I suppose they figured that I was a tough guy because I had stood up to them, that I was tough enough to deal with their producers and make them conform to American and Canadian production patterns."

After some hesitation, he decided to go—it would mean being separated from Edna and his daughter for the duration of the war (that was the length of the appointment, according to a confidential memo that he had received), but Ernie regarded this as his duty and part of the sacrifice that so many Canadians were making to win the war. The BBC agreed to pay Bushnell's salary, then $7,100 a year, into his Canadian bank account while giving him a subsistence allowance of four hundred pounds a year; a wire to Rendall in response said that Bush was "ready to set sail at ten days notice".

On August 4, he left New York City on the *Britannic*. It was the third time that he was to make the wartime crossing of the Atlantic on this ship and, as he boarded her, the purser said: "Look here, Bushnell, don't you get the idea this is a ferry boat." It was a pleasant, uneventful voyage, and he whiled away much of the time playing bridge with his fellow first-class passengers; they included a secret-service agent returning to England from Japan, and Frank Fisher, a great hulking man with a dark saturnine appearance who was head of British

United Press, as it was then called, in Canada. Bush's main recollection of that trip was bidding and making a grand slam in no trumps, doubled and vulnerable.

The morning after the *Britannic* docked in Liverpool found Bushnell in Broadcasting House, meeting the officials with whom he was to be closely associated in the months ahead, when the air-raid siren sounded. It was the first time that he had heard its banshee wail, and he doesn't mind admitting that it sent a shiver down his spine. He was with the director general of the BBC and, at Ogilvie's suggestion, they left his office and made their way to the concert studio, a large studio in the middle of the building that served as a bomb shelter. It was piled high with mattresses which had been provided for the staff in case they could not get home because of the raids that were expected but had not begun yet. Bushnell wondered idly whether the siren was some kind of a warning to him, whether Hitler was trying to frighten him away from reorganizing the North American service. That evening he was taken down to the sub-basement and shown his bunk.

However, after spending one night in that "prison cell" Bushnell decided to get the hell out bombs or no bombs, and he and Bob Bowman found quarters above ground. They changed their domicile a couple of times and ended up in a furnished apartment on the third floor of a luxury block for which they paid five pounds a week—the lessee had fled at the time of Dunkirk and was glad to sublet at any price. The apartment, which was only a short distance up Portland Street from Broadcasting House, became a headquarters for all CBC personnel in London at the time. Although the buildings around—including their favorite pub—were bombed and blasted, their block somehow escaped a direct hit.

Before he made any changes, Bushnell had to know what was being produced on the North American service, so night after night he listened on a pair of earphones to the transmission. His listening post was a corner of the underground canteen at Broadcasting House; since the short-wave program didn't start till midnight and continued into the small hours of the morning, he was assaulted by the penetrating odours of fried kippers and the wartime "sawdust" sausages. There was also the stench of Brussels sprouts left stewing in the pot from the dinner meal— ever since, he hasn't been able to face a Brussels sprout. (Another British culinary favourite that he became hardened against had the whimsical name of Bubble and Squeak and was, as he recalls, a fried hash of left-over potatoes and cabbage.)

When he returned to Canada, the weekly periodical *Saturday Night* asserted that Bushnell was to blame for cutting out the classic abject apology of BBC announcers on fluffing, the way they blurted out: "Oh, I say, I'm so awfully sorry. I read that badly. I'll read the item again." Undoubtedly Bush had done so, and his argument was that, while this might be considered delightfully quaint and terribly-terribly British, such an interruption would spoil the average listener's concentration on the message that was being broadcast. However, that was a very small part of his job of making the BBC programs acceptable to Canadian and American radio stations for rebroadcasting. And that was the aim of the short-wave service, not so much to be heard by listeners in Canada and the United States on their own receiving sets, but to have its programs recorded by stations in both countries and put out again at a good listening time.

In order to make that possible, Bushnell had also to see that BBC programs could be fitted into the rigid North American time slots. He pointed out that a fifteen-minute program was just thirteen minutes long, and that a half-hour program must be twenty-seven minutes long—no more, no less. It was easier said than done as the British producers had had no experience in timing programs—a drama could run to one hour and thirty-two minutes or two hours and one minute, while talks might be five minutes long, or nine, sixteen, or twenty-five minutes, and musical programs were as long as the artist took to play the numbers. Who would dare to tell Myra Hess, the concert pianist, that she must tailor Beethoven to fit into so many minutes? Some of the BBC producers went so far as to say that it could not be done and should not be done; that, if it weren't immoral, it was at least a violation of artistic freedom. After many conferences, Ernie, in his down-to-earth manner, said that they'd better bloody well subscribe or they'd be sabotaging the war effort, and most of the producers came to recognize the need for timing; then he had to tackle the famous authors and artists, such as J. B. Priestley, Leslie Howard, Wickham Steed, Sir Phillip Joubert, Sir Hugh Walpole, Vernon Bartlett, and others who had never heard of this bit of North American "nonsense" and resented having their scripts cut or expanded. However, they came to accept "Bush's new rules", especially when they began receiving congratulatory letters, and even fan mail, from the rebroadcasts of their programs in Canada and the United States. After that, there was no more trouble about the length of a program and actually, as Bushnell pointed out, the time limitation often had the effect of "sharpening up" a commentary.

Bushnell was responsible, too, for the content of the broadcasts and, while he didn't have as much of a struggle over this as over timing, he did insist that there should be more American voices on the short wave. The United States had a large and competent corps of war correspondents on hand and they were only too eager to report what was happening. "Americans, British and Canadians alike, each in his own way, and each melded into a well-co-ordinated, well-balanced and well-conceived schedule of programs, gave freely and enthusiastically of their talents to report hour by hour, day by day, events and incidents . . . which might have the effect of enlightening important people who listened across the Atlantic, and of eventually stirring them up to the point of joining those who were determined at all costs to ensure survival and a future freed from Nazi domination."

From that statement, it is evident that Ernie Bushnell was as much a propagandist for the British as the Minister of Information, Brendan Bracken. In fact, years later, he was to say: "What we were trying to do was to drag America into the war." They were helped in this effort, which proved to be entirely successful, by Edward R. Murrow, the celebrated correspondent of the Columbia Broadcasting System; Ed Murrow lived across the way from Broadcasting House and Bush recalls seeing him after he had been bombed out, and all his papers destroyed. "Murrow was heartbroken," he said. "He was supposed to have written the book about Hitler's Reich instead of William Shirer, and would have done so if his papers had not been burned up."

There was one crisis over content—it occurred when J. B. Priestley was sent to Scotland to report on the whiskey industry. At the time, exports were of prime importance to the United Kingdom. "Naturally," Bushnell says, "to give an authentic report, J. B. had to sample the product. His broadcast originated in Glasgow and was sent down the line to London. I was asked to listen to it before it was to be transmitted. I cancelled it because I was quite sure that the temperance people and their ilk in Canada and the United States wouldn't understand how an author of world-wide fame could become quite so incoherent. Later, J. B. and I had a good laugh about this incident and he readily admitted that it had been a wise decision."

By forcing the BBC programs to fit into the North American quarter- and half-hour time slots, Bushnell was getting wide rebroadcast distribution throughout Canada and the United States. So successful was he that, as one wag put it, Bushnell outdid Goebbels, and there was no doubt that British propaganda put German propaganda in the shade on the North American continent during the Second World War. The *Ottawa Journal* ran an editorial that claimed: "Since Ernest L. Bushnell went over from Canadian Broadcasting headquarters in Toronto to direct the BBC's Empire [sic] Service, short-wave broadcasting from London has eclipsed German broadcasting or the short-wave service of any other country."

All of this was accomplished during the Blitz, with its disruptions and bombings. On many a night, Bushnell and Bob Bowman would crawl up the fire escape to the top of their ten-storey apartment block to see the fearful fireworks; they didn't like standing on the roof watching the flashes of explosions and the tracer making patterns in the sky while the shrapnel from the "ack-ack" guns came clattering down, but they didn't like huddling in the basement shelter any better. There was something that drove them to the apartment-block roof, the reporter's compulsion to see history in the making, and it was from this vantage point that they saw the second great fire of London on a Sunday night, December 29, 1940. Bushnell described it in a national broadcast he made on returning to Canada:

> . . . there was an amazing, almost incredible sight. Certainly, we had never seen a fire like that before. We couldn't tell just where it was but judged it wasn't far from Fleet Street. They must have dropped thousands of incendiaries. We came down and had dinner. Bowman called Holmes and asked him to drive us down toward the fire. Holmes agreed and brought two friends along. They called for us about 9:15. Our fighters had been up and chased the enemy away—the gunfire had ceased. A great pall of smoke, lit by a lurid glow, overhung the capital. Big buildings looked like ghosts—church spires like ivory spears. We left our car at the Haymarket and walked through Trafalgar Square, down the Strand, turned toward the river, and along the Embankment to Blackfriars Bridge. Dozens of fire engines roared by. I had forgotten my helmet so kept an eye peeled for a handy shelter in case the bombers returned. We wondered why they didn't. By then we could see the dome of St. Paul's silhouetted against the flames. The church itself didn't seem to be on fire but it appeared as if only a miracle could save it. Silently I cursed the Nazis. We walked along and saw another church—this one already gutted. I thought of the Christmas service there had been there last Wednesday—"Peace on earth, good will toward men," the little choir boys sang. We asked ourselves when they would sing it again, and where. We walked on toward Fleet Street, scrambling over thousands of feet of hose lying everywhere six to eight inches deep and looking like snakes that had crawled out of the river. St. Bride's Church, too, was on fire but the spire still stood. Again we wondered why they always seemed to hit churches and hospitals. We talked to bystanders, for there were hundreds about. One old chap said, "Rare show tonight guv'ner—'e was throwin' them down like cans of condensed milk 'e was." An old woman, who looked like Apple Annie in the movie, ran in and out of her basement doorway with cups of hot tea for

the firemen. Plenty of canteens about but I guess she wanted to do her bit too. But her action struck me as odd. Where would she get a fresh supply, with tea rationed? I couldn't get the old lady out of my mind for it seemed to me she understood the true meaning of equality of sacrifice. The firemen understood too and they were grateful to her, for the night was cold. For almost two hours we wandered rather aimlessly in and about those narrow streets. Then the AA guns barked, and we scurried for shelter—but the firemen didn't. We struck out at a brisk pace to pick up our automobile and while walking down the Strand the "All Clear" sounded and Big Ben chimed a quarter to twelve.

Art Holmes was a most enterprising engineer: he was determined to get a recording of a direct bomb hit, and set out night after night in the CBC recording van for Hyde Park. There, in that open space in the midst of London, he felt sure he would capture in permanent form the whole ghastly symphony: the wailing of the sirens, the drone of the approaching enemy bombers, the crack and crunch of the anti-aircraft artillery and the slap and splatter of the shrapnel falling on the roofs, mixed with the whistling scream of the five-hundred-pound or thousand-pound bombs and the earth-shattering crash of the explosions, near enough and loud enough to frighten but not so near or so loud that the needle would jump. Art made a lot of recordings and finally got the perfect one that satisfied him, but nobody was interested and the recordings remained piled up in the CBC office. This was a time when most people considered radio a medium for speech and music and ignored its capacity to capture other sounds. Then one day, Bushnell, seized with an idea for a program, came round to the CBC office and asked Holmes if he thought it would be possible to take the van out some night and record a raid. The engineer almost exploded and pointed to the pile of unwanted bomb recordings. From then on, they would be reverberating in programs short-waved across the Atlantic, and dubbings of them would be used in many films. In fact, Holmes's recordings became classics, though he was never given any credit for them—they were always referred to as part of the BBC "Blitz collection".

It was after the Nazis scored a direct hit on Broadcasting House, killing some of the staff, that the North American Service was evacuated to Evesham in the green and pleasant Malvern Hills. Bushnell was billetted in a large stone house reserved for BBC executives as the village was the technical headquarters of the Overseas Service. It was also the hideaway for the BBC's remarkable Intelligence Service; there, some hundreds of foreign-language experts, many of them refugees from Germany, recorded and transcribed the war of words that was raging over the short waves.

"Every day—and sometimes several times a day—an analysis of these short-wave programs was made and copies rushed to Winston Churchill, the head of the air force, the head of the admiralty, the head of the army and many other key people," Bushnell remembers. "One of them came to me every day. At a glance you could see what every country in the world was saying, for outside consumption. If you wanted a complete copy of any transmission you made your request, and in a short time it was on your desk. You can readily see how valuable a service like that would be."

However, the beautiful Vale of Evesham was not a retreat that appealed to Bushnell and his confrères of the North American Service, who included J. B. "Hamish" McGeachy—he had been the *Winnipeg Free Press* correspondent in London. They complained bitterly that it was an impossible place to work, that they couldn't get anyone to go there, that they were out of touch with reality. Although in the countryside, Evesham was on the flight path to Birmingham, and Bush often lay in bed at night listening to the ugly drone of German bombers on their way to blast the Midland city. After six weeks, their pleas were heeded and the North American Service moved back to London, to 200 Oxford Street, the bombed-out annex of the Peter Robinson department store which the indefatigable housing officials of the BBC had had repaired and renovated for them.

Before leaving for London to take up the BBC job, Bushnell had turned over some program ideas in his mind and wondered whether a wartime "soap opera" wouldn't have a propaganda impact—they were all the rage then in Canada and the United States. Accordingly, he had taken some of the serial scripts with him, including an episode from "Ma Perkins". Then came the difficult task of selling his idea to the BBC mandarins, who were horrified at such "fearful bilge, like the comics, old boy, and we wouldn't want them"; Archie Harding, who was second in charge of drama at the BBC (number two to Val Gielgud) but the actual operating chief, would have nothing to do with such "awful tripe". However, Tony Rendall had visited North America and had heard soap operas; he agreed that a wartime serial might go over. Rendall had the final say, and he encouraged Bush to find an author to write a couple of episodes as a pilot project. After much searching around, Ernie found an up-and-coming playwright, Allan Melville, who was ready to try his hand. It took some "blood, sweat and tears" on Bushnell's part, but the writer finally acquired the knack, and thus was born "The British Family Robinson" which entertained Canadian and American listeners for the duration; after about six months on short wave, the serial was carried on the BBC Home Service and continued long after the war. Thus Bush, who had originated the singing commercial, now had to plead guilty to introducing the soap opera to British air waves.

In January of 1941, Ernie Bushnell received a message from Gladstone Murray asking him to return to the CBC. He didn't want to go back—in fact, "I was almost in tears"—but Gladstone Murray, in deepening trouble back home, was adamant and insisted on his return.

13 Fate and Murray's Ouster

Bushnell had been away so long that he hadn't been able to keep up with the political infighting in Ottawa. It was some weeks after his return that Donald Manson, who as secretary of the CBC board acted as a liaison officer between W. E. Gladstone Murray, Alan Plaunt and other members of the board, "tipped me off that Alan was after Bill's hide". Manson was distressed at this development because he was fond of both of them. It was a case of idealists falling out, of the revolution devouring its young, since Alan Plaunt had fought hard for the appointment of Gladstone Murray, and the Radio League and its supporters considered Murray one of their own, eminently well qualified to head public broadcasting in Canada. Plaunt had stopped at nothing, and even had Murray sign "the pledge" in a letter that was made public. That letter, in Bush's view, did more to sour relations than anything else, and even Plaunt's friends admit that the cause of Plaunt's eventual disillusionment with his protegé was Murray's drinking.

Meanwhile, Ernie returned to the task of organizing the war-time programming of the CBC. In a New Year's Day message, Gladstone Murray announced the formation of the national news service which Bush had urged some two and a half years before in a special memo he had written after his first trip to Europe. Bush was being called on more and more to represent the general manager at conferences and functions across the country and in the United States; at Columbus, Ohio, he spoke of the wartime role of radio and said that, while broadcasting in Canada was being conducted in a "somewhat different

100

atmosphere" from that of the United Kingdom, "as I see it, the job of both broadcasting systems, the BBC and CBC, is to animate war fervour but to repress war fever—to encourage rational, clear-headed thinking and to discourage irrational, falsely conceived patriotism or jingoism. . . ." There were still eight months to go until Pearl Harbour and the United States was technically neutral, but Bushnell was taking part in a University of Ohio symposium on the role of radio in America in case of war. He put the broadcasting of news first in wartime programming and said:

> . . . the most important function of any station or network is to broadcast news at frequent and regular intervals, thereby keeping the public properly informed on current events—to broadcast news that is factual and objective—not scare news, not speculation, but news that is the latest and most authentic available from thoroughly dependable sources.

This was more a presentation than a speech, since Bush included recorded excerpts of the CBC's wartime programming as illustrations. After mentioning that the CBC had its own national news service (without saying how short a time it had been in operation) and that the Canadian newscasts had a different style, "something between" the completely impersonal British format and the personalized American style, he played two or three lead items from the National Bulletin, with Lorne Greene as reader. Bushnell returned again and again to the key role of news in broadcasting:

> In a country at war the greatest conceivable care must be taken to present the news completely and fairly, without any false emphasis. Efforts to sugar-coat news that is bad, even if attempted by our editors, would be dangerous; conversely, if enemy successes were overstated, an atmosphere of defeatism might be created. I can say with complete frankness that no effort has been made, either by the official censorship or voluntarily by our editors, to suppress or distort news that may not be palatable. For one thing, it would be senseless in view of the easy accessibility of news broadcasts from the

United States. The official censorship, insofar as it deals with radio news, has been concerned principally with news of troop movements and concentrations, news of ship sailings or news that might give too-detailed information about our vital war industries. News, in short, that would be of obvious value to the enemy and which, for the most part, is not of vital concern to listeners.

In Ottawa, Bushnell found the atmosphere of suspicion and intrigue doubly distressing as he hated anything underhand or conspiratorial and had developed a high regard and real affection for Bill Murray. Later he was to denounce those responsible, "for a not-so-subtle form of treachery and sabotage" of the war effort; "the executioners were sharpening the guillotine and for the second time in the short but hectic history of national broadcasting, another head was being prepared to roll."

The Plaunt-Murray feud came to a head with the war, when it became apparent that Alan Plaunt, like so many other idealists of the time, was at heart a pacifist. He seemed to believe that the period of one week between the British declaration of war and the passage through the Canadian Parliament of a resolution of concurrence was not simply a rather hollow demonstration of Canadian sovereignty but a time of true neutrality, and he therefore protested at BBC programs being carried by the CBC. His pacifism, or anti-imperialism as he would have preferred to call it, led him to support American programs which he had so roundly condemned short years before; he questioned the CBC ruling that Canadian stations should no longer carry news or commentaries originating in the United States.

Although Alan Plaunt, Gladstone Murray and Leonard W. Brockington, who did so much to shape the early days of the CBC, were fellow intellectuals, they were very different: Murray had won the MC and the DFC when he switched from the infantry to the Royal Flying Corps during the First World War, and was the very essence of a British imperial officer (retired); Brockington, who had inherited the oratory of his Welsh forebears, had all the idiosyncrasies and pomposities of a Law Lord and was more British than Canadian. Plaunt had a British veneer from going to Oxford but it was only a veneer; above all, he was a Canadian nationalist and a North American, and when the war came, he found his roots counted. He was on the side of American neutrality . . . but he was to die before Pearl Harbor.

What made Plaunt furious was the way that Murray, at CBC expense, went regularly to New York to consort with an old friend named Stevenson, who was a British agent. Bushnell knew about this and expressed the view that the two of them were engaged in trying to get the United States into the war; he would have seen nothing wrong with that since he had been doing the same thing, directing the BBC's North American Service. Between February and May of 1941, a series of articles on Canadian broadcasting appeared in the *Canadian Forum,* under the by-line of "V. R. Hill" who was one of the faceless supporters of Plaunt and the Radio League; these articles attacked Gladstone Murray as a public relations man who had "the faculty of being all things to all men", who was not firm enough and could not say "No." But the real charge against him in *Forum* was that he was capricious: "Caprice is a luxury not to be indulged in during wartime; when that caprice is shown to be definitely illiberal, it becomes even more of a luxury in a war devoted to preserving democratic processes."

However, it was Gladstone Murray's drinking which was the cause of his downfall and the loss of his friends; in the end, everyone admitted this, although there was a tendency to try to hide it by saying that he was "not doing his job". Then too, Alan Plaunt was suffering from terminal cancer, and that might have contributed to the way he hounded the man he had worked so hard to get as general manager. Plaunt may also have felt that he had been deceived, because he got a letter from Murray assuring him that he was not drinking, only to find that within a year or so of his appointment, Murray was drinking more than ever. Still, in reviewing this period, Bush was to write:

"In my judgment Bill Murray was a great man. Put his weaknesses on the one side of the scales and his virtues on the other and there can be no doubt of the result: they weighed heavily on the right side—on the side of justice, on the side of inspired leadership, on the side of devotion to a principle in which he believed and for which he prepared himself and many of those who were privileged to work with him to defend at all costs. William Ewart Gladstone Murray had, I believe, the qualities and qualifications of a fine architect and the skills of a master mason. Maybe his trowel slipped occasionally, but not often enough to warrant the ignominious treatment he received of being kicked downstairs, of being transferred from the post of general manager to the hastily conceived and meaningless job of director general. Director general of what? Nothing. After less than a year of doing nothing, of being put on a lonely shelf and of being ignored, Mr. Murray resigned—and who could blame him?"

The ouster of Gladstone Murray might have looked to Bushnell at first like a horrible example of another's adversity advancing one's own career. Even if he hadn't listened to the gossip that he was being considered for the top job, there was a good chance of his becoming assistant general manager in the event that Dr. Augustin Frigon was made general manager—and, as far as Bush was concerned, Dr. Frigon was the logical choice. However, by a curious quirk of fate, "one of those crazy, mixed-up situations", Bush calls it, the Murray dismissal did not improve his fortunes but turned out to be a grave setback, and Bushnell was never to become general manager of the CBC.

One Saturday morning in November 1942, Rev. Canon W. E. Fuller, a member of the CBC Board of Governors, visited him in his office at 55 York Street, Toronto. Bushnell, in recounting this, imitated the way that the Anglican minister paced back and forth in front of his desk, wagging a finger at him, and saying repeatedly:

"We're not going to have that man, Frigon.

"With the French Canadians opposing the war, it would be disastrous. You know, Bush, all the unrest this would create in wartime, all the fuss over conscription. We're not going to have that man, Frigon. I know that the chairman is going to propose him, but we'll move an amendment, and we'll make you general manager."

104

All that Bushnell could do was to splutter his protest. He argued that such a move would only add fuel to the fires of dissension in Quebec. He remonstrated with Canon Fuller, he pleaded with him. He pointed out that Dr. Frigon was one of the pillars on which the CBC had been built, that he had been a member of the Aird Commission that recommended a system of publicly owned broadcasting, that he was a personal friend of Ernest Lapointe, Prime Minister Mackenzie King's trusted right-hand man and Quebec deputy—but to no avail. He tried blasphemy and shouted at the reverend gentleman who was wearing his clerical collar: "You must be out of your bloody mind!"

But Canon Fuller stood firm. He said there were two other members of the board, J. Wilfred Godfrey, KC, of Halifax, and Rowe Holland of Vancouver, who supported him and would be seconding the amendment to have Bushnell named general manager. The minister's parting shot was to order Bush to be in Ottawa "bright and early" Monday morning when the board was to meet.

After what Bush described as a "sleepless weekend"—he knew that the action of the three board members would put him in an extremely awkward position and might prove to be disastrous—he arrived in Ottawa on the night train and went directly to 140 Wellington Street and the executive suite on the third floor. At half past eight, Dr. Frigon stepped off the elevator, "chipper, cheerful and full of his usual graciousness". He smiled and asked Bush to come to his office for a few minutes before the board met. There, he told him that he confidently expected to be named general manager, and invited him to be his assistant general manager. For Ernie, this was one of life's most embarrassing moments. What should he do? What should he say? In the end, he stammered a hesitant thanks, and he recalls Dr. Frigon replying:

"Now, now, Bush, I know how you feel but I'm sure the two of us can make a fine job of running Radio Canada together. You run along and I'll ask you to join us in the boardroom in about half an hour."

While he was in Dr. Frigon's office, Bushnell's three

advocates had slipped into the boardroom, and there was no chance of reaching them to tell them. Bushnell could only assume what happened at the board meeting, but he did know that at a quarter to ten, Dr. Frigon left the meeting, and walked past him on his way to the office. "He looked pale, he hadn't lifted his eyes when he passed by, he hadn't spoken," Bush wrote in his memoirs. "I think I knew his thoughts—the double-crossing so-and-so. And who could blame him? I couldn't and didn't."

It was really an indecisive meeting of the board. Dr. James Thomson, the president of the University of Saskatchewan and a member of the board, was made acting general manager, and Dr. Frigon continued as assistant general manager. Although Messrs Fuller, Godfrey and Holland had succeeded in preventing Dr. Frigon from becoming general manager, their success was not only partial but temporary. However, the incident had a lasting effect on Bushnell.

During the next few months the situation was not a happy one for Bush, who had a genuine fondness for Dr. Frigon and had been an innocent victim of the antipathy between the English and French Canadians that had been whipped into a frenzy by the war. From then on, "Dr. Frigon was cordial but coolish, never mean, as he wasn't made that way, never unkind, as he wasn't made that way either, but he didn't smile at me as he once did. He didn't confide in me anymore."

The next summer, Dr. Thomson told Bushnell that he would be resigning shortly, that he wanted to return to the ministry (United Church), and that broadcasting was not his cup of tea; but he asked Bush to say nothing as his resignation would be given to the board at its upcoming meeting in Vancouver. Bush spent that weekend at his cottage in the Gatineau Hills. While he was playing golf nearby at the Larrimac course, he heard the familiar voice of Donald Manson, the secretary of the CBC Board of Governors, who said that he wanted to talk to him. So he went over to Don's Packard to chat. Manson too had heard that Dr. Thomson was fed up and would likely resign; he was leaving that night for the board meeting in Vancouver.

"I just wanted to let you know that I'm sure you will be

appointed assistant general manager and Dr. Frigon general manager," Manson said. "Won't that be great! Won't that be nice to be all working together again!"

Bushnell asserts that he never asked anyone what took place at the Vancouver meeting of the board, nor was he ever told, nor did he want to know. Dr. Frigon was named general manager with Donald Manson as assistant general manager. Apparently, the board was afraid that he might resign, so they made him director general of programming and gave him the same salary as Manson's, which was eleven thousand dollars a year.

On Dr. Frigon's retirement, and death shortly thereafter, Donald Manson became general manager and was so for a brief period at the beginning of the fifties; the assistant general manager was J. Alphonse Ouimet, a brilliant engineer who had developed the first workable television in Canada twenty years before. Bushnell was left in charge of programming which, he said, was "what I wanted, for that was the part of the CBC that fascinated me, that was the vocation I had chosen, and that was where I felt most at home".

The ouster of Gladstone Murray, aside from the effect that it had on Bushnell's own career, marked a turning point in the affairs of the Canadian Broadcasting Corporation. It was the end of the beginning, the end of the first rapturous enthusiasm that had made radio such a joyful and thrilling occupation: in his report on the BBC, Bush had noted that in the beginning of any public enterprise, such as the beginning of television at Alexandra Palace, there was an especially high and creative *esprit de corps*. All the politics and plotting that had gone into the dismissal of Murray had left a bad taste in the mouths of the CBC staff for, as Bush says, there was "never more loyalty to a chief executive than to Bill Murray—everyone loved Bill Murray". There were to be new programs; the war reporting was certainly the CBC's "finest hour", and there were sparks of genius struck again, but generally speaking, the war was a kind of watershed—after that, the corporation grew only in size and was to become more and more laden down with the red tape of bureaucracy and the feather-bedding of unionism. Gladstone

Murray was the first "program man" to run the CBC and the last; he was to be succeeded by engineers and technicians, Frigon, Manson, Ouimet, and by a top civil servant, Dr. George Davidson.

14 The False VJ-Day Broadcast

No better example of the overwhelming importance of the news broadcasts in wartime was provided than by what might be called "the case of the news reader who was too good". That is what Ernie Bushnell dubs it; he describes Lorne Green as a perfectionist who was "too good for an important and highly specialized national service". The uproar over the portentous way that he read the news and his deep sonorous voice made Bush realize what a sensitive and intimate instrument radio was; he quotes Brockington, the former chairman of the CBC Board of Governors, who called it "the thing that purrs like a kitten and sings like a kettle on every hearth".

Lorne Green was the announcer from Ottawa who read the late-night national news, and it would be no exaggeration to say that, during wartime, he had the nation as his audience. His rich bass-baritone voice, the care that he took with both enunciation and pronunciation, the hours that he spent on rehearsal, all contributed to his success. However, the very quality of his voice began to grate on the nerves of many people who listened to him night after night describe one Allied disaster after another. He became known as the Voice of Doom and, more because of a sense of uneasiness than of any mass protest, Bushnell decided "most reluctantly" that someone else "whose tones and overtones were not quite so disturbing in periods of anxiety" would be better suited for this all important job. However, by the time that Lorne Green had been replaced, eventually by Earl Cameron, the course of the war had changed completely. Instead of disasters, there were now victories to report.

The time of the national news was moved from eleven to ten pm at the insistence of C. D. Howe, the minister of Munitions and Supply, who said that eleven o'clock was much too late in the industrialized areas of Ontario and Quebec, that everyone should be asleep by then so that he or she could contribute a full day's work to the war effort. This was one case of government interference which was neither resisted nor resented; the only annoyance that Bush felt was that he hadn't thought of it in the first place.

All combat areas were now covered by voice-reporting CBC war correspondents. After the D-Day landing in Normandy there were two separate teams in Italy and Western Europe with their own portable recording equipment, which was transported on jeeps and the huge recording vans that were big enough to accommodate a talks studio, as well as the engineers (accredited as war correspondents) to service them. For the first time in history, reporters described a battle as it happened with all its sound and fury in the living rooms of the nation; it was a new kind of journalism, unmatched by the BBC or the American networks. *Maclean's* was so impressed with the coverage of the Sicilian landing that it compared the CBC correspondent to Pheidippides, who ran to Athens to cry out that the Greeks had won over the Persians at Marathon. Bushnell adds that "all those who from time to time were allocated front-line reporting duties performed a notable and distinguished job" of which the CBC could always be proud.

In March 1945 Bushnell went overseas again, to attend the Commonwealth Broadcasting Conference in London and to visit the CBC war correspondents on the Western Front. By then, the First Canadian Corps had left Italy and rejoined the First Canadian Army at Nijmegen. Howard Chase, the chairman of the CBC Board, accompanied him to London, while Roy Cahoon, the senior engineer in the new International Short-wave Service, went with him to the scene of the fiercest fighting of the war, the crossing of the Rhine. When he returned in mid-April, Bushnell made another coast-to-coast broadcast and again he showed himself to be a perceptive reporter. He paid tribute to the CBC war correspondents, who were "not tin soldiers" but had been in the thick of battle. While Paris was still Paris in many ways, with the women still chic—"their clothes made of goodness knows what"—Bushnell noted that it was, in reality, "a pretty grim-looking city just emerging from a cold winter", where there was a shortage of everything.

Why? Transportation facilities were meagre, indeed they are totally inadequate. Flying low over the coast of France at Calais I was able to see both the arterial highways and the bisecting country roads. Not one truck or vehicle of any kind was visible for the first twenty minutes of flying time—a distance of sixty to seventy miles—and then one here and one there began to pop up. As we got closer to Paris there were a few more but not many. One train was all I could see in that flight from Calais to Paris. A country lives not only on its natural resources but on its ability to transport them. No wonder Paris food shops are bare—almost empty.

In contrast, there was the heavy traffic on the roads leading to the front, and Bush's broadcast, without saying so, pointed up the difference in priorities during wartime. Civilians, mostly women and children, were being left to starve in Paris while every vehicle was being used to feed the armies fighting on the Rhine:

Hundreds of thousands of motor vehicles rushed along the arterial highways leading to the sector held by the 21st Army Group. No words can adequately describe the flow. Swish, swish, swish—every two to three seconds, twenty-four hours of the day they went. Trucks, tanks, Weasels, Buffalos, Jeeps, motorcycles and goodness-knows-what kind of strange thing passed along the road in a continuous stream. And how do they get the gasoline? It comes out of a pipeline that runs along the side of the road for hundreds of miles. This is the supply line that feeds our planes as well as the thousands of vehicles carrying men and munitions to the front—not only carrying them up but down again. Down for a rest—down to base hospitals. Red Cross signs are plentiful and in the back of each Red Cross lorry is someone who has been

111

wounded—someone who probably has been treated in a casualty-clearing station and is being rushed back to hospital where he has a good chance of recovery. Think well of your doctors, nurses and the Red Cross, for all are doing a magnificent job.

There was a period of six months when Bushnell was seconded to the Wartime Information Board to be in charge of radio. He was nicknamed the Czar of Radio, but he did practically nothing. It was farcical, a wartime comedy of errors. In the whole half year of service on the board, he says that he wrote a couple of announcements. He seldom left the Victoria building for the WIB headquarters, as he found the place chaotic. He continued working for the CBC; the only difference was that he was being paid by another government agency. One day, he bumped into Donald Gordon, the wartime prices controller, on the street.

"Are you going to the meeting?" Donald Gordon asked.

"What meeting?"

"You know what meeting," Donald Gordon said—wartime secrecy prevented him from saying what it was.

"No, I don't," Bushnell said, and that was the end of the conversation.

He did visit the WIB headquarters when it had been moved to the Supreme Court building and found that there was not only no office and no desk for the Czar of Radio, but no telephones anywhere—not one for the Wartime Information Board. The whole thing was ludicrous.

All the pent-up tensions and frustrations of wartime exploded like a thunderclap in an unseemly row he had with Brooke Claxton, then an up-and-coming Liberal MP and parliamentary secretary to the prime minister. A new program called "Of Things to Come" had started in the fall of 1942, when the tide of war was beginning to turn; it led to some lively discussions on the future, but these were not appreciated by the government which had become authoritarian and frightened by the inroads that the socialist CCF were making. In the summer of 1943, Morley Callaghan, the program chairman, and Neil

Morrison, who had launched the highly successful "Farm Forum" and at the age of twenty-eight had just been named head of talks and public affairs, visited Ottawa to discuss the next season's "Of Things to Come" with the government and opposition parties. They called on Brooke Claxton, who was regarded as a friend in court because of the prominent part he had played in the Radio League and the founding of the CBC. However, they soon found that his idealism was no deeper than his political affiliation, and Claxton seemed to resent the fact that they had seen the opposition leaders first, although he was told that this was because he was out of the office when they first called. And he blew up when he heard that they had discussed the possibility of a controversial labour leader, J. L. Cohen, and the CCF lawyer, David Lewis, participating in the fall series.

"We're not going to stand for this," Claxton said angrily. "There are too many CCFers. The government is not going to stand for this."

Morley Callaghan became indignant at the peremptory manner of the parliamentary secretary, and Morrison recalls him shouting that he wasn't a CBC official and wouldn't be ordered around by anyone like Claxton.

It was a disastrous meeting, and all due to a misunderstanding, as Morrison reported to Ernie Bushnell. Claxton seemed to think they had done rather more than discuss their plans with the opposition leaders, although it had only been "a scouting expedition" they were on, a conciliatory effort to consult the politicians. However, Ernie had suffered for too long from the throttling hold that the government applied in wartime to believe that there could have been any misunderstanding; he was inclined to regard Claxton as the evil genius who manipulated broadcasting for the benefit of the Liberal party and the government from his office in the East Block. Bushnell was furious over the way that the CBC board, most of whose members were well-known Liberals, had knuckled under to the government's demand that there should be no broadcasting of the Conservative party's leadership convention in December of 1942, not even on the private stations. Arthur Meighen, the retiring leader, subsequently used half his speech at the convention to denounce the CBC as an "effective monopoly, tool and instrument of a partisan government". Bushnell, with his political sixth sense, realized the damage that had been done—the Conservatives never forgave the CBC and, years later, when they came to power, one of the first things they did was to break off the regulatory functions of the corporation and give them to an "impartial" and separate Board of Broadcast Governors. Although Bush was no radical and might have agreed with Claxton that there were too many CCFers on the air, he fought for their right to broadcast because he believed in the independence of the corporation above all—that was his credo.

As they were all staying in the Chateau Laurier, Morrison arranged for a further meeting with Claxton in his room on the seventh floor the following night. It was meant to be a reconciliation, but Bushnell heard about it and insisted on participating. From the moment he entered the room he fought with Claxton, accusing him of being responsible for the number of occasions on which the government had interfered in the affairs of the CBC. Perhaps it was the heat, for it was a remarkably hot night, or the accumulation of irritations, for Bush admits now that he was in a foul mood. Morley Callaghan was present and wrote an amusing piece on the Billingsgate that ensued. According to Morrison, Bush set out to humiliate Claxton, and the meeting broke up in sweaty and angry disorder. There was no doubt that Claxton would report the whole matter to Mackenzie King, and Morrison thought: "There go Bush's chances of becoming general manager"; he was sure that this acrimonious clash with authority represented by Brooke Claxton would have serious repercussions. Bushnell is inclined to believe that his loss of temper on this occasion was one of two factors that cost him the OBE—the other was the false VJ-Day broadcast.

It was obvious that the Second World War was petering out, especially after the atom bombing of Hiroshima and Nagasaki which had a curiously numbing effect on the Canadian conscience, conditioned by years of horror and slaughter. When the prime minister's private secretary, Jack Pickersgill, advised the corporation to have ready a nation-wide network (which was to include not only the CBC stations and affiliates but every radio station in the land) as Mr. Mackenzie King had a statement of importance to make, Bushnell concluded that this would be the announcement of the Japanese surrender. He presumed that the prime minister was irked by the fact that Canadians had learned about VE-Day from Prime Minister Churchill and President Truman, and was making sure that they would hear about VJ-Day from the lips of their own glorious leader.

On Saturday, August 11, 1945, the Associated Press carried a "confidential to editors" advice that a special White House press conference was being called for half past eight the following morning. This information was passed on to the prime minister's office, and Bushnell ordered the extended network to be ready from 7:30 am the next day. Early Sunday morning, Mr. Mackenzie King drove in from his country residence at Kingsmere to the CBC's Ottawa studios on the seventh floor of the Chateau Laurier; he arrived a few minutes before the eight o'clock news bulletin, while his faithful secretary, Pickersgill, didn't reach the studios till 8:15 am. Of course, Bushnell was there to greet the prime minister; in his detailed report on the incident to the general manager, he said that Mackenzie King listened carefully to the eight o'clock news bulletin and the others that followed and expressed his confidence that this was the day, as "otherwise President Truman would not have called a press conference".

However, the hours went by—nine o'clock, ten o'clock, eleven o'clock, noon—and there was no "flash", no excited voice saying "Now we interrupt the program to bring you a special announcement." The prime minister paced back and forth in the carpeted corridor outside the CBC studios. According to Bush's report, Mackenzie King and Pickersgill spent much of the morning "editing a statement the prime minister said he had written between eleven and one o'clock on Saturday night and Sunday morning". The report quotes Mackenzie King as making it very clear that he wished to follow President Truman's announcement (it was taken for granted that the president would announce the Japanese surrender) "as soon as he possibly could do so". It goes on to say:

> At about twelve noon, Mr. Pickersgill suggested that the prime minister might like to rest, and he arranged with the Chateau Laurier hotel management to provide him with room 748, just three doors away from the CBC studios.
> At approximately 12:30, Mr. King retired to his room, and lunch was ordered for him. He left instructions that he was to be called the moment anything of importance happened. A radio was put in his room so he could hear the CBC news bulletins. Before retiring, Mr. King again emphasized that he was certain the news of Japan's acceptance of the Potsdam terms would be received that day.

The afternoon went by without any development. Pickersgill sat with Bushnell and Charlie Wright, the station manager, making desultory conversation in CBC's small reception room. At six o'clock, the prime minister emerged from his room and called Bush aside to tell him that he was in a great quandary; he was determined to broadcast immediately after the president's announcement of the Japanese surrender but he had accepted an invitation to dine with the Governor-General, the Earl of Athlone, at seven o'clock that evening, and since Rideau Hall was a good two miles from the Chateau Laurier, he would never be able to get back in time. Bushnell suggested that he might record his message. At first Mr. King, who was the soul of propriety and caution, demurred, but then he decided that the only thing to do under the circumstances was to have it "put on wax". A recording was made and played back, and at quarter to seven, the prime minister and Pickersgill left, after repeated assurances that the recorded message would be used immediately after the announcement of the official end of the war.

Seven o'clock passed, then eight o'clock, nine o'clock, and Bush began to wonder if he were in for an all-night vigil. At half past nine, the CBC began broadcasting "The Album of Familiar Music", which originated with the NBC; a few minutes later, the program was interrupted by an NBC announcer saying: "Flash! President Truman has just announced that Japan has accepted the surrender terms of the Allies." The announcer then repeated the bulletin and said, "The war is over"; a commentary followed. By this time, Bushnell was talking to Charles Jennings in Toronto on the closed-circuit telephone, and Bush's report to the general manager described what happened:

> He [Jennings] informed me that the Toronto newsroom had received a flash which read: "Washington—President Truman has just announced that Japan has accepted the surrender terms of the Allies." I told him that seemed to be authentic and to stand by to broadcast the prime minister's statement. We cut out of the NBC commentary at 9.36.20, played a short musical interlude, flashed the news item from the Toronto studios to the network, and at 9.37.10 we transferred to Ottawa studios and played the recording the prime minister made earlier in the day.
>
> We had not played more than ten seconds of it when Mr. Jennings told me that a further message had come over our news teletype asking editors to hold the item that had been transmitted about three minutes previously. By this time the prime minister's broadcast was well under way and it did not seem advisable to me to stop it. It concluded at 9.42.41. At about 9.40, British United Press denied the original report and stated they had no knowledge of its source.

For a moment, Bush recalled, there was a state of confusion and panic. What to do? Should an apology be made? Should the CBC put the blame on the BUP? Should they repeat the prime minister's message when the news was official? VJ-Day did not occur till August 15, 1945. Nothing much was done as everyone was too stunned to act. It was not long after the broadcast that Mackenzie King ascended to the seventh floor of the Chateau Laurier and appeared in the studios like an angel of wrath; he let Bushnell know that he was furious, that he had been made a laughing stock. What would Parliament say, he asked: the answer to that question was too horrible to contemplate. Bush showed the prime minister the wire copy in the sequence that it had been received, and expressed his deepest regrets. What more could he do? He thought that his explanation had been accepted and that he had been forgiven.

However, "Hell hath no fury like a politician scorned," and the next day's Hansard showed that Mr. King had been seriously embarrassed by the false VJ-Day broadcast. Bushnell feels sure that it was because of this blunder that his name was removed from the postwar honours list. Dr. Augustin Frigon, the general manager, received the CBE, and six of Bush's colleagues the OBE. In retrospect, it seems incredible that the man who was responsible for reorganizing the BBC's North American Service and for moulding the CBC's war reporting so that it was unequalled should have been given no award, while those junior to him in the corporation, some of whom had not contributed to the war effort, were honoured. Bushnell comforted himself with the thought that "You can't buy ham and eggs with an OBE."

If, as he believes, the clash with Brooke Claxton and the blunder over the false VJ-Day broadcast were the reasons his name was struck off the honours list, then it is clear that awards, whether British or Canadian, are the favours of politicians in power and subject to their every whim and spleen. There was also the fact that Bushnell was not part of the Liberal intellectual establishment in Canada—in fact, the establishment regarded him as crude and commercial, an entertainer who had trod the boards of the chautauqua circuit and definitely not the kind of chap to be invited to a garden party; at the same time, the establishment resented the fact that it had to have him running the CBC.

15 The Postwar Red Scare

After his experience in running the BBC's North American Service, it was natural for Bushnell to want the CBC to have its own short-wave service. There was talk of Canada joining in the "war of words" raging in the ether, untouched by the shot and shell of the battle below, but the government had been too busy prosecuting the real war effort to bother with such electronic frills. However, aside from keeping up with the international Joneses, the telling argument was that short wave was needed to keep the troops in touch with home, and this became more self-evident with the passage of each contingent of Canadians overseas. Then, there were the frequencies that Canada had reserved by international agreement and had not used—there was a danger that they might be pirated by other nations. Finally, the government relented and in September 1942 authorized the CBC to proceed with the construction of a modern short-wave transmitter and facilities, although C. D. Howe still grumbled about the expense. "It may cost only a half a million dollars to get this thing started," he said, "but it will cost five million before you are through with it." He was right.

Peter Aylen, the manager of CBO, was named the first supervisor of the International Short-wave Service; he was to serve "under the supervision of Mr. E. L. Bushnell", according to the minutes of the General Administrative Conference of September 27 to 29, 1944. As might be expected, Bush was much more concerned with programming than with transmission; in fact, the high fence of steel towers that flung the CBC signal across the Atlantic was as remarkable and incomprehensible to him as the technical and scientific jargon with which the engineers praised their new toys. The two 50,000-watt transmitters on the Tantramar Marshes near Sackville, Nova Scotia, while not the most powerful short-wave stations in the world, did put a clearer signal into Great Britain and many parts of Europe than any other North American transmitters.

The International Service's programming was largely composed of news; an appendix entitled *CBC Programming* published in 1949 described Canadian news as "the kernel of the whole service forming a part of every language section's transmissions", and put in second place "news features, news talks (prepared regionally on items of special regional interest), reviews of Canadian editorial opinion, commentaries (midweek and weekend)". The aim of the IS was primarily to keep Canadian servicemen overseas in touch with what was happening at home—the first test transmission on Christmas Day 1944 consisted of messages to the troops—and only secondarily to answer the enemy's propaganda. There was a constant exchange with the Voice of America so that the two North American allies should not be saying different things.

After the war, the character of the International Service changed somewhat. No longer was it concerned with Canadians overseas; in Bush's words, its programming "became a reflection of Canadian life, portraying the good life of the people of Canada, especially the life of the immigrants". He found that he was gradually required to exercise less of a supervisory function than an advisory one, as the External Affairs Department became more interested in the Voice of Canada and particularly in its political broadcasts; there grew up a close liaison between the department's East Block offices in Ottawa and the IS headquarters in Montreal. Then, as a backlash of the Gouzenko spy trials, a Red witch-hunt developed which almost reached the virulence of McCarthyism in the United States, and the International Service was wracked by charges of Communist infiltration. This occurred after Peter Aylen had left to become head of the United Nations radio division, and had been succeeded in the International Service by Professor Ira Dilworth.

Bushnell by then was very fond of Dilworth, but he recalls that he had seriously considered resigning when the British Columbia educationist was originally taken on by the CBC—that was back in 1938 and was a direct result of what became known as the "Lotus Leaves" scandal. When Jack Radford (who was one of the original CKNC boys and had started in radio as the blood-curdling cry in the commercial of Sappho the Killer) was named manager of CBV, the CBC station in Vancouver, Horace Stovin, the regional representative in the West, decided that he should be welcomed with a band. This was in the hearty back-slapping tradition of the chautauqua circuit. The only trouble was that Stovin didn't know which route Radford was taking to cross the continent; nothing deterred, he hired two bands, one to greet Radford at the CPR station if he arrived there, and one to greet him at the CNR station. The bands fees were charged to a program called "Lotus Leaves"; however, a check of the log showed that no such program had been broadcast. Bush explains that musicians were paid much less for meeting a train than for playing on air, and when an explanation was demanded of Stovin, he frankly admitted that he had spent $180 to $200 of CBC funds to welcome Jack Radford to his new post.

It was a scandalous situation, and the rather pompous representatives of the establishment on the CBC board didn't consider such high jinks funny. Leonard Brockington, the chairman of the board, took the first train to Vancouver to investigate and, without any reference to management, appointed Ira Dilworth, then professor of English at the University of British Columbia but better known as the principal of Victoria High School, to be in charge of the CBC on the Pacific Coast and "to clean up the mess". Bushnell was indignant. Not only had Brockington taken it on himself to name a senior official but he had altered the executive structure of the CBC, since there was but one regional director for the West who was answerable to the supervisor of programs, and that was Horace Stovin. Bush considered resigning but decided that it was not he who should quit on this issue but the general manager, Gladstone Murray.

However, Bushnell never held a grudge for long; he soon got over his resentment and came to appreciate Dilworth's unusual and varied talents. There was no doubt that Dilworth was different—for one thing, he was a scholar, which made him a rare bird indeed in the early days of radio, with a passionate interest not only in English but also in music. He conducted the Vancouver Bach Choir for seven years, and he was the leading interpreter of the famous British Columbia artist, Emily Carr, whom he regarded as a remarkable writer as well as a fine painter, "a truly great Canadian"—it was he who edited the four books that Emily Carr published before her death. Both English and music are among the foundation stones of radio programming, and it could be said that Ira provided a highbrow balance for Ernie's rather lowbrow view of broadcasting, as the common denominator of entertainment.

When Professor Dilworth was persuaded to go into broadcasting and join the CBC, he was so uncertain about his new career that he only took a leave of absence from the university. At first, he felt like a fish out of water—in his own words, like "a pedagogue who was really rather pompous and precious among the buskers and hucksters of radio." However, he enjoyed the challenge of broadcasting; he liked being at the "centre of things" after the remote life of the campus, and he resigned from the university. Once having taken this decision, he was determined to make a clean break with his academic past and to become accepted in the new electronic order, even to the extent of matching the rather vivid language that his new colleagues were wont to use. The only problem, Bush remarks, was that when Ira used a cuss word, he made it sound so literary that he might have been a Shakespearean actor declaiming: "Out, damned spot."

Although Bushnell was not much involved with the programming of the International Service after the war, Dilworth nevertheless consulted him regularly as his immediate boss; he complained about the vagaries of the External Affairs officials as far as the short-wave was concerned, and about their interference in programming. He referred to them as "those buggahs in Ottawa" in a gentle but exasperated tone: "Bush, those buggahs in Ottawa are going to be the death of me yet."

It was inevitable that the International Service should be one of the first victims of the anti-communist hysteria aroused by the Gouzenko spy trials. The liberals were running scared, and some of the CCFers, including a prominent academic at McGill University, turned informer; the Liberal party took its cue from Prime Minister Mackenzie King, who asserted that the Gouzenko affair revealed "a diabolical, planned effort to produce a fifth column within a friendly country and to have all plans laid in readiness for another war". At the same time, Mr. King couldn't help praising himself for the courage he showed in saving the Christian (sic) world from Russian intrigue by his fearless handling of the case. The members of the establishment were badly frightened and suffering from an atomic guilt complex, and it was therefore not surprising that they should have visions of Reds broadcasting nuclear secrets, in code naturally, over the Sackville transmitters to agents behind the Iron Curtain. As a result, the atmosphere in the old Ford Hotel in Montreal (where the IS had its offices along with the rest of Radio Canada) was stiff with fear and suspicion, as a witch-hunt was organized and whipped to greater excesses by the English- and French-language newspapers.

"You can't imagine how horrible it was," one of the foreign-language officials said years later. "I hated to come to work. I wanted to quit—but all 'foreigners' were suspect then, and there wasn't another job to be had."

Who should be put in charge of the International Service during this auto-da-fe but Ira Dilworth, who was among the most conscientious of men and whose soul had been badly burned by another case of mass hysteria, the disgraceful treatment of the British Columbia Japanese. He had been on a wartime committee that supervised the forced removal of these wretched people (most of them were Canadian born) from their homes on the Pacific Coast to concentration camps in the interior of the province. Now, here he was faced with another irrational attack on human dignity and civil rights. Dilworth consulted Bushnell: he pointed out that the police reports were based on hearsay and that there was no conclusive evidence that any of the staff members under surveillance were communists or "fellow travellers".

On January 8, 1949, he wrote, at Bushnell's suggestion, a secret memorandum to the general manager in which he said that one of the first things he learned on taking up his appointment as supervisor of the International Service was that there were RCMP reports on certain members of his staff. He realized that "we are in a very vulnerable position in the International Service", but added: "I now feel that I am able to say that the claim made concerning this service, namely that it is fairly uniformly radical, if it were ever justified, does not seem to me to be so now." Dilworth went on to say that the IS had attracted "people of unusual ability who have unusual interest in social and political affairs, particularly in the international field" and compared the political attitude of his staff, which he described as "liberalism so far left as to verge on socialism", with that prevailing in an academic institution. He added this observation: "It is very difficult to determine at what point such a liberal attitude goes too far, becomes dangerous to our democratic way of life, and should be restrained."

He took up individual cases and pointed out that the only evidence in one police report was that the person's parents were known to be "either communists or supporters of movements which are related to communist activity". Such guilt by association was repugnant to Ira, but what he found even more distressing was the McCarthyist mentality of the Mounties with whom he dealt.

Shortly after he wrote the secret memorandum, Dilworth had a severe heart attack from which he never really recovered—he was a casualty of the cold war, and Bushnell agreed that the virulent anti-communist witch-hunt at the IS might well have led to the heavy coronary seizure that almost killed him. "Ira," he said, "was the kind who felt those things very deeply." Although Dilworth was to return to his office and continued as supervisor of the International Service for some time, the question of a replacement had to be considered. Bushnell favored Stuart W. Griffiths, the head of the key English-language service from which the other language services took their direction, and pressed for his appointment as supervisor.

However, Griffiths was one of the individuals named in the secret memorandum who were being questioned by the police. Again, Dilworth felt that the information in the RCMP file was not enough to warrant branding him a communist or a "fellow traveller"; furthermore, Griffiths had denied that he was or had ever been a party member. What was of concern was that the contents of the police file had been divulged to Griffiths, who had raised the question of his civil rights and suggested that they would be infringed if the security reports were to hinder his professional advancement. Dilworth, therefore, warned management in the secret memorandum that his dismissal or transfer to a lower job "may precipitate an extremely critical situation"—in other words, Griffiths would make a civil rights case out of it and take the CBC to court.

Dilworth had a very high regard for Griffiths's ability. He wrote that Griffiths had a very keen interest in international affairs, that he had done his work very well, that he would be difficult to replace, but that he "was not always a comfortable person to work with"; he was "extremely persistent" and wouldn't take *no* for an answer. "This was the chief reason," Dilworth wrote in his secret memorandum, "that I was unwilling that he should become my assistant in the supervision of this service."

Things had reached such a stage that the External Affairs Department, according to his memo, "expressed itself on several occasions as being worried, particularly about Griffiths, and Mr. [Saul] Rae has gone so far as to say to me and others that as long as Griffiths is at International Service there can never be the free flow of information from External Affairs which we require nor can there be complete confidence on the part of External Affairs in our service." Dilworth felt that "every effort should be made to clear up Griffiths's case one way or the other." Under the circumstances, there was not a chance that Dr. Frigon, who was not the most broad-minded man, would agree to appoint Griffiths supervisor of the International Service.

This was not the first time that Stu Griffiths had come to Bushnell's attention, although the so-called security crisis at the IS helped to fix him in his mind. The pudgy young man had a great deal of drive; he was dynamic, an eager beaver full of ideas, and there was this go-ahead aggressiveness. Furthermore, Bush never had any doubts about his loyalty and had accepted his denial: "He was not a communist; he was an advanced thinker, but there was nothing disloyal about him," Bush says. Stu had made an impression on Bushnell from the moment he joined the CBC in Toronto. What Bush liked most about him was the way he never stopped working: even in the days of the International Service, when a cloud of suspicion hung over his head, Griffiths spent fifteen and sixteen hours a day at his desk.

Finally, after a two-year search, a diplomat, Jean Desy, who insisted on keeping his rank and title of Ambassador, was named to head the IS. In the interim, Ira Dilworth recovered sufficiently to return to his office for a few hours work a day, and continued as the crippled chief of a sick service. As his doctors insisted that he lie down and have a rest after lunch, he asked for a couch to be installed in his office and Donald Manson broke the rules to get him one: only those with the rank of director or above were entitled to a couch or a sofa in their offices, the assistant general manager explained, and Dilworth was just a supervisor. The executive order, with all its rigid rules and regulations about the number of windows for an office, whether there should be a carpet on the floor, when an official could have his own vacuum flask and not have to drink from the water cooler in the hall, was taking over—until CBC headquarters moved into a modern, Y-shaped building on Confederation Heights in Ottawa which met all the proprieties of a managerial society.

Jean Desy's appointment was the ultimate triumph of External Affairs, but Bushnell was happy enough; now he could wash his hands of the International Service with a clear conscience. Desy was supposed "to clean up the mess in the IS" but he made very few changes in personnel; all he really did was to cut down on programming, and fire most of the foreign-language commentators for being unreliable. The ambassador also ingratiated himself with the Latin Americans by inviting their artists to come to Canada at enormous public expense, a move that was not appreciated in Parliament and put the International Service onto the legislative chopping block. By the time Desy left to return to the fields of diplomacy, nobody cared very much whether there were subversives in the IS or not. Although the Voice of Canada had been temporarily muffled by External Affairs, it is still being heard and, thanks to the great transmitters at Sackville, its accent is loud and clear.

At the end of 1951, Bushnell was able to fix up a job for Dilworth which was not too demanding on him but had the resounding title of director of Program Production—now he could have a couch in his Toronto office without breaking any of the managerial rules.

That the International Short-wave Service, which was regarded as a propaganda weapon, should have been started in wartime was to have been expected, but what was extraordinary at that time was the expansion of the domestic service and the formation of a second national network. The first public proposal for a second network was made during the 1942 hearing of the House of Commons Radio Broadcasting Committee: Gladstone Murray said that there should be alternative facilities available so that listeners could have a choice of two programs; he envisaged "the taking over of a great many privately owned stations" for this second network or the construction of a number of 50,000-watt transmitters. The general manager's utterance must have sent a cold shiver down the spine of a government that was already hard pressed by war spending. But the suggestion had to be made, because already there were more commercial programs than the single network of the CBC could handle.

It was E. A. Weir who was largely responsible for the idea of a second network; he had returned to broadcasting with the CBC after his dismissal from the old CRBC, and had become the corporation's commercial sales manager. Bushnell finds it ironic that Austin Weir, who was to blame most of the ills of the CBC on commercialism in his book *The Struggle for National Broadcasting in Canada,* should have been the one who pleaded with management for the creation of a second network in order to take care of his excess commercials. There was "so damn much business", Bush says, that he "didn't really know where to put it". Radio broadcasting as an advertising medium had come into its own with the full employment and prosperity of wartime, and "sponsors were waiting in line to buy time and programs— not just spot announcements but half-hour and sixty-minute programs". The original Aird Commission had recommended that only institutional advertising should be permitted and that the pure Canadian air should not be defiled by the cries of hucksters, but Bush notes that "lack of dollars and United States broadcasting policies had blown to smithereens the dreams of those stout protagonists, who included the Canadian Radio League, of fully nationalized radio".

As general supervisor of programs, Bushnell was an ardent supporter of the idea of a second network. He felt that the single CBC network, which was known as the Trans-Canada Network, "was overcrowded with commercially sponsored programs and that the creation of a second network would give us more time and greater scope to build programs of our own— programs on which, with some degree of pride, we could pin the label 'Made in Canada by the Canadian Broadcasting Corporation'." So he ordered his senior program officers to work closely with Mr. Weir and his sales force in planning the second network.

For a time, there was discussion of CFRB as the anchor station of the new Dominion Network, and in the detailed report which Austin Weir prepared for the general manager, he included the big private station as the Toronto Outlet because it had the same power (10,000 watts) as CBL, the anchor station of the Trans-Canada Network. However, CFRB objected and raised such a howl that the idea was dropped, and it was decided to use the low-powered CBY (which had the former CKNC transmitter of hallowed Canadian National Carbon Company memory) as the originating station. The call letters were to be changed, and Bushnell was given the task of selecting new ones: he wanted to honour the memory of his father, James Bushnell, so he put J among the new call letters, CJBC—C for Canadian, J for James, B for Bushnell or Broadcasting, and C for Corporation. He was proud of his handiwork, of memorializing his family without being too obvious about it—only later did he realize that this very set of call letters had been assigned in the early days of broadcasting to the phantom station of the Jarvis Street Baptist Church, whose pastor was a fire-and-brimstone preacher known as "Tilly" Shields. CJBC was the only station owned and operated by the CBC among some thirty private stations which made up the Dominion network.

In his report, Austin Weir proposed that the second network begin with three hours programming nightly, ultimately to be extended to sixteen hours daily. He recommended that operations should commence on January 1, 1944. In a covering memo, dated April 6, 1943, Weir wrote: "There is one important point and that is, when a decision is reached to operate this network . . . at least six months prior notice should be given to [private] stations [which were to become affiliates] and sponsors. It would also afford adequate time to adjust any business as between the two networks."

As Weir wished, the Dominion Network began broadcasting on January 1, 1944, with twenty-five member stations from Victoria, BC, to Sherbrooke, Quebec; the Maritime stations were added on October 1, 1944, and the network began providing a limited service from coast to coast. By April 1948, the new network had contracts for twenty-six commercially sponsored programs with a net revenue of three hundred thousand dollars. It became the mainstay of many small stations across the country, and it lasted long after the advent of television and the virtual demise of the American radio networks. But the Dominion Network finally ran its course, and officially ceased operations on September 30, 1962.

16 Euphoria and "Wednesday Night"

In retrospect, Ernie Bushnell was to avow that the late forties and early fifties were the best years of his life; he was speaking of the century although he might have been speaking of himself, for he was as old as the century. They proved to be productive years that saw the development of new and more sophisticated programming, including the incomparable "Wednesday Night", which was culture for the highest brow, and also the beginning of television. But more than anything else they were easy and happy years.

Shortly after VJ-Day and the war's end, a youthful Montreal newspaper editor with a sharp nose and a boyish look, A. Davidson Dunton, was appointed as the salaried chairman of the CBC board, a position that Leonard Brockington had proposed and hankered after. Although Dunton was a prime representative of the establishment, with impeccable Liberal connections, he had never been involved in broadcasting and hadn't even belonged to the Canadian Radio League. The story went the rounds that Prime Minister Mackenzie King, on one of the few occasions that he read the papers, noted an article by Dunton describing what was wrong with the CBC and how it could be fixed up; King, on one of those whims that prime ministers can indulge, decided to let him put his words into action. There was some trepidation among the older CBC officials about what this "young squirt" would do but there was no need to have worried. He went around saying, with a chuckle that verged on a nervous giggle, "I'm Davie Dunton. I'm sure we're going to have a lot of fun working together," and he proved to be a born conciliator, a man who was adept at smoothing things over with an unerring ability to gain a concensus. He was the sort of slick public relations officer that the corporation needed. Bushnell wrote of the period following Dunton's appointment as "an era of relative peace, harmony and progress for the CBC".

Although Bushnell had not achieved the position nor the honours that might have been expected, he emerged from the war with a greatly enhanced reputation: as director general of programs, he was responsible for every broadcast, commercial and sustaining, on the CBC's two English-language networks. Everything from the fumings of a parliamentary committee to a spat between two stenographers landed on his desk; it was no wonder that Jean Tweed, writing in *Saturday Night* for August 31, 1946, should have noted that he was comparatively sane— "because no sensible man would touch his job with a ten-foot pole".

He was fast becoming known as Mr. Broadcasting in Canada, and was regarded as a rich and earthy character by his colleagues and confrères. The way he would bang the table at a program meeting and explode with "Wait a minute, goddamit," was the subject of good-humoured joshing at conferences with CBC affiliates from coast to coast. His profanity and his sentimentality, which was a common enough trait in show business, were matched by a patent honesty and sincerity, and by what was described as a "hair-raising frankness"—it was this more than anything else that made him call a spade "a bloody shovel". There was his Irish temper which would flare up and subside just as quickly, but, above all, Bush had the sublime quality of being able to make subordinates feel like equals, and getting everyone to work together as a team.

Neither the privileges nor the perquisites of power meant much to him. When he moved into a spacious office in the Kremlin, as the executive building at 354 Jarvis Street was irreverently called, Georgie Appleby, who had a separate office of her own, hoped that she would now be summoned into his presence with a buzzer. Instead, he shouted louder—"Hey, Georgie." His memos were usually terse and to the point or, as one recipient remarked, they read as if he were speaking in

131

good, straight Canadian English, without any of the four-letter words. However, Bush remembers one exception: "I got a little fancy once and dictated a long memo to editors berating them for splitting infinitives in our news bulletins. The only trouble was that the memo itself contained no less than six split infinitives. That ended it. From then on I stuck to scribbled notes."

The key to Bushnell's success was that he had been in broadcasting from the beginning and knew every aspect of it. In a *Liberty* magazine "profile" of October 5, 1946, Max Braithwaite quoted an associate as saying: "Bush never asks people to do things he doesn't know all about himself." His profanity was entertaining more than offensive, and a friend remarked with real admiration, "I don't know of anybody who can say what he thinks without pulling his punches and with as little offense as Bush."

As the head of the large and growing production centre in Toronto, he had become identified with the CBC, or at least with its main English-language networks; Dunton and Dr. Frigon, the general manager, were far away and were concerned with policy rather than programming. "Nothing goes on in the organization that Bush doesn't know about," a radio producer said. "Even the most infinitesimal upset gets to him. He doesn't spy, he just listens. He's always willing to hear what you have to say, and he never crosses you up. In private, he may give you the devil, but in public he backs his employees to the hilt. And once he's had his say, it's all over. There's no grudge carrying."

One of his greatest virtues was an ability to delegate authority, as Neil Morrison was to point out years later; that was the basis of his all-embracing grasp of the corporation's affairs. "Bush allowed you a great deal of autonomy," Morrison said. "He let you have your head. Mind you, if you made a mess of it, he would be down on you and bawl you out—and the four-letter words would fly." Mavor Moore, the actor and drama producer, commented in *The Arts in Canada** that Bushnell's term as program director was distinguished for "a rare combination of intellectual vision and common touch. . . ."

*Toronto: Macmillan, 1958.

Bushnell's view of broadcasting had not changed much with the years. "Basically and fundamentally it is show business—or entertainment if you like that term better," he wrote in the tenth anniversary edition of *Radio,* the CBC staff magazine. The way to rile him was to refer to "the longhairs of the CBC", and he sought to assure a parliamentary committee that "our policy most definitely is to give the listeners what they want, keeping in mind the rights of minorities." He spoke of "not-too-thinly veiled suggestions" that the "intellectuals" or the "longhairs" of the CBC program division were determined to see that the public got what they, the planners and producers, thought the public should hear. "That, Mr. Chairman," he said flatly, "is nonsense."

However, Bush was aware of the educational possibilities of broadcasting, and he told the parliamentary committee that "national radio, more than any other means available, is contributing through its day-to-day presentation of programs in Canadian homes to the development of a truly Canadian outlook—and I mean that in the broadest sense, without political or other special implications. . . ." His attitude seemed to be that education and even information must be secondary to entertainment, for without entertainment there would be no audience to educate or inform. There is a parable in a remark that Bush made in 1946 to his only daughter, Marilyn, who was then fifteen. Marilyn was agitating to go to another school with higher scholastic standards and even higher fees; at the same time, she had to have some expensive dental work done. Bush ended the family argument by saying: "Listen dearie, we'll get you beautiful first and worry about your education afterward."

Undoubtedly, his was a practical approach to broadcasting, but while he was concerned with the vast majority and its desire to be amused and entertained at the end of a day's work, he did keep in mind the rights of minorities, and "Wednesday Night" was his gift to intellectuals. According to the minutes for the program meeting on March 12, 1947, R. S. Lambert first made the suggestion that the CBC "should devote one evening per week to block programming somewhat along the lines of the BBC's 'Third Programme' "; Bushnell liked the idea and cleared

133

the time for it—he also named it "Wednesday Night".

A decade before this, Richard Stanton Lambert had been awarded £7,500 ($37,000) in damages, the largest amount ever given in a slander action in Britain according to his famous counsel, Sir Patrick Hastings: this was "The Talking Mongoose Case". Lambert, editor of the BBC magazine, the *Listener,* and author of a number of books, had joined with Harry Price, secretary of the University of London Council for Psychical Research, in investigating the story of an Isle of Man farmer who claimed his house was haunted by a mongoose that spoke English and several foreign languages, could sing and dance and change itself into a cat, was eighty-six years old and answered to the name of Gef. Lambert and Price visited the remote farm but did not see the mongoose. However, they wrote a popular book entitled *The Haunting of Cashen's Gap* in which they cast doubts about Gef, although they did not entirely dismiss the phenomenon; in fact, in the introduction to the book the co-authors describe it as "an essay in the Veracious but Unaccountable". It was this which led Sir Cecil Levita, a man of considerable influence who had acted as Lambert's sponsor, to. doubt his sanity, and he said so to Gladstone Murray, who was then Lambert's immediate superior in the BBC. Murray informed Lambert, who was incensed and demanded an apology; instead of complying, Sir Cecil repeated the alleged slander to the top executives of the BBC. One of them, Sir Stephen Tallents, was unwise enough to warn Lambert that he faced possible dismissal if he continued with his action. It was a memorandum written by Sir Stephen on this incident that Sir Patrick Hastings was able to introduce as evidence resulting in the record award for slander; the case also led the government to appoint a parliamentary commission to inquire into the BBC.

Shortly before the war, Lambert left the BBC—he had learned that the publication of the *Listener* would probably be suspended on the outbreak of hostilities—and immigrated to Canada where his former boss and good friend, Gladstone Murray, got him a job with the CBC. Ernie Bushnell complained that he'd had little advance notice of this new employee in his department when Lambert arrived on his doorstep. "I was disturbed," he says, "but after a session with the general manager I realized that Rex Lambert must be a person of wide experience and if we could find the proper niche for his talents, he could well become a useful colleague." Bush put Lambert, who had a deep interest in education, in charge of school broadcasting, much to the dismay and resentment of the heads of the provincial departments of education. Who was this Englishman who had been foisted on them, and what did he know about education in this country? Bush did his best to smooth ruffled feathers; in no time at all Rex Lambert had not only been accepted, but was regarded by the education officials as a most loyal ally and far-sighted protagonist.

Lambert participated in all the CBC program meetings and it was at one of those meetings, in the early spring of 1947, that he made the proposal which resulted in "Wednesday Night". According to the minutes: "He felt that it would be an excellent thing for the CBC to lead the continent in a program policy of this nature. The programming should aim perhaps at those people who are tending to turn from radio to records as their form of home entertainment."

It was clear from the thorough discussion that followed that those participating in the conference were in favour of the proposal and were excited by its prospects. The fact that there were two networks now, and that listeners had a choice, made it possible to consider an evening of heavy culture. The roots of an idea and an ideal had been firmly planted by Lambert; then came the practical task of clearing the commercially sponsored programs from the schedule for one night of the week, and finding the money to produce grand operas, modern verse plays and the other expensive items that were envisaged. A committee to plan the programming was set up: the chairman was Harry J. Boyle, and among the members were the supervisor of drama Andrew Allan, Neil Morrison, professors Ira Dilworth and Arthur Phelps, and Lambert.

As the 1947-1948 schedule began to take shape, it became apparent that there was really only one night in the week— Wednesday night—on the Trans-Canada Network when all sponsored programs might be removed. The last obstacle was an

NBC origination, "The Album of Familiar Music", which Bush had no reason to like since it was the program that had led to the false VJ-Day broadcast. But Austin Weir and his commercial department protested that it would be disastrous to move this popular program to another night or to the Dominion Network. Finally, Bush blew up and in a fine flurry of expletives demanded that Austin "get the goddam show to hell out of there." In December of 1947, "Wednesday Night" began its long history of programming "for the mind", as Davie Dunton described it.

Many titles were suggested for this evening of block programming, and Bushnell himself proposed that the main hour, between nine and ten o'clock at night, be called the "CBC National Hour"; some of the titles put forward were derisory, and none seemed quite right. One morning while shaving, Bush had an inspiration. Why not call it what it was, "Wednesday Night"?

Harry Boyle's committee had worked hard and come up with proposed schedules for most of the first season—they were included in the agenda of the National Program Conference of October 7 to 9, 1947, which set December 3, 1947, as the starting date. Charles Jennings told the conference that there was one "absolute must", and that was that the new venture avoid being dull. Here, in a condensed version, is the proposed schedule for the first season:

7:30 to 8 pm: The first half-hour was to be devoted to light classical music by the Parlow String Quartet or the CBC Symphonette, a thirty-man ensemble under the baton of Samuel Hersenhorn, or to a music appreciation series with a narrator and small orchestra.

8 to 9 pm: This period was mainly for the spoken word. Andrew Allan had staked out a claim with such modern verse plays as T. S. Eliot's *Murder in the Cathedral* and W. H. Auden's *For the Time Being*, and there were to be citizens' forums on such subjects as atomic power and whether it would destroy the world. A series of three "Great Moments from the Operas" was also planned for this time, an expensive undertaking as a "good-sized orchestra" would be needed as well as "three vocal principals".

9 to 10 pm: The main hour, which Bush had wanted to call the "CBC National Hour", was for the big orchestral productions with guest artists of the calibre of Heifetz and Rubinstein; it would be leavened with adaptations from contemporary literature, such as *Penrod* by Booth Tarkington, *Anna Christie* by Eugene O'Neill and *Hedda Gabler* by Ibsen.

10 to 10:30 pm: News and "News Roundup" were to remain in this slot.

10:30 to 11 pm: Choral groups, cantatas, contemporary music and recitals by distinguished Canadian artists.

11 to 12 midnight: The final hour would be filled by recorded concerts and operas, and the works of Ravel, Bach, Greig, Mozart, Verdi and Puccini were listed in the proposed schedules.

In less than two years, Bushnell was able to claim that "CBC Wednesday Night" was an outstanding success. He wrote in "CBC Programming", an appendix to the report on the autumn program conference of 1949: "We have come to feel a strong bond with a constantly growing body of listeners who have appreciated an honest and sincere attempt by the CBC to satisfy what one person called 'a nutritional deficiency in radio programs'. Listeners tell us that they are not always in agreement with everything we present, but the vast majority say they do get many things from the program which they feel they cannot get anywhere else. 'CBC Wednesday Night' is valuable to everyone who likes a better type of entertainment but it is especially valued by listeners to whom the stage, lectures, concerts, libraries, museums and similar facilities to be found in the larger cities are not available."

Not only were the immediate postwar years a time of euphoria for Ernie, but they were a time for rethinking, for reassessing his own role and reappraising his ideas and views—he would have considered "philosophy" too pretentious a word. While Bushnell still believed that broadcasting was basically show business or entertainment and that radio was "the poor man's theatre", he told a summer course at Queen's University in July 1945 that there were three essentials of programming: knowledge, sincerity and showmanship. As far as the latter was concerned, he admitted that some show-business people who had got into radio in the early years were carrying on with the traditional means of appealing to a mass audience. They didn't seem to understand that "noise, fanfares, drum rolls and the raised voice" had a very different impact on the individual listener or the family group which formed the normal radio audience. "The best kind of showmanship, whether for the theatre or the broadcasting studio," Bush said, "consists rather of a sense of timing of entertainment values, and of the balance and shape of a program. Without showmanship of this kind even the best program material may lose its audience. In exactly the same way, the very best of books will not easily find readers unless it is well and clearly printed and logically spaced."

His major speeches were filed in a ring binder with a black leather cover that he keeps in his desk. In the binder he also put the statements of others on broadcasting: interspersed with his own speeches are those of CBC Chairman Davidson Dunton, as well as articles by Edward R. Murrow and Clifford J. Durr of the Federal Communications Commission, and predictions ("Radio: Next 25 Years") by such notables as Niles Trammell, the president of the NBC; Paul W. Kesten, an executive vice-president of the CBS; Mark Woods, the president of the ABC; and Edgar Kobak, the president of Mutual. There are also odd items like "The Canons of Good Broadcasting" and a *Fortune* magazine survey of soap operas. Thus, the black binder became a sort of bible on broadcasting which Bushnell would read like a Gideon Bible in a hotel room, taking it out of his desk drawer and perusing it at random. For the good of his soul, he included a report from *Variety* dated December 26, 1945, which began by quoting unnamed "Canadian showmen visiting New York" as saying that "Canadian broadcasters suffer from a horrible inferiority complex" and that Canadian radio had about it "a drabness and mediocrity". Bush ridiculed that paragraph:

These Canadian showmen are of the opinion that the CBC should first of all install an American broadcaster to manage the operation, and let him in turn surround himself with good programming. Such a guy at the helm, they point out, might command fifty thousand a year, which in terms of radio in Canada is fabulous coin, but they're equally convinced that such vision can pay off.

The black binder included what was really a pep talk Bushnell delivered at the October 1948 National Program Conference. He warned that, with television on the horizon, "we cannot—we must not stand still," and added: "Either CBC program service will become a more dynamic, living and vital service to a larger body of listeners or inevitably it will hit the skids. How far distant is that danger point today—not tomorrow nor next spring nor next autumn, but right now." Bush posed another question. He wanted to know whether the producers, the participants in this conference, were engaged in putting on programs: "Are we—and when I say we I mean everyone of us—are we thinking, eating and sleeping with program ideas? Or, conversely, are the regenerative and creative wells of thought going dry?" Not for nothing had Bush sung in the choir of the Methodist church in Omemee—some of the revivalist rhetoric had rubbed off on him. He admitted that he and his colleagues had the heavy task of programming three networks (Trans-Canada, Dominion, French), as well as thirteen—soon to be fourteen—CBC-owned and operated stations. More staff and money would be a help, but Bush averred: "The most important thing of all is just good, honest, hard thinking. We have to dig deeper and longer and harder if we are to achieve really satisfying results."

On many occasions, Ernie Bushnell spoke of the CBC as a "unifying force", but he was worried that its pervasive impact on the country at large would result in a common Canadian culture that would be "uniform or characterless". He told a parliamentary committee:

It seems to me far more desirable that the music and songs of Quebec, for instance, should continue to preserve their distinctiveness and local quality; the same is true of the Gaelic tradition of Cape Breton or the Fraser Valley, the Ukranian songs and dances of the prairies, the seafaring songs and tales of the Maritimes and so on. The important thing is not

139

uniformity but diversity, provided that all of us, no matter where we live in Canada, have the common privilege of sharing—of vying with one another in developing music and drama and other programs that will draw on these local cultures for the enjoyment of all.

Perhaps this statement more than any other summed up his broadcasting philosophy: at any rate, there is more than one speech in the black binder that ends on this note of the need for cultural diversity.

Young Ernie Bushnell (third from left) sang tenor with the Adanac quartet on the Chatauqua circuit in the early twenties.

Charles Jennings, Ernie Bushnell and Stan Hamilton (left to right) beside the Bomber *during the Royal Tour, 1939.*

Gladstone Murray presents an award to Lorne Greene with Bushnell standing by at the Davenport Road studios in Toronto at the beginning of the war.

Bushnell Visits Canadian fighter squadron in Britain during the war, with broadcaster Don Fairbairn (right) and CBC engineer, R. G. Cahoon.

CBC executive meeting 1945. Front row: Jack Rodford, E.A. Weir, Donald Manson, Dr. Augustin Frigon, E.L. Bushnell, G.W. Olive.

Ernie Bushnell at the sod turning ceremony for CJOH studios in 1961— on his right, Miss Appleby and Stu Griffiths.

Lord Sidney Bernstein and J. Alphonse Ouimet (at opening of CJOH studios, 1961).

Stu Griffiths and Ernie Bushnell in 1971.

17 How Television Began

On March 28, 1949, the government brought out its long-awaited policy statement on television. As might have been expected, this 1,250-word document caused quite a stir in the upper echelons of the CBC. Reading its two and a half closely typed foolscap pages, Ernie Bushnell got the distinct impression that the government would have much preferred to delay its decision until the Royal Commission on National Development in the Arts, Letters and Sciences (the Massey commission) had been able to advise on the sort of TV that Canada should have. He notes that the statement said the government proposed to include television among the subjects of inquiry for the commission, but "in the meantime" had decided to give the go-ahead signal for the development of a Canadian television system "on an interim basis". It would seem that the government had given in to the demands of the electronic industry, and some of its Liberal supporters in Parliament were alarmed at the threats of lay-offs in the industry; but in Bush's view, the greatest influence in hurrying Ottawa was the forest of TV aerials to be seen in the Bathurst and Spadina areas of Toronto. The inactivity of the government had meant that thousands of Canadians were tuned into American TV stations, and it was a moot question whether the CBC or Canadian television would ever get them back.

While the statement said that the CBC was the government's main instrument for television, it did allow for the licensing of private stations, "the operations of which [will be] co-ordinated with those of the national facilities." The corporation was to set up national television production centres in Toronto and Montreal; it was to provide a "service of television programmes for broadcasting by stations which may be established in other areas of Canada"—in other words, a TV network—and to establish "transmitting stations in Montreal and Toronto". It would be necessary for the government to grant the CBC loans to cover the capital costs of the new studios and equipment as well as the first operating costs, and "Parliament will be asked to approve a loan of four million dollars this year." The statement went on to say that "the national television operation will become self-sufficient from licence fees and commercial revenues in a few years".

Such a claim was simply political eyewash; the licence fee, which was never more than $2.50 for a radio receiving set, had already proved difficult to collect and was suspended in 1953, a short time after the first Canadian television station went on the air. It was estimated that the proposed licence fee for television would have had to be around fifteen dollars a year, and that would have been totally impractical since the first Canadian viewers were tuned in to commercially supported American stations and would have resisted any attempt to collect money. For a time, the CBC was maintained by a fifteen per cent excise tax on new television and radio sets, but that was a diminishing return and in the end the government had to make grants to the corporation of one hundred million dollars a year and more.

The publication of the policy statement on television started a chain reaction of internal memorandums in the corporation. Ernie Bushnell was worried about the inroads that the advertising agencies and sponsors might make in the new medium of television, and petitioned the general manager about that; Dr. Frigon was concerned about whether the commercials from the United States would be suitable for re-broadcast by the CBC, and wrote to the director general of programs that there should be a "review committee" of three persons, whose decisions would be final, to "assure a proper control of commercial programs offered to us from outside".

As might be expected, Bushnell was nominated as the one indispensable person to initiate the medium that would become, according to the government statement, "one of the most effective means of mass communication yet devised". He went again to London—the British had, after all, been the pioneers of television, and Bush, during his prewar trip to Britain, had had his first look at TV on an early set with a postcard-sized picture tube. He also visited a handful of American stations, WWJ and WXYZ in Detroit, WNBK and WEWS in Cleveland, and WBEN in Buffalo. Since Canadian television would have to have the same video standard of 525 lines as the US networks, CBC TV was likely to be much more closely tied to the American system than radio was—the British, at the time of his visit, still had 405 lines.

Norman Collins, the best-selling author of *London Belongs To Me*, was the head of BBC television at Alexandra Palace. In those days, so many people wanted to see the marvels of TV that Bush recommended that every new studio built should be equipped with a visitors' gallery. He attended a rehearsal and was thrilled by "a bigger six-ringed circus than was ever staged by Barnum and Bailey". The rehearsal, he wrote in his report, "continues all day (with time out for coffee and tea, of course) until 'THE END' has disappeared over the final turn of the caption roller. Nothing has changed in my twenty-five years' absence from the stage. Confusion still reigns supreme. Grease paint and powder neither look nor smell different. Language is practically the same: 'Curtain'—'Lights'—'Music full up'—and 'On with the show'."

It was obvious that Bush considered BBC television worthy of much greater attention than the American private TV stations; he spent three weeks in London, making almost daily visits to Alexandra Palace and viewing television production on a set in his hotel room, whereas his study of the five stations in Detroit, Cleveland and Buffalo took only five days. His report on the BBC operations was a full account, often glowingly written as he himself admits, with ten chapters and a like number of appendices, whereas the report on his brief swing around the American stations was based largely on a transcript of notes taken. However, a comparison would be misleading, and Bushnell was aware of this when he wrote: "The approach to television by the BBC is quite different from anything we have seen on our side of the Atlantic." As a program director, he could not be blamed for preferring the big four-camera dramatic productions of Alexandra Palace to the two-camera quiz or games shows in the US TV studios. There were only 160,000 sets in Britain then, and the BBC was spending a million pounds a year on television. Bush worried: "How present applicants for private station licences hope to produce a television service that will in any way measure up to the requirements of either the medium itself or the demands of a reasonably intelligent audience has become an increasingly deep mystery to me."

His American observations did not make him any more sanguine. The operation of WBEN in Buffalo, a station watched by thousands in Toronto, was a "revelation to me": it had one studio no bigger than a large living room with two cameras, and the full-time staff numbered thirty-three, many of whom were salesmen. WBEN drew support from the *Buffalo Evening News* (which owned it and a radio station) and was run on the most economical lines possible. The lack of studio facilities was a severe handicap, and Bush wrote: "It has five flats [sets] and properties that could be bought at any auction sale for fifty dollars. If this station had any more equipment, it would not know where to put it. . . ." Yet, despite extravagant penny pinching, he reported that the station was operating in the red and expected to be doing so for many months to come. For that matter, none of the American stations that he visited was making money. WWJ in Detroit was trying every conceivable means of making ends meet, "even to the point of selling time on its test-pattern periods at twenty per cent of its card rate".

In his report on BBC television, Bushnell asked the question: "What is television?" He wanted to know whether it stemmed from the theatre or vaudeville or Hollywood, or was it "photographed radio", as Alistair Cooke had described American television? In any case, what was television in Canada to become? Bush ended this report, which was filed on June 17, 1949, by repeating the question. While admitting that he did not yet know the answer, he said: "One answer could be and maybe should be: 'It is a mirror reflecting life—life while it is happening.' "

The first TV appointments were made in December 1949 when Fergus Mutrie was named director of television, Toronto, and Aurèle Séguin, director of television, Montreal; they began the long and arduous task of organizing staff, acquiring facilities and preparing for TV production and transmission in the two cities to which the government's policy statement had given priority in television. The fact that it took three years to get the first TV stations on the air was due to red tape and the corporation's cautious and deliberate bureaucracy. Also, it was made clear, Bushnell recorded, that radio would continue to be the most important function of the CBC, and "for years to come must be accepted by everyone as 'the senior service' "; the effect of this policy decision, which was taken at the highest level by Dr. Frigon himself, was to make it even more difficult for those who were planning the development of television, especially in the recruitment of staff from radio.

For some time, Stuart Griffiths had been asking to be transferred to television—he was at a standstill in the International Service and he knew it. In 1951 Bushnell was able to get him appointed director of programs for CBLT, the call letters for the projected CBC television station in Toronto. Almost immediately there was a spurt of activity at 354 Jarvis Street as Griffiths went to work; he began hiring producers, directors, performers, cameramen and technicians; he tried to persuade such CBC radio greats as Andrew Allan and Frank Willis "to get in and pitch in this wonderful new ball game", as he put it, but they refused. Undoubtedly, they were influenced by the policy decision that radio would remain Number One; they were also accustomed to a network and a nation-wide audience, and the beginning of television must have seemed like going back to single-station broadcasting. However, when they were ready to get into TV there was no place for them, as the young men and women that Griffiths and his assistant, Mavor Moore, had taken on and trained were now highly professional and running things very well. Some of that younger generation went on to make names for themselves in television and films in Britain and the

United States; among them were Norman Campbell, Joyce Davidson, Elaine Grand, Harvey Hart, Arthur Hiller, Norman Jewison, Peter Macdonald and Sidney Newman.

The first studio was in a wooden shack that had been used by the CWACs, the Canadian Women's Army Corps, during the war when 354 Jarvis Street was Havergal Ladies College. A 500-foot steel tower was erected hard by the shack and "the Kremlin", that dignified Victorian annex where Bush had his office; Dan McArthur, the chief news editor, called the transmitter "a shorter and uglier Eiffel Tower". Behind that monstrous pylon, a warehouse of a building was put up to house the television offices and studios.

Shortly before CBLT was due to open, Griffiths came to see Bushnell; he was completely broken in spirit and even had tears in his eyes.

"Bush," Stu said, "I've had it—I'm licked." Then he launched into an almost incoherent review of the difficulties he'd had in obtaining head-office approval for hiring sufficient staff to get the station on the air. He cursed "those stupid bastards in Ottawa" who had sat on his recommendations and requirements for over a month and had not yet come through "with a bloody one of them".

Since the official opening was only a week away something had to be done, and Bush asked what he needed in the way of help.

"Carpenters, painters, designers, and one or two video operators," Stu replied.

"Could these people be considered artists?" Bush put on an air of pretended ignorance.

"Of course, they're artists," Stu said. "Otherwise we wouldn't need them."

The director general of programs fully expected that, at the most, four or five were required, and when Stu said that he needed thirty-two "bods", Bushnell was thunderstruck.

"Holy-be-Jesus," Bush said. "We *are* in a predicament, but the blasted station has to open next Wednesday and if these people are artists, as you tell me they are, there's nothing for it but to hire them and pay them via the artists' weekly payroll route."

So the thirty-two were hired and put on the artists' payroll. Bushnell knew there would be trouble, as the artists' payroll was meant to pay only musicians and actors and such like, not carpenters and painters and video operators. Sure enough, when the payroll list reached Ottawa, he was called on the telephone for an explanation; since his replies were not understood, he was asked to come to headquarters to explain. (Bush had suggested that one reason for the extraordinary alarm was the public outcry over the "horses on the payroll" scandal. That was a case of malfeasance or corruption in the Department of National Defence, when horses were discovered on the armed forces' payroll.)

When Bush arrived in Ottawa, he found the general manager, Donald Manson, and the treasurer, Harry Bramah, as well as the head of personnel and administration, Colonel Landry, all trembling in their respective britches over a situation that could wreck the CBC—or so they said. After about two hours of badgering, Bush got fed up, turned to the general manager and said:

"Look, I've had enough of this. Did we or did we not get your goddamn television on the air on time, and did we or did we not make a pretty goddamn good job of it?"

The answer was in the affirmative.

"Well then, there was no misappropriation of funds. A critical situation arose and I took what I considered to be the only kind of action I could take to resolve the problem. Maybe what I did was somewhat irregular and contravened some of your bloody regulations and cut across the furrows of the bum sitters here in head office. But if you don't like it, you can all go to hell—or alternatively, fire me."

With that, Bush stalked out, and it was the last he ever heard of the incident.

Aside from the fact that the call letters, CBLT, came on upside down when the station went on the air—and the corporation took an unmerciful ribbing over that—the opening ceremony went off without a hitch on September 8, 1952.

At the end of that year, there was a major shuffle of the corporation's top executives. Donald Manson, who had succeeded Dr. Frigon as general manager, retired; J. Alphonse Ouimet took his place and E. L. Bushnell became assistant general manager and was also named co-ordinator of television. The new appointment meant that Bush had to leave Toronto and his spacious office in the Kremlin, where he was boss of English-language broadcasting, for the third-floor executive suite at 140 Wellington Street, almost directly across the lawn of Parliament Hill from the Peace Tower in Ottawa.

When he moved to the capital, he found that the corporation's plans for erecting a two-hundred- to three-hundred-foot-high television tower had fallen afoul of Ottawa's formidable mayor, Dr. Charlotte Whitton. The CBC was negotiating to purchase a large stone house on Richmond Road as a site for the Ottawa studios and transmitter, and when Mayor Whitton heard about it via the grapevine, she let out a blast that could be heard twenty miles away in Carp, according to Bush. "No bloody big tower like that will ever be allowed to deface the horizon of the nation's capital," Charlotte said.

It was an unseemly and unequal match: the CBC triumvirate of Dunton, Ouimet and Manson (who had been retained as a consultant after his retirement as general manager) was thoroughly cowed by this ferocious female, and their last resort was to ask Ernie Bushnell if he couldn't use his influence. He had known her for a long time and was a friend; surely he could persuade this diminutive dragon of a woman that they had to have the tower up in time for the coronation.

So Ernie phoned as an old friend to request an interview, but Her Worship suspected his motives and refused to grant it, at the same time launching into a vitriolic denunciation of the CBC and its "Grit" advisors. Davie Dunton was "listening in" on an extension, something Bush didn't discover till after the hour-long telephone call was over. The language used at both ends of the line, according to his own understatement, "was, to say the least, not generally acceptable in either social or business circles". Her Worship quieted down enough to allow Bush to threaten publicly to put the blame on her if the CBC could not find an alternative site on which to build studios and tower in time to show the coronation ceremonies to Ottawa viewers. This hit Charlotte Whitton, an ardent royalist, right in the solar plexus.

"Ernie," she yelled over the phone, "you wouldn't do that to me, would you?"

"I sure as hell would," he replied. According to his account, her retort was: "You're a dirty bugger."

At which he issued an ultimatum: "I'll give you twenty-four hours to find a suitable city-owned parcel of land, and at a cost of not more than eighteen thousand dollars."

This sparked another outburst: "Why I just turned down sixty thousand dollars for a piece of land that might be suitable—do you think I'm going to sell it to you for eighteen?"

That was the top price, he said, knowing full well as he did that Charlotte was "a pretty sharp horse trader".

"Alright, you so-and-so," Charlotte blurted out. "I'll call a meeting of the Board of Control for tonight and have a special resolution passed, but even if I do that, the Ontario Municipal Board may not approve."

"That's up to you," Bush said, pressing his advantage, "but remember, no deal, no coronation on television in Ottawa. If I have to, I'll go to see Prime Minister St. Laurent and put the blame where it belongs—right on you."

"OK, OK," a subdued Mayor Whitton muttered. "You file a letter with the city's chief engineer by four o'clock this afternoon and I'll do my best."

Bushnell felt that he had won a victory and went into the chairman's office to report the result, only to find that Dunton knew all about it. He was sitting, as he often did, with his feet on his desk; there was a quizzical but admiring grin on his face.

"I've never heard anything like that in my life," he said with a chuckle, "but for God's sake, get that letter down to Her Worship before she changes her mind."

Charlotte Whitton was as good as her word; the CBC engineers got the television station ready for the coronation, but only just—CBOT was officially opened on June 1, 1953, the day before the big event. However, Ernie feels sure that Charlotte never forgave him for the not-so-subtle form of blackmail he had used on her. Eight years later, when she was again mayor and he was starting his own station, CJOH-TV, in a temporary studio located in an Ottawa lumberyard, he needed a hundred-foot tower to beam the signal to his transmitter at Hazeldean, and went ahead with its construction before receiving the city's approval. Dr. Whitton insisted that the tower be inspected, and engaged a consultant in Toronto to come to Ottawa for that purpose; subsequently, she sent his bill for $250 to CJOH. At first, Bush refused to pay; he said her action had not been authorized by the Board of Control, but his lawyer, G. E. "Ted" Beament, persuaded him that it would be foolish to carry on a feud with Her Worship. So he paid the $250.

A few years later, Stuart Griffiths as general manager of CJOH engaged Dr. Whitton as one of the station's commentators, and Ernie and Charlotte buried the hatchet and became friends again. It was about time, too, since it had been more than a decade since their no-words-barred battle over the telephone, but they were, by their own admission, a couple of "stubborn old mules".

In its first statement on television policy (March 28, 1970), the government had announced an interim plan for the development of Canadian television, pending the report and the recommendations of the Massey commission. The report, which was a monumental work and the first survey of the Canadian cultural scene, came out in due course, and the government made a further statement on television (December 8, 1952), in which it said:

> The Commission recommended that the Canadian Broadcasting Corporation proceed with the production of television programs and with plans for national coverage. It spoke of extension of national coverage through publicly and privately owned stations. It said that no private station should be licensed until the CBC had available national television programs, and that all private stations established should be required to serve as outlets for national programs. It emphasized the need for direction and control of television broadcasting in Canada to prevent Canadian stations from

150

becoming mere channels for broadcasting material from outside Canada, and to encourage Canadian content.

Since a national television service had been started, the government felt that it should be extended as widely and as quickly as possible to other areas; the statement said that Parliament would be asked to approve a loan to the CBC for the purpose of building stations in Vancouver, Winnipeg and Halifax. In addition, the government was now "ready to receive applications for licences for private stations to serve areas not now served or to be served by publicly owned facilities already announced". The statement went on to say: "Since the objective will be to extend services as widely throughout Canada as is practicable, no two stations will be licensed at the present to serve the same area." In other words, there were to be no competing Canadian TV stations, and that was the way it was to remain until the government changed and a new regulatory body was established . . . by which time Ernie Bushnell had left the CBC, and was ready to apply for a second station licence.

18 The Great Coronation Sweepstakes

The coronation of Queen Elizabeth II on June 2, 1953, came at the very beginning of Canadian television; CBMT in Montreal and CBLT in Toronto had been on the air only a few months, while the Ottawa station was rushed to completion specifically for the event. Furthermore, the crowning of the new monarch occurred in the decade before the communications satellite with its possibilities for live transmission from any part of the globe; it therefore gave rise to a fantastic trans-Atlantic race by the fastest jet planes available. It developed into "the Great Coronation Sweepstakes", and the Canadian Broadcasting Corporation with its three new stations, which would have been rated by any handicapper as complete outsiders compared with the huge American networks and their hundreds of affiliates, won easily. However, there were all kinds of chills and thrills before the film was clipped into the television projector in Montreal, and Bushnell describes the episode as an amazing mixture of international intrigue and co-operation, of bad faith, even blackmail, as well as of wild enthusiasm and rapturous good luck. He feels that the broadcast was one of the greatest achievements of the CBC, if not the greatest.

It began with a long-distance telephone call one day in December 1952. On the line was J. B. Clark (the late Sir Beresford Clark) who had been Bush's old boss and friend when he ran the BBC's North American Service. Clark had been put in charge of televising the coronation; TV cameras were to be allowed to cover the whole ceremony, within and without Westminster Abbey, but they were to be only BBC cameras.

That much was known in Canada, but where did the CBC fit in or, for that matter, the American networks and other foreign broadcasting organizations?

"Bush," J. B. said, his familiar voice only slightly blurred by long distance, "a certain problem has arisen which I find very difficult to discuss with you be telephone. Could you by any chance hop over to see us soon? Naturally, I presume you have some idea of what it is all about but it's of such importance and magnitude that I'm most reluctant—indeed, I cannot—discuss it with you either be telephone or letter. Do you think you could possibly spare the time, there's a good fellow, to visit us in London for a week or so?"

"You betcha," Bush said, or something to that effect. "When do you want me to be there?"

"I'm terribly sorry, but could you possibly make it the day after tomorrow?"

On the following day, Bushnell flew to London. Since he had already been appointed co-ordinator and supervisor of coronation broadcasts, and there had been some discussions in Ottawa and tentative plans laid, he was empowered to negotiate with the British. Clark met him at London Airport and told him while they were driving into town that they would be meeting with a strong delegation from the American networks who were quite prepared to take over the telecasting of this historic event and make it available not only to their own viewers but to Canadian viewers as well—and at no cost to the CBC, J. B. added with a grin.

"Very nice of them," Bush said. "We appreciate their thoughtfulness, but they can go to hell. We have our own plans."

This was really a bluff, but Clark was intrigued and wanted to know more. Bushnell tried to stall, saying that he had to have further confirmation from Canada which he hoped to get before his return, but his old CBC boss was insistent and he finally blurted out:

"OK, OK. I'll tell you—in confidence, of course . . . we're trying to persuade the RCAF to fly our films from London to Montreal."

"*Your* films—where do you think *you're* to get any films?" Clark spluttered. Only BBC cameras were to be allowed to cover the ceremony, and Bush knew this. But his explanation of what he meant fortunately was cut short as the car arrived at the Dorchester Hotel.

Both NBC and CBS had sent over some of their top executives for the meeting that was held in the BBC boardroom in Broadcasting House on the day after Bushnell arrived. ABC, then a comparatively small television network, relied on its London representative; he appeared to show only mild interest in the proceedings, which was ironic in the light of what finally happened. J. B. Clark was in the chair and swore everyone to secrecy before beginning his presentation; essentially, what it amounted to was that the BBC would process dozens of 35-millimeter prints of the spectacle inside Westminster Abbey, to be made available at no cost to any country or foreign broadcasting organization that wanted a copy.

"Wonderful."

"Magnificent."

The murmur of applause from the conference table was followed by nagging questions:

"How are we going to get the films?"

"When can we expect delivery?"

"Obviously," said someone stating the obvious, "distribution is the hard core of the problem."

"Gentlemen," said J. B., looking rather smug, "I believe we have that matter well in hand. The BBC has arranged with the British Air Ministry to have a Comet aircraft placed at its disposal for the purpose of flying processed film to America."

The use of the term "America" always burned Bushnell's hide, and he interrupted to say:

"You mean to the United States, I presume."

Clark apologized and averred that Bush was right.

There followed a long and sometimes heated discussion about who was going to get what, when and where. None of the American networks wanted a pooled service, either in Britain or at home; they were competitors, not partners, and each of them, with the exception of ABC, put forward a plea to have their own commentators in the Abbey. One network wanted its print delivered to Boston, another to New York. At that time, the Comet was one of the fastest commercial aircraft in existence, capable of flying the Atlantic in ten hours. Since the coronation ceremony began at three pm London time—ten am Eastern Daylight Time—there was a slim chance of getting the program on the air late that night. But there were more questions:

"How long would it take to process the 35-mm film?"

"How long would it take to make dupes?"

If the CBC could get the RCAF to fly its film to Montreal, Bush thought, "we'll beat the hell out of those damn Yankees," but he was worried about the 35-mm prints as CBMT had no 35-mm projector, nor could one be installed. However, any mention of 16-mm prints was greeted with derisory scorn by the BBC engineers. "Impossible, old boy, the quality is not good enough for the reproduction of such a historic event as the coronation. No, really, nothing doing." It will be a historic event, Bush thought glumly, by the time we get it on the air. The BBC's 35-mm film took hours to develop and print, whereas Bush knew that there was a "hot-kine" method which processed 16-mm film almost instantaneously. But he wasn't going to say anything about this at the conference table with all those American network sharks around.

It was Stu Griffiths who had put the CBC on to the hot kine. On one of his trips in search of material for television, he had visited New York and the United Nations which had just moved into its glass tower on the East River; it wasn't the UN General Assembly or the fact that Canada's Lester B. Pearson was president that fascinated him so much as a new piece of equipment in a basement darkroom which produced television recordings in a matter of minutes. This, thought Stu, was just the thing for the coronation and, without consulting anyone, he talked General Precision Laboratory into giving the CBC an option on two or three of these "film recorders and hot processors". (The only way to record television in those pre-video tape days was to "film it off the tube", and General Precision's machine passed through processing vats and over racks at a higher speed.)

When he got back to Ottawa, Griffiths told his superiors what he had done; Bushnell remembers that "the reaction was a cool one indeed". The attitude seemed to be "who was this young whippersnapper to make such a commitment?" Then came a barrage of questions: How good was this new gadget? What would it cost? Would it be sufficiently reliable for the purpose of recording the coronation? Would the BBC allow it to be used? And how could it be got to London? Griffiths remained calm and unruffled, and suggested the sensible thing to do was to send CBC engineers to New York to take a look. At the same time, he said that televising the coronation within a reasonable time of its occurrence would mean that the film would have to be flown from London to Montreal.

"I guess maybe I shouldn't have done it," Stu admitted meekly, as though confessing to a felony. "But I've already talked to Avro Aircraft and they think that they can arrange to furnish us with a few fast planes—at least enough to do the job—that is if we can sell the idea of flying them over and back to the RCAF."

"The RCAF wouldn't touch it with a ten-foot pole," Bushnell interjected. "They got into a fine mess when they just happened to be flying a squadron to Vancouver on Grey Cup Day and we persuaded them to carry some film for us. They got hell for that on the floor of the House of Commons. Once burned, twice shy. I'll bet there's nothing doing."

"Well, I thought I'd just mention it," was Griffiths' laconic rejoinder. However, he had started a train of thought, which was probably his intention: the engineers realized that they would have to examine the hot-kine process not by their exacting standard but on the basis of whether it would work in the situation; it made Bush reconsider the whole question of having the RCAF deliver the film. In fact, in the lively account that he wrote about televising the coronation, he gave Stu full credit for being the spark that started the CBC "on the road to success".

During his visit to London, Bushnell bumped into Sir Francis Charles McLean, who was one of the top men in the BBC engineering department and an old friend from war days; it was at a cocktail party, and after the usual small talk and reminiscences, Bush hesitatingly told McLean that the CBC was considering a 16-mm hot-kine process and asked his opinion of it. The BBC engineer allowed that it might work but added that, as a matter of policy, they did not use any equipment which had not been tested and approved by his department. However, he would look into it further as he had heard about the process and was interested. He did that and, at Bush's request, wrote to say that if the CBC were willing to take full responsibility for the quality of reproduction of the hot kine, the BBC was prepared to provide the necessary space for the installation of the General Precision machine at Alexandra Palace and would also provide a direct television feed of the coronation coverage.

That was a weight off his mind, and Bushnell sighed with relief, but there was still the problem of delivery. He began negotiations with the Department of National Defence; he found the minister, then Brooke Claxton, sympathetic and anxious to help but reluctant to commit the RCAF to such a hazardous and costly adventure. However, Claxton said that "he would keep trying".

Meanwhile, Davidson Taylor, who was in charge of public-affairs broadcasting for the NBC, kept coming to Ottawa and visiting CBC headquarters; he must have shrewdly suspected that the British were going to see that Canadian television would get the films of the coronation first, and he pleaded for co-operation. Since there had been no approach by either CBS or ABC, Bushnell was prepared to bargain. "Co-operation is a two-way street," he told Taylor, who agreed that CBC and NBC would work as a team.

Once again, "London calling Mr. Bushnell" on the telephone, and the familiar and mellifluous voice of J. B. Clark, who said that he had some good news for Bush. "I think—now I'm not positive, mind you—but I believe I have solved the difficulties of the transportation of films for you." J. B. went rambling on in his unhurried, circumlocutory manner, about the importance of Commonwealth relations and especially of Canada getting the TV broadcasts of the coronation procession and ceremony before any other country, including the USA, all the while driving Bush almost frantic. "Yes, yes," he would interrupt, "but for God's sake, tell me how." In the end, Clark confessed he was calling to alert Bush to a letter: "I can't tell you over the phone. . . . I'll be writing you today and will try to send my letter via the Canada House diplomatic pouch."

When External Affairs phoned to say that they had a private and confidential letter for him, Bushnell himself went to the East Block on Parliament Hill to pick it up. He was overjoyed by its contents: J. B. wrote that the British Air Ministry had assigned a squadron of Canberras, the latest and fastest jet aircraft, to ferry the coronation films to Montreal, and that the most experienced RAF pilots would be flying the planes; they had even given the operation a name: Pony Express. Since this information was completely confidential, Bush knew that Dave Taylor and the National Broadcasting Company could not be told, and he was in favour of breaking the agreement. But Dunton said they would have to stick to their side of the bargain, and asked Bush to leave it to him to find some way around the difficulty.

By this time, the hot-kine process had been tested and found workable; the CBC had made a deal with the General Precision Laboratory and arrangements had been made to air freight this cumbersome and complex bit of machinery to London. With it went an installation crew from the corporation's engineering staff; they assembled their machine at Alexandra Palace, then lived and slept with it until the coronation was over and it was dismantled.

From the trade press, Bushnell found out that the CBC blueprint was being copied. The plot was thickening. NBC too had a hot kine, obtained undoubtedly from General Precision who were the only people making it, but what seemed incredible was that they too had arranged for Canberras to fly their film across the Atlantic. "Where on God's green earth did they get those aircraft?" Bushnell wondered. "Has the British Air Ministry let us down? Has political pressure, too hot to resist, been applied?" Finally, the full story was published: several Canberras, which were made by the English Electric Company, had been ordered by the Venezuelan government for its air force, and it so

158

happened that the delivery of the first of these fast planes would be made on June 2, Coronation Day; NBC therefore persuaded the Venezuelan government to fly them home by way of Boston. When he learned this, Bush, who was always a keen competitor, was thoroughly disgusted. The delivery date of June 2 was a pure coincidence, he was told, a lucky break for NBC. "Like hell it was," and Bush was furious over the way in which the CBC's carefully guarded plans and secrets had become known to its American rivals. At the same time, he learned that the Columbia Broadcasting System, which had been suspiciously silent, had entered the race. They had engaged the movie star, Jimmy Stewart, who had a fast private plane, to fly their film across the Atlantic. This, however, turned out to be a cover for a much more ambitious scheme.

The azimuthal maps were brought out, and distances carefully measured—London turned out to be a tiny bit closer to Montreal than to Boston. "With luck and with care," Bushnell thought, "we can still beat them." Dave Taylor of NBC was back on the corporation's doorstep, seeking full and friendly co-operation and agreeing that it was a two-way street. Bush was tempted, as he said, to throw him out of a third-floor window at CBC headquarters in Ottawa, but he was persuaded to renew the agreement, "just in case something unforeseen should happen."

Just a few days prior to June 2, Bushnell received a telephone call from an old friend at ABC, Phil Carlin, who asked if the CBC would give them "its feed of the coronation".

"No can do, my friend," Bush said. "We have an agreement with NBC which entitles them to an exclusive feed."

"But this is history," Carlin protested. "You can't do that, or there is bound to be a stink raised which will impair our good old international relations."

"You go to blazes. Good relations or bad relations, we simply can't do it. We gave our word—and anyway, this is a fine time for you to come up with such a request. Cripes, are you all asleep down there? What's wrong with you?"

"But, but . . ."

"But nothing, I'm too damn busy to listen to any more of your wailing."

"Hey, wait a minute, brother," Carlin said. "Maybe you don't know it but you can't feed NBC because we have contracted for the only available microwave circuit between Toronto and Buffalo."

"You *what*?" Bushnell cried out. "You're a bloody liar. I don't believe it."

"Well, if you won't take my word for it, call the Bell Telephone Company and they'll confirm it for you. Now what are you going to do?"

It was "a hell of a picklement", as Bush wrote in his account of the coronation broadcast; after all the careful planning, after everything seemed to be going so well, there was one hitch, one omission—they had forgotten about the only microwave circuit between Toronto and Buffalo. In the end, the CBC had to agree to give its coronation feed to ABC.

J. P. "Jimmy" Gilmore, an up-and-coming young CBC executive, was named Bushnell's assistant on the coronation broadcast and was sent to London to supervise operations there. Shortly after he arrived, he heard that the Columbia Broadcasting System had made arrangements to have Britain's latest and most advanced jet bomber, the Vulcan, which was a good deal faster than the Canberra, deliver their kine recordings. Ed Murrow had approached Prime Minister Churchill on the matter while doing a "Person-to-Person" program with him. At the time, the prototype Vulcan was with the British Ministry of Supply but was to be returned to its manufacturers, the De Havilland Company, for tests during the week of June 1: the plan was for one of these tests to be a flight to Boston carrying some early CBS film. As might be expected, the CBC was upset and so was the BBC; they argued that it would not look right for the British government to seem to be favouring an American network in such a manner. Whether their protestations had an effect, or whether there were technical problems as the Air Ministry claimed, the net result was that the Vulcan flight across the Atlantic was cancelled.

Thus, CBS was scratched. Only NBC, with its Venezuela-bound Canberra, was going to make a race of it—although there was the likelihood of a secondary race as it was decided that it would be safer for the RAF Canberra, which was a pool plane carrying the CBC, NBC and CBS films, to land at Goose Bay, Labrador, or Gander, Newfoundland, and transfer the American prints to P 51 fighters which would fly them the rest of the way to the United States. (NBC had only one Canberra ready to fly the Atlantic; it would leave early and, according to the agreement reached in Ottawa, would carry both NBC and CBC films.) CF 100s of the RCAF were standing by in both Goose and Gander to fly the recordings to Montreal in case the Canberra didn't go on.

Coronation Day came. Jimmy Gilmore and the CBC crew manning the hot kine were in Alexandra Palace, London; Ernie Bushnell and many of the corporation's top executives were in the Radio Canada building in Montreal. Every loophole had been plugged, everything had been done that could be done, but it was a tense time and Bush prayed: "Dear God, be kind to us." He knew that the CBC would win the race from Goose or Gander because, aside from the fact that the Canberra or the CF 100 were faster than the P 51s, Montreal was just that bit closer. There were helicopters to fly the film from St. Hubert Airport to the rooftop of the Northern Electric building, and a squad of motorcycle police to rush it across the one short block to the Radio Canada building. But there was that NBC Canberra, and he had a feeling in his bones that they were going to be in for "a beautiful doublecross".

It was nevertheless a shock to hear Gilmore, on the trans-Atlantic telephone, report that the NBC Canberra had taken off with the first twenty minutes of the NBC kine instead of the first thirty minutes, although it had waited for the delivery of the first thirty minutes of the CBC film. What were they up to? Jimmy was distraught; he figured that waiting for the CBC film was a cover because the plane was carrying wingtanks with enough fuel to fly to Boston. He suspected the worst. What was to prevent them flying straight to Boston without first stopping off at Montreal? Nothing but an agreement with Dave Taylor, and it was a moot question whether Taylor knew anything about the finagling that was going on. Bushnell put down the receiver and cursed. He felt so depressed that he slunk away to brood alone.

An hour or so later, Gilmore was on the phone again. Bush expected more bad news but noted that Jimmy sounded different, and he said that he had "what might be considered good news". The NBC Canberra had got out over the Atlantic but had been forced to turn back because of the loss of a wing tank. Meanwhile the first of the RAF Canberras had left—"keep your fingers crossed", Gilmore said. Bushnell whooped with joy. God had answered his prayer.

Now, there was nothing else to do but to listen to the radio which was describing the coronation ceremony as it happened: this was the way that most of the country would follow the event since Canadian television was still confined to the tri-city Montreal-Ottawa-Toronto hook-up. In his account of the coronation broadcast, Bushnell wrote that his only reason for not relating more fully the important role radio played was that "this part of our job was comparatively easy". Radio had had the experience of two royal tours (1939 and 1951); it had the equipment and the men who knew what to do and how to do it. The CBC executives could sit back in their chairs in the Radio Canada building in Montreal and glow with quiet pride as they listened to Ted Briggs and Marcel Ouimet speaking from the abbey, describing in fulsome phrases all the pomp and dignity and religious circumstance of the historic ceremony.

There was another alarm. The second RAF Canberra had been forced to turn back, but Gilmore was not downhearted; he said that he had "dupes" of the film on the second plane and would put them on the third Canberra together with the rest of the film—there was a possibility of it arriving in time but, "if not, you can repeat a part of the first half-hour until number three arrives".

At about two o'clock in the afternoon, the news was received that the first RAF Canberra had landed at Goose Bay. The films for the American networks were unloaded and put aboard the P 51s; the secondary race was on, with the CBC having the advantage of a faster plane and a shorter distance. Bushnell waited as the aircraft, with their throttles wide open, screamed southward. Three o'clock, three-thirty, and the tense wait went on—then came a message quickly relayed to Bush: "Aircraft approaching St. Hubert, will land at approximately 1555 hours." The excitement mounted. Was the helicopter ready? Yes, it had taken off. Was there a CBC man on the roof of the Northern Electric Building? Yes, Bush reported, "We could see him standing there from a window in the Radio Canada building." Then the chopper hove into view and moments later the police sirens blared as the film was rushed across the block, carried to the projection room, the reel taken out of its container and clipped into the machine. An announcer said: "The Canadian Broadcasting Corporation is proud to present a filmed portion of the Coronation ceremony which began in London, England, this morning."

Time: 4:13 pm, June 2, 1953.

The officials in the Radio Canada building were, of course, monitoring NBC; a set was tuned into Channel 5 at Plattsburg, and Bushnell noted that the regular programmes were still on. The CBC had scooped the NBC and CBS, while ABC, having had the foresight to reserve the only microwave link between Canada and the United States, had joined the CBC in being the first to show pictures of the coronation. Five minutes passed, and the telephone rang: it was Merle Jones, a senior vice-president of CBS and another old friend of Bush's who wanted to know:

"What are you guys up to? You must be showing pictures of yesterday's rehearsal."

"Like hell we are," Bush trumpeted. "These are the authentic pictures of today's ceremonies."

After ten minutes, the NBC gave up and accepted the humiliation of taking a feed from ABC of the CBC broadcast. It was not till some time later that the American networks got their films and both NBC and CBS could show the coronation with their own commentators describing the ceremonies. The third RAF Canberra arrived in good time, and there was no need for the CBC to re-run any of the first hot-kine recordings.

During the celebrations in Montreal that night, Bush learned that there was a near accident at the Goose Bay airstrip. In the scramble to get away, one of the American planes had not waited for authorization from the control tower to take off and had cut across the nose of the Canberra, which *had* been authorized to take off. "Just three or four seconds," the RAF pilot said, "and bang-oh, there would have been no television." As it was, Operation Pony Express was a great success, and Ernie Bushnell, who inherited a liking for horse races from his father, James, was to describe the Great Coronation Sweepstake as his most thrilling experience in broadcasting.

19 The Years of Discontent

With the appointment of J. Alphonse Ouimet as general manager of the CBC on January 1, 1953, Ernie Bushnell had been passed over for the third time. Davie Dunton "explained the necessity of the rotating principle of French- and English-speaking 'top brass' "; the CBC chairman had a long session with him and "seemed to suggest that if it had not been for that, I might well have been named general manager." Bush added that he "accepted this line of reasoning and felt that as long as Mr. Dunton remained chairman of the board, Mr. Ouimet and I could work together in harmony."

Actually, the "rotating principle", which the Liberal government had devised as a pattern of power politics, resulted in the Canadian Broadcasting Corporation being headed by a French Canadian for most of the mid-century. At the time of Gladstone Murray's ouster, three members of the board, alarmed at the prospect of a French Canadian heading the CBC in wartime, had tried to get Ernie Bushnell made general manager; although they had failed in this endeavour (and, in the process, done him a lot of harm), they did succeed in stalling Dr. Frigon's appointment for a while. There was the brief interlude of Thomson's temporary regime. When Dr. Frigon became general manager, Donald Manson was named assistant general manager and, on the doctor's retirement in 1951 because of ill health, Manson succeeded him for a very brief time in office. Thus, both the "rotating principle" of French- and English-speaking chief executives and the practice of elevating the assistant general manager to the general manager's job had been established. The

165

wiley Dr. Frigon saw to it that another engineer and a French Canadian, Al Ouimet, was appointed assistant general manager and would be in the right slot when the next rotation occurred, which it did a little more than a year later.

To some extent, Bushnell had been outmanoeuvred, but partly it was his own fault, as he himself admits: he had been drinking, perhaps not excessively but too publicly and, he wrote, "My behaviour on some rather notable occasions had not been all that it should have been." The establishment's disregard for him, and his dislike and mistrust of them hadn't helped. If it had been at all possible, the powers that be would not have made him assistant general manager, but there was his great contribution to broadcasting to consider; what was more important was that he had come to epitomize broadcasting in English Canada, not only as far as the private operators were concerned but for ordinary listeners. Bush himself wondered whether he should have accepted the appointment which was really only a consolation prize, and years later he wrote:

> On reflection, I believe that I should have refused promotion and asked to be permitted to keep the job I was most interested in—director general of programs. There were two temptations: firstly, a small increase in salary, and secondly, the opportunity of moving back to the centre of things, to Ottawa, the nation's capital, where for five years and some twenty summers I had enjoyed the environmental advantages of a smaller city. In the new job, I could still keep an eye on programs (besides being assistant general manager, Bushnell was named co-ordinator of television); I could still meet with broadcasters; I could have lunch at the Rideau Club with important people, and from May to October I could live on the banks of the Gatineau River. What I didn't realize was that I would have to live in a professional climate far different from any I had so far experienced. In Toronto, I was the boss, reporting to Ottawa but left almost entirely free—in fact, too free—to make decisions and to see they were carried out. When the decisions were right, I accepted the praise, and when they were wrong, I took the blame. I

was tightly associated with those who understood me and those whom I understood. We spoke the same language. We shared both our ideas and our ideals. While we did not always agree, we made it our business to resolve our disagreements. We were for the most part, a happy family, concerned with only one thing and that was, within the limits of human frailty and ability, to make the best damned programs we could dream up and produce and at the same time to live within what we always felt were insufficient financial means to do a better job. We hated to see so much money being wasted on a lot of administrative nonsense, not only at 140 Wellington Street but even in our respective bailiwicks, be it Toronto, Winnipeg, Vancouver, Montreal or Halifax. That was the climate I left. Suddenly I was thrust into a new atmosphere, a chilly climate, not cold in a personal sense for I had many friends in head office, but chilly from the perpetual fog that, to me seemed to pervade many of the offices.

If it had not been for the leadership of Mr. A. Davidson Dunton and the long and happy personal association with Mr. Donald Manson, whom I first met in 1927, I daresay I would have called it quits.

One of Alphonse Ouimet's first actions on becoming general manager was to move the department heads and program supervisors to Ottawa, with the idea of making the capital not only the official headquarters but its operational headquarters as well. There was a very good reason for reversing the 1938 decision that had spread the corporation over three cities, leaving the official headquarters in Ottawa but putting French-language broadcasting in Montreal and English-language broadcasting in Toronto. The French- and English-language broadcasting programs were growing farther and farther apart. Ouimet considered that this disparate development made a travesty of the Broadcasting Act, which identified the CBC as an instrument for national unity. By bringing the operating heads of the corporation to Ottawa, he reasoned that the two ever-widening streams could be merged into one great bicultural river.

That, at least, was the theory, and most of the program supervisors bought it; they had become increasingly concerned with Bushnell's behaviour, with his drinking and irrational acts when he was away from home base, and they were beginning to be afraid, as one of them said, that he was going the way of Gladstone Murray. They were ready to welcome Al Ouimet, who seemed to them to be the best kind of French Canadian executive, with his modern outlook, and were prepared to give him their unstinting support. Not everyone would come to Ottawa: the engineers stolidly refused to be budged from Montreal while some program people like Rex Lambert would not leave Toronto. However, most officials heeded the call, sold their homes and moved families and furniture to the capital.

The attempt to centralize the CBC in Ottawa and to unify its direction proved to be a costly failure. What happened, Bush says, was that the department heads found themselves cut off from their departments and the program supervisors could not supervise at such a distance from the main production centres of Montreal and Toronto. There was a loss of effective control, and the producers, left on their own, quickly seized power and became virtually autonomous. Instead of bringing together his chiefs in the capital in order to give imperial direction to the corporation, Ouimet had created a number of semi-independent satraps who tended to disregard his authority and to insist on the freedom to act on their own. The reorganization resulted in more red tape: instead of forms being in triplicate, they had to be in quadruplicate with a specially coloured one for the absentee executive at headquarters; furthermore, as so often happens with such a move, new positions were created and co-ordinators multiplied until there were co-ordinators of co-ordinators. All the while, the main production centres in Montreal and Toronto went on producing, and French- and English-language broadcasting went their own separate ways.

From the moment he became general manager, Alphonse Ouimet was constantly reorganizing the corporate structure of the CBC, so much so that it became almost an obsession with him. Despite the fact that his first effort to concentrate the CBC's top brass in Ottawa had turned out to be "completely non-productive" (to use the organizational jargon), he persisted in drawing up management charts and tables and working out new executive patterns. Al Ouimet had been a brilliant engineer; he was one of the real pioneers of television who had made the first TV receiver in the very early thirties. However, when he was appointed chief engineer in the CBC, he had become an administrator and got the management bug. His first triumph in his new job was a wage analysis of his department; it was such a success that it forced Bushnell, who was scornful of such accounting nonsense, to delegate Neil Morrison to make a similar survey of the program department. Ouimet became a devotee of big business methods; he took a managerial course and constantly studied textbooks on administration.

Between 1953 and 1958, there must have been half a dozen reorganizations of the CBC. When anything went wrong, Bush recalls, Al never blamed the person or persons responsible but would decide that it was due to a flaw in the organizational structure. It was the approach of an engineer: if a machine was properly constructed or repaired, then it should work. But the CBC was not simply a piece of machinery. So Ouimet kept on redrawing his charts, and adjusting and readjusting the corporate structure of the CBC; he had a board made in which there were pegs representing various posts, and with strings and elastic bands he showed how they derived their authority—it was his plaything, and he kept moving the strings and the elastic bands around to form different alignments. He divided the CBC executives into "staff officers" and "line officers" (using military rather than business terminology): the staff officers were his advisors and were concerned with policy while the line officers were the program producers and the station and network supervisors. Ouimet loved to lecture his staff on the intricacies of the latest reorganization, and he would take his board with its pegs and strings and rubber bands with him when he visited the regional offices. Once he even brought the board to a news conference in Ottawa and used it to illustrate the significance of the changes that he was making. The correspondents appeared bemused.

Of his relations with the general manager, Ernie Bushnell had this to say:

It was not that I disliked Mr. J. Alphonse Ouimet, nor that I felt he disliked me, but we were two entirely different breeds of animal. He was an engineer, had a disciplined mind, and rather prided himself on being a top-flight administrator. Although we had been colleagues for some twenty years, I question whether he ever understood me or that I completely understood him. I respected him. . . . But we just did not fit into the same set of harness. With him, the reins must always be tightly held while I felt intuitively that good people should be given authority with responsibility and, vice versa, if they didn't respond to give them a kick on the backside—or fire them. He had the authority and the responsibility which I didn't have. It was not an envious position I was in, and it created in me a sense of frustration which, on occasion, led me to express my opinions in a manner and a style quite different from any he had previously experienced. Criticism, whether from me or others seemed to offend him and indeed to worry him.

He was by nature a shy, sensitive man, a brilliant man in many respects, but, to me, he took a much more lively interest in playing with charts or a slide rule than in trying to assess and evaluate human relationships and human qualities. It was all very well to move strings around the pegs on an administrative chart, but the thought that most frequently rose in my mind was "Who in the hell will you eventually decide on to fill those slots?" He was a voracious reader of textbooks on administration. I was not. I could not believe or accept the principle that a broadcasting organization should be run on precisely the same set of administrative principles and guidelines as a motor-car company or a boot-and-shoe factory. In both cases, theirs was a tangible product to make and to sell. Ours was an ephemeral thing called programs, some of which evolved from a dream of some creative idiot in Vancouver, Halifax, Toronto, Montreal, or where have you—or occasionally popped out of a bottle of whiskey about midnight when the program "nuts" got together to bellyache and to console one another on the hardness of their lot and how little their efforts were appreciated. J. Alphonse seldom if ever joined in these after-work revelries. He didn't drink, he didn't smoke, he didn't swear—not because he considered any of these immoral. He couldn't for health reasons and, I suspect, for another reason as well: he couldn't relax and enjoy himself—he could not and did not "let his hair down".

In time, Al Ouimet was to lose the loyalty and respect of the intellectuals and program people who had rallied to his support when Bushnell had seemed to them to have become a spent force and to be hitting the bottle. They found that the modest manner of the new general manager, which sometimes verged on humility, hid an arrogance that would brook no opposition and that his desire for a dialogue was a cover for his own decisions which seldom took into account the opinions others had expressed at his request. Neil Morrison wondered whether Al Ouimet was not the precursor of a type of French Canadian who emerged with the Quiet Revolution in Quebec, an authoritarian, élitist technocrat who worshipped charts and believed in a rigid management theory. Neil had been supervisor of talks and was one of the program people to become disillusioned with the general manager; another was the late D. C. McArthur, the chief news editor, who had admired Ouimet as a modern French Canadian, a man who had broken with the past. However, after days of grinding consultations with him, including one non-stop discussion that continued over lunch in the Rideau Club and lasted twelve hours, Dan came to the sad conclusion that the general manager did not understand broadcasting and, what was worse, would not accept advice. As one of the inventors of television, Ouimet considered himself a "video" man; he told Morrison in the early days of Canadian TV that "there won't be any room for talks and public affairs on television". He liked specialists, and didn't understand anyone who claimed not to be a specialist but simply a program organizer.

Since the days of Gladstone Murray and the temporary Thomson regime, the direction of the CBC had been in the hands of engineers or technicians (Manson, who had worked with Marconi on the first trans-Atlantic wireless broadcast from Newfoundland, was really a technician) who were more interested in "housekeeping" than anything else. Bush recalls that the discussions at committee meetings—and the CBC was run by committees—when Murray was general manager were mainly about programming; afterwards, they were mainly about facilities. There was no doubt that the Board of Governors and the executive had to be concerned with keeping their house in order immediately after the beginning of television in Canada because of the overwhelming demand for TV from every part of the country. Bushnell wrote:

> During the '53 to '58 period, a great deal of our time at head office was occupied in planning and developing the more-or-less new monster of television, the appetite of which in a monetary sense was seemingly inexhaustible. Public demand and clamour for TV service here, there and everywhere was terrific, and the dollars provided . . . were far from being adequate. New privately owned companies in such cities as Sudbury, Port Arthur, Regina, Saskatoon, Moncton, Quebec City and a host of others had applied for TV licences. The CBC was both judge and jury and, at its frequent board meetings, hour after hour was spent in listening to and deciding on the applications of private operators or entrepreneurs as to who should or should not be given a licence.

Although the government's policy statement on television made no mention of it, the original plan was for the CBC to have its own TV stations in each of the provincial capitals. The first stations in Montreal and in Ottawa were bilingual but, as Ouimet told a parliamentary committee, this proved to be disastrous. Such broadcasting simply irritated and infuriated both language groups. Presumably, the plan would have had to be amended to allow for two TV stations, one English and the other French, in Montreal, Ottawa and Quebec City, but the original scheme could not be implemented because the business-oriented government of Prime Minister St. Laurent, with its annual budgetary surpluses, refused to provide the necessary funds.

The CBC Board of Governors was in a dilemma: most of its members were idealists who believed in the public ownership of television—and, at the time, Ernie Bushnell was among them—but were being forced to license private stations in many provincial capitals where the corporation was supposed to have its own stations. Not only that, but the board had to provide the microwave network to connect these privately owned stations with the basic publicly owned stations in Montreal and Toronto—in Bush's opinion, "the cost of connecting them to unite Canada was astronomically high". During the formative years of television the board was subject to mounting political pressure, but the board members knew full well that if they gave in to the demand for a station in a relatively remote northern area, as they sometimes did, they would have to pay the formidable cost of connecting it with the rest of the microwave network. Bush noted that, in order to meet these extraordinary expenses, the CBC began borrowing money that it would never pay back; actually, this was a system of financing which the St. Laurent government devised because it was easier and looked better, as far as the business community was concerned, to provide loans rather than to make grants.

No wonder Bushnell was to say that "this period of tremendous growth, while exciting in one sense, was also one of frustration for those who had the authority and the responsibility to determine both the near- and long-term means by which a demanding public could best be served."

Television also brought about a CBC staff explosion: the number of employees doubled and tripled and quadrupled and quintupled, until the CBC had grown from what Bush described as "a comparatively small family" to a vast impersonal corporation where there were so many faceless names on the payroll and no feeling of solidarity among them. A special management meeting held in September 1958 blamed "the serious lack of loyalty" among employees on a failure to assimilate them. At its endless meetings, the CBC Board of Governors struggled with new administrative problems and the growing demands of an increasing number of trade unions. Some idea of the enormity of the task facing the members of the board is shown in the following table (between 1949 and 1950, the last fiscal year before television, and 1958 and 1959, the staff multiplied by more than five and expenditures increased more than tenfold):

fiscal years	staff numbers	EXPENDITURES net	gross	capital
1949-50	1375	$5,725,000	$8,241,000	$387,000
1952-53	2075	$10,920,000	$14,304,000	$2,588,000
1955-56	5022	$30,409,000	$40,301,000	$5,247,000
1958-59	7065	$53,152,000	$86,346,000	$5,325,000

Gross expenditures included the revenue which the CBC received from advertising, which generally amounted to about a third of the operating costs and seldom exceeded forty per cent; net expenditures were the moneys provided by the government in grants or in never-pay-back loans.

When Bushnell spoke to the Radio Pioneers in New York City on November 20, 1956, he faced the usual problem of explaining why Canadians should have a publicly owned broadcasting corporation. ("It was not *government* owned or controlled", as he reiterated time and again in the United States. There was the size of the country, Canada's wide-open spaces, a comparatively small population strung like beads along the border of a great and wealthy neighbour. Furthermore, he told the Radio Pioneers, in the language they understood, "there are not enough advertising dollars to go around". That made this weird un-American set-up of the CBC comprehensible: advertising dollars would not support the full cost of a Canadian TV or radio system; public financial support in some form was essential if the system were to be preserved and allowed to develop in a natural, healthy way. Bush said: "Our system is one born of necessity."

Staff recruitment absorbed much management and executive time and energy in those years of television's growth. Where to find capable engineers and technicians and programmers without denuding the radio service (and thereby defying government policy)? There was a reservoir of experience and talent not far away in New York City, and inevitably a number of Canadians who had gone to the US to train in the new medium were taken on. They were used to the harsh competitive ways of commercial television, and the only security they had known on Madison Avenue was provided by the trade unions; they brought their affinity for unions with them when they returned north. Up till then, there had been little labour activity in the CBC—there had been little need for it since a job with the corporation like a job with the government provided security of tenure. The unions found themselves in a totally different milieu, a fat and flabby milieu, and they began to treat the CBC as if it were a milch cow.

At first, the board and the management tried to resist the union demands but, Bushnell says, "We got damn little support from the government." The board decided on a limit of four to five per cent for wage increases, which led to protracted negotiations; after a long session of hard bargaining, a senior official from the Labour Department who had been acting as a conciliator drew Bush aside in order to speak to him privately. "There's only one or one and a half per cent separating you," the department man said. "Why are you putting up such a fight about this? After all, you're not going to pay for it. The government will foot the bill. So why not settle?" Bushnell threw up his hands. What was the use of trying to keep expenditures down? It was obvious that the government would not support the CBC if it held out against union demands, that Parliament would not allow a strike or anything that threatened to interrupt the service.

Such an irresolute stand at the negotiating table was bound to lead to scandalous "feather-bedding" practices which were not so evident as long as the CBC retained its monopoly of network television production. However, once the second stations were licensed and the CTV network was formed, a comparison could be made; Bushnell was to assert that there were three times as many crew members on a CBC mobile unit as there were on a comparable CTV unit, and that they took three times as long to set up their equipment and break it down. The same was true in the studios, and woe betide a performer if he touched a mike or moved a glass of water—there would be a grievance filed. Overtime became a racket and, as a result of its excessive and often fraudulent use, a technician belonging to NABET or a reporter who was a member of the American Newspaper Guild would be getting more take-home pay than his boss, the supervisor. Then, the supervisors' pay had to be raised. Bush recognized that there would be no stopping the way that this vicious pay circle added to the spiralling costs of television.

During those years, the CBC head office in Ottawa tended to divide into two camps: there were the organization men who rallied around Alphonse Ouimet and acted as his sword carriers and courtiers, and there were the programmers who had at first seen him as the new saviour but were now bitterly disillusioned. Ernie Bushnell sided with the programmers, who were his kind of people; most of them had worked with him and many had been appointed by him. However, he didn't want to seem to be allied with them against the general manager; he didn't want to be the leader of an opposition, even a loyal opposition, within the corporation. He would talk to them in his office and listen to their complaints about the lack of inspiration or direction. The only person to whom *he* could unburden his soul was Davidson Dunton, who would put both of his feet on his desk when Bush came in for a little chat and puff judiciously on his pipe. The chairman had a sympathetic ear, and Bush says today: "To me, Davie was a source of comfort and a man of great judgment. The longer I worked with him and for him the greater became my admiration and respect."

However, he found the atmosphere at head office altogether too oppressive and tense, and his happiest days in those years of discontent were when he was on the road, visiting the regional offices and renewing acquaintances with old friends. There was, though, Bush wrote, one great danger in being "a travelling man":

The danger was the hospitality, the well-meant kindness of my hosts in putting 'just one for the road' in my unreluctant hands, which occasionally led me to say far too much that I should not have said and, more often, in a way that it should not have been said. I accept the fact that at times I have a sharp tongue. Too much of the grape certainly did not lessen

176

its abrasiveness. As a result, the odd report began to filter back to head office that my personal behaviour had not been quite in keeping with that of a person in my top-level executive position. I knew about these reports but being a stubborn Irishman I suppose I thought I could ride out any squall or even a storm.

I was and still am a diabetic. I knew that on some occasions I could take five or six drinks in an evening and feel cold sober. On other occasions, two drinks of any alcoholic beverage and I assumed all the characteristics of a drunk. It was not until I became the vice-president, and spent a calamitous six months trying to run the CBC as its chief executive officer, that I came to my senses.

20 The Disastrous Months

When Davidson Dunton resigned as chairman of the CBC Board of Governors at the beginning of July 1958, Ernie Bushnell felt the chilly draught of isolation. Not only was he losing an old colleague, but he would no longer be able to consult the chairman and talk over his problems behind the closed doors of his office. That gave him cause for concern bordering on alarm, for Davie had acted the part of an arbiter and had been able to settle so many of the differences and disputes that Bush had had with Al Ouimet. From then on, Bush was on his own.

The chairman's resignation came as a surprise to him, although he admits that it should have been expected. More than a year had passed since John Diefenbaker and the Conservatives had come to power, ending twenty-two years of Liberal rule that had encompassed the whole corporate life of the CBC; the first minority government was followed by the landslide of the 1958 election and the greatest parliamentary majority in Canadian history. There was no doubt now that the Diefenbaker government would carry out its stated intention of redrawing the Broadcasting Act and of splitting off the corporation's regulatory functions and giving them to another agency. It was not right that the CBC should be judge and competitor, the Tories said repeatedly, and added that they were simply implementing the recommendations of the Fowler commission, which the Liberals had appointed. The job of chairman of the CBC Board of Governors was to disappear when the regulatory functions were given to the Board of Broadcast Governors, while the corporation's board became merely a board of directors. Dunton was astute enough politically to realize that he could not expect any favours of a Conservative government. So, when the opportunity arose for him to become president of Carlton University, he seized it.

On November 1, 1958, J. Alphonse Ouimet and Ernest L. Bushnell were appointed president and vice-president of the reconstituted Canadian Broadcasting Corporation; they were officially installed at the first meeting of the new board of directors in Montreal on December 8. A week later, Ouimet left for a three-week vacation in Florida and Bushnell became acting president.

From time to time, rumblings of trouble among the Radio Canada employees in Montreal had reached the ears of those in head office. André Ouimet, who was Al's brother and director of television for the French network, had been rather high handed in his dealings with the producers and hadn't renewed the contracts of eight or nine of them; in fact, he had let it be known that he didn't think they were any good and he would just as soon fire them—or so Bush heard. At any rate, there was a newspaper report that the producers were organizing. On December 21, André came to Ottawa to attend a meeting about a General Motors-sponsored program which was to be carried on the French network; afterwards, he visited the acting president's office to wish him the compliments of the season and was asked whether there was any trouble among the producers. André "firmly assured" Bush that "everything was peaceful and normal". Although the television director was treating the matter with unjustifiable disdain, it must be said that he didn't learn that the situation had reached the point of a threatened strike until Christmas Eve: the producers had had a meeting the day before and voted to give their executive the power to call a strike at an "opportune moment".

On Sunday, December 28, Bushnell was telephoned at home by Gerard Lamarche, the Quebec regional representative (technically André's boss, although André was inclined to report directly to big brother Al), who said that serious trouble was brewing between André and the TV producers and that he feared there would be a strike which could close down

French-language television; he was appealing for help. The acting president dispatched Jimmy Gilmore, the controller of operations, to Montreal to act as a trouble shooter, on the understanding that the producers would take no action until the holiday season was over.

Aside from André Ouimet whose harsh attitude had led to the dispute, the main obstacle to a quick settlement was the fact that the producers were considered to be part of management and, as such, could not have any affiliation with a trade union or any right to collective bargaining. The CBC had no objection to them forming an association within the management area; however, the producers were insistent on a union, a professional association under the Professional Syndicates Act of Quebec, and they had already voted to affiliate with the CCCL, the Canadian and Catholic Confederation of Labor (now the CNTU). At the same time, they wished to retain their management status. In the corporation's view, this was tantamount to having their cake and eating it too, but no amount of arguing by Gilmore at the meetings that continued throughout most of Monday could persuade them to change their stand. There were overtones of Quebec nationalism in the discussions, and the Montreal producers were resentful of what they claimed were the better pay and working conditions enjoyed by the English-language producers in Toronto. An impasse had been reached, and the negotiations were broken off in the afternoon. At five o'clock, the eighty producers went on strike and set up a picket line in front of the Radio Canada Building.

The situation was critical: a mass meeting of all the broadcasting unions had voted overwhelmingly to support the producers and not to cross their picket lines. Bushnell cabled Alphonse Ouimet at Key Biscayne and advised him of what had happened but added, as he wanted Ouimet to have as much of his holiday as possible, that he didn't see any point in his returning before the weekend. (New Year's Day 1959 was on a Thursday.) However, the president decided to return immediately to Ottawa and on December 31, he and a number of other key executives, including Bushnell, took the train to Montreal.

Mr. Ouimet felt "completely confident that this unfortunate affair could be settled within a few hours", Bush writes. And the omens seemed good that evening when their train pulled into the station, as there were a large number of striking employees on the platform to greet the president, and they marched with him in what seemed like a conciliatory if not triumphant procession to the hotel. There were many old friends among the crowd that met Ouimet, some of whom had known him since 1933. However, Al Ouimet was not dealing with them but with a union that was determined to win at all costs and which was backed by the emerging personalities and forces of what became known as the Quiet Revolution in Quebec. In fact, Bush asserted that the producers' strike was "one of the first, if not the first, indication of an attempt by a 'power bloc' to gain control of an important medium of communications."

And there they were, the revolutionaries of yesteryear, on the picket line or supporting the picket line: René Lévesque, the magnificent broadcaster in either language, who became the ranting, raging spokesman for the producers and was to demand equal time for them on the air; Jean Marchand, the powerful general secretary of the CCCL, who was to finance the strike and provide the "muscle" the producers lacked; Claude Ryan, the influential journalist who, as president of l'Institut Canadien d'Education des Adultes, deplored the dilatory tactics of the CBC in the negotiations and then offered the good offices of the institute as a mediator—an offer that was rejected; Marc Lalonde, the legal advisor of the institute and president of the committee of "Les Idées en Marche"; Gérard Pelletier, the editor of *La Presse*, who used the editorial columns of the biggest French-language paper to argue the case of the producers.

During the first few days of January, Al Ouimet had a series of meetings with the producers and tried vainly to persuade "his old friends" to understand the corporation's position. As most of these negotiations were conducted exclusively in French, Bushnell found himself left on his own and returned to Ottawa. Little or no progress was being made. Although the president did not participate in all the discussions, he was in full charge of negotiations; at the same time, he had to deal with the refusal of many CBC employees, members of the various broadcasting unions, to cross the producers' picket lines. At a hastily called meeting, it was made abundantly clear to the officers of these unions that they were breaking their collective agreements with the corporation and that their members would be considered to be absent without permission and without pay. Shortly afterwards, ARTEC ordered its members back to work. However, this slight glimmer of light was obscured by Al Ouimet's sudden collapse; the president suffered from a gall bladder ailment which may have been aggravated by all the tensions and worries of the strike; the doctor called it a heart attack. At any rate, he was rushed to hospital.

Bushnell was acting president again, and was to continue as chief executive of the corporation during the first six months of 1959. They proved to be disastrous months—illness kept Ouimet away from his desk for all that time and more. As far as the negotiations with the Montreal producers were concerned, Bush was aided and guided by an executive committee of the CBC board; the committee was headed by R. L. Dunsmore, the chairman of the board, and included the Montreal department-store owner, Raymond Dupuis. The discussions had to be conducted in English since neither the acting president nor the chairman could speak French, and that was resented by the Quebec nationalists and trade unionists on the other side. Bush had the highest praise for the assistance given him by Bob Dunsmore, a former oil-company executive, and for the "indefatigable spirits" of Egan Chambers, a Conservative MP from Montreal who acted as an unofficial intermediary. Most of the producers happened to live in Mr. Chambers's St. Lawrence/St. George riding, and the member felt that it was his duty to help his constituents find a settlement; he did not speak or act in any way for the government.

In fact, the Diefenbaker government deliberately kept out of this dispute. George Nowlan, the minister through whom the CBC reported to Parliament, refused to become involved and would have nothing to do with any decision making whatsoever.

Michael Starr, the Labour minister, would not intervene despite pleas not only from the opposition benches but from Quebec Conservative members. He got more than one wire from Jean Marchand, the general secretary of the CCCL, calling on him to use his good offices and charging that his Labour department was aiding and abetting the CBC in the dispute. Starr's reply was to refer Marchand to the Canada Labour Relations Board, which was set up to dispose of disputes relating to representation and bargaining rights; the minister added coldly that there was nothing to prevent the producers' association from applying to the board. But he was not going to intervene.

A remarkable and perhaps significant feature of the strike was the extraordinary amount of violence that it generated. Bushnell said that the producers' picket lines around the various Radio Canada locations were "on many, many occasions joined by paid goon squads recruited from the Montreal docks" who roughed up employees trying to enter the premises. He charged that these strong-arm men were hired by the unions belonging to the CCCL, as the producers, while relatively well off when employed, didn't have a strike fund or money for such activities. There were attempts to break into the Radio Canada building; tires were slashed; soft drinks were poured into gas tanks; paint was splashed on cars, and automobiles were damaged in other ways. On March 2, several producers and their supporters, including René Lévesque and Jean Marchand, were arrested and charged by the police with "refusing to move on". Those CBC employees, mainly supervisory personnel, who remained on the job, were threatened with physical violence to themselves and their families; some were beaten up, and there was a documented case of the wife of an announcer-producer who was attacked by goons in her house at night and had to be treated in hospital for bruises on her face, cut lips and broken teeth. Occasionally bystanders suffered, and there was a remarkable instance of mistaken identity mentioned in the report to the acting president prepared by Maxwell Henderson, then comptroller of the CBC: the house of a Montreal businessman, J. Alfred Ouimet, was ransacked in error for that of J. André Ouimet. The damage done was estimated at $2,500.

The CBC had to protect its facilities and its staff; in fact, those employees who were maintaining a semblance of a French-language television service "threatened to suspend operations unless some provisions were made for the protection of their families and homes". Guards were hired from various private agencies and, according to Mr. Henderson's detailed report, "the cost of protection reached the level of $174,500 by February", after which it continued at $6,750 per day—the total cost would have been around $400,000 including the smaller bill for damages. (The estimate of $4,355 for damages was probably slightly lower than the final amount as the report was dated February 24, 1959, two weeks before the strike ended.) The report noted that the tension continued high among the CBC's Montreal working staff. "Since the guards were assigned to the homes of certain of the working employees, it has been noted that several automobiles gather outside three or four of the locations every night . . . as a consequence homes believed to be targets remain under a twenty-four-hour watch."

Finally, a settlement was reached. The CBC agreed to grant the Montreal producers full trade unionism—the corporation was able to do this by removing the management functions of the producers and creating a new job category for them as "directors". Early in the strike the producers had suggested such a solution, but the CBC had said then that it would take time to rearrange the structure of the corporation, that it was a complicated business and, in any case, the producers didn't seem to want to relinquish their management functions. It took almost ten weeks (sixty-nine days) for both sides to realize that this was the only possible solution; after that, the other details of a collective agreement were easy to work out.

However, the producers insisted on one further condition which they seemed to consider to be as important as belonging to a union affiliated with the CCCL: the dismissal of J. André Ouimet as director of television and his physical removal from the Radio Canada building. It was Bushnell's unpleasant task to have to ask Al's brother for his resignation; it was made clear to him that it would be in the best interests of the corporation that he should retire gracefully and without any fuss, but André would not see it that way and refused. So the executive committee of the board had to find some gesture, some sort of golden handshake, to ease his departure, and they hit on the job of director of planning. In making the offer, the acting president pointed out that the position was recently created and bore no relationship whatsoever to the sinecure of the same title that Dr. Frigon had held from the time he had quit as general manager because of ill health until his death; it was all a white lie, as Bush admitted later. André remained in that nebulous, completely isolated position for a few months until he got a job in private enterprise.

Altogether, the producers' strike had been a severe test for the acting president and, in the judgment of his colleagues, he had passed it with flying colours. H. G. "Bud" Walker sent him a telegram of congratulation and admiration for his "astute and thoughtful guidance and leadership in what surely will prove to be the most challenging and frustrating segment of corporation history". Professor Ira Dilworth, who was in semi-retirement in Vancouver, wrote to Bush: "I want to congratulate you and all those associated with you in dealing with this distressing incident." Ted Briggs, the Maritimes regional director, offered congratulations on behalf of all regional officers and said: "I should just like you to know and be able to pass on to those concerned, that all of us here were one hundred per cent behind you, and it has been most gratifying to all of us to witness the fair, just, but at the same time, firm stand which the corporation, through you, maintained." However, the event was viewed differently by much of the press and public. There were protests in Parliament about the French-language television service and how it had been reduced to screening old films, and criticism of management for fumbling the strike; when the settlement was reached, there was grumbling in parts of the country that the CBC had given in to the French Canadians. Furthermore, the Montreal producers' strike was the first of a series of disasters that befell the accident-prone corporation that year.

On May 3, 1959, the French TV network marked the

beatification of Marguerite d'Youville, the founder of the Grey Nuns, by putting on a play called *La Plus Belle de Ceans* (The Prettiest Girl in Town), which could only be likened to a licentious Restoration romp. Blair Fraser, writing in *Maclean's* magazine, described the saintly Marguerite "bounding around with [her lover] on a double bed in a startlingly low-cut night-gown". Several other shots, he said, were "memorable for what Hollywood delicately calls 'cleavage' ". Such a program would have drawn protests at any time, and this was long before Quebec had been introduced to the permissive society. Besides that, it was supposed to have been a religious show, not an exposé of the saint's early sex life, and parish priests had told their congregations not to miss this sacred play. Little girls were allowed to sit up late to see it. Convents borrowed or rented TV sets for the occasion. Of course, there was a furious reaction: the Roman Catholic hierarchy in the province condemned not only *La Plus Belle de Ceans* but "numerous French-language televsion productions which flout as if deliberately the highest values of Christian faith and ethics". Bushnell told the parlia-mentary committee on broadcasting which began its meetings a week later: "We have offered our abject apologies." He said there were no excuses, although CBC spokesmen did try to put some of the blame on the confusion resulting from the pro-ducers' strike.

Early in the parliamentary committee's hearings, Art Smith, a prominent young Conservative from Calgary, raised the issue of the government subsidising advertising on television through the corporation; he suggested that the CBC was only recovering twenty per cent of a commercial production, and wanted a breakdown of the cost of the General Motors Show. Despite the fact that Smith had a resolution adopted by the committee asking for these figures, the corporation kept stalling . . . all of which annoyed the MPs who were members of the committee and added to their suspicion that the CBC was wasteful or, at the best, spent too freely with too little accounting.

Then, after the June election in Ontario which he won handily, Premier Leslie Frost wheeled around and blasted the CBC for what he called "slanted" news coverage. His angry outburst might have been an expression of the pent-up frustration and resentment that he and a number of other Conservatives felt about what they regarded as the corporation's Liberal bias. (The CBC was a Liberal creation, the Tories argued, and had known no other masters until the Diefenbaker government came to power.) What had infuriated the premier was that the CBC had been unable to put him on the air from his Lindsay home on election night. The corporation's explanation had been that it was technically "unfeasible" to do this; that Lindsay, which is only some eighty miles from Toronto, was too much of a backwater for a television origination. Yet a live telecast was arranged from the Kitchener home of the defeated Liberal leader, John Wintermeyer. Mr. Frost asserted that the whole principle of the CBC was wrong. "The government's part in TV and broadcasting ought to be regulatory," he said. "It should not be in the [broadcasting] business." Although Leslie Frost, Old Mr. Ontario as he was called, was highly regarded in Ottawa, the federal Conservatives were somewhat embarrassed by his all-out attack; while they themselves had misgivings about the CBC, they didn't want it abolished and they didn't want anyone to think that they wanted it abolished. Jack Pickersgill, a Liberal member of the parliamentary committee, tried to make political capital by having Premier Frost invited to appear as a witness; his move was quashed.

To add to the corporation's miseries that spring, there was wide-eyed Joyce Davidson saying on television, "I, like most Canadians, am rather indifferent to the Queen's visit." with exquisite timing, she made the remark just as the 1959 royal tour began. "An insult," cried Mayor Nathan Phillips of Toronto, and there was another row in which the CBC was clobbered by irate Empire Loyalists, who may have been a minority, but not a silent one. "How dare she?" "Keep that beep-beep little beep off the air!" The CBC switchboard in Toronto was bombarded by 593 calls, almost all of which were, to say the least, critical. Miss Davidson had become an early Canadian television star by doing interviews on an evening public-affairs program called *Tabloid*; she had the wholesome good looks that the IODE (Imperial Order Daughters of the Empire) might have admired. Bushnell ordered her suspended until the furor died down. In the end, Joyce Davidson went to the United States and quit CBC television.

It was now mid-June 1959, and the scene had been set in those disastrous months for the tragicomedy of the *Preview Commentary* scandal, and the parliamentary committee's hearings into Bushnell's foreboding that "heads will roll".

21 *"Heads Will Roll" (the warning)*

It was on the evening of June 23, 1959, during a telephone conversation with Al Ouimet, that Ernie Bushnell was to utter the portentous warning: "Heads will roll." Ever since, he has indignantly maintained that this was his choice of phrase and his alone, that no one else made this remark to him nor even suggested it, that it was a "Bushnellism", as the *Toronto Telegram* called it, like his riposte that day to a *Telegram* reporter that the only headaches he was likely to have, and he didn't have many, would be if he were to mix rye and scotch—the reporter had said something to the effect that as acting president of the CBC he must have a great many headaches.

That day, the corporation had been host to the parliamentary committee on broadcasting which was on a field trip visiting the Toronto studios; most of the MPs had never seen television production before and were suitably impressed by the lights, cameras and rehearsals, but there was carping criticism of past errors, and astonishment, even alarm at the news that most of the talks and public-affairs producers had resigned because of the cancellation of the daily radio program "Preview Commentary". The members were photographed reading the scare headlines in the papers about CBC employees quitting. The day had been a full and exhausting one for all concerned, and especially for the acting president who had had to fend off newsmen. He then had to entertain the committee members to dinner at the Celebrity Club, which was conveniently located across Jarvis Street from the main Toronto studios.

They were in the midst of drinks when Bushnell was paged;

he asked Charles Jennings, the controller of broadcasting, and H. G. "Bud" Walker, the director of Ontario and English networks, to accompany him to a private room in the club where he took the telephone call—he knew who would be on the other end. Although Al Ouimet was confined to his home in Ottawa, he was not so much of an invalid that he could not keep in close touch with what was going on in the corporation. He had learned about the mass resignations of the producers in the papers that day; actually, Walker had phoned him the day before and told him that trouble was brewing in Toronto. It was obvious that Alphonse was "more than a little upset" about the latest events which, with the unhappy occurrences of the past, had been "casting an unfavourable shadow on the management of the CBC". Bush could not but agree with this, although he resented the implication that the blame was his.

He was only too conscious of the disasters of the past months. During the whole of this critical period, while Ouimet was absent sick, Bushnell had had to keep George Nowlan, the minister of National Revenue and minister responsible for the CBC, informed on all matters pertaining to the corporation and what was described in Parliament as its "disgraceful conduct". "Certainly, I talked to Mr. Nowlan," Bush writes.

Certainly, I had answers prepared for him to a lot of questions [in the House], many of which were stupid and for the most part irrelevant, largely founded on articles appearing in the newspapers. In case there is any doubt about it, let me make it perfectly clear that there was nothing new about this kind of procedure or the action that I was required to take. How can any minister reporting to Parliament for any crown corporation provide proper answers to questions, valid or silly, if he doesn't consult with the principals concerned and hasn't been given either a reasonable explanation or the facts?

To my knowledge, every general manager of the CBC from Mr. Gladstone Murray, Dr. Thomson, Dr. Frigon, Mr. Manson, was obliged to consult with the appropriate minister from time to time. If the problem had to do with programs, I

190

was quite often asked to prepare a written reply or to go along with the general manager to relate just what had happened and why. Mr. Dunton, as chairman of the board, was either called to Parliament Hill when the necessity arose, or the private line or a letter asking for the facts was employed by the minister, the minister's executive secretary, or any responsible officer of his department, to provide relevant information.

Does this suggest or imply control or a misuse of authority? It does not, and to my knowledge this kind of day-to-day communicating with extremely rare exceptions has never been abused or taken advantage of by any minister, and the chances are that no matter who the minister may be or who the president of the CBC may be, this getting together in one form or another will go on. . . . Proper channels of communicating are one thing; interference is another.

So what happened in the stormy first six months of 1959? Did Mr. Nowlan keep in touch with me or Mr. Dunsmore [the chairman of the CBC board]? He did. Did Mr. Nowlan ever at any time give me an instruction or an order or even make a request to do this or that? He did not. Did Mr. Allister Grossart (national director of the Progressive Conservative party) give me an order, make a request, or suggest how any tricky situation should be dealt with? He did not. Although Mr. Grossart and I had been on quite friendly terms in Toronto over a period of years, I saw him on the street twice after he moved to Ottawa, and talked to him once over the telephone about the division of free time for political parties in a non-election year.

One complaint that Bushnell had was the difficulty of getting to see Nowlan or even talking to him on the telephone. Mrs. Ruby Meabry, who was only doing her job as an efficient executive secretary fended off those importuning the minister and acted as a barrier to his office. George Nowlan himself, who had the greatest appreciation of the CBC and the contribution it was making to Canada's national life, wanted at all costs to preserve its independence; he refused to interfere in the corporation's management or even to give the appearance of interfering, as he demonstrated during the Montreal producers' strike. Bushnell considers Nowlan to be the greatest minister that the CBC ever had: "If there ever was or is likely to be a minister reporting to Parliament for the CBC who has tried or will try to promote the welfare of the corporation more sincerely than the Honorable George Nowlan, I don't know who it was or who it could be or is likely to be."

However, there were occasions when Bushnell was able to get past Mrs. Meabry and have a session with Nowlan in his big office where the lights always appeared to be subdued. On those occasions the minister would not mix words but would express to Bush the concern that he felt about the corporation and its lack of responsibility and restraint. Why was a program like the one on Marguerite d'Youville ever even considered, let alone put on the air? Didn't management have any control over what was broadcast? If it didn't, then something should be done about it quickly, otherwise there would be serious consequences, and Nowlan hinted at the pressure that he was under from the cabinet to put the CBC in its place. Bush could not but nod his head in agreement. But whenever he sought the minister's advice on what he should do, Nowlan would rise to his full six-foot-five-inch height and, with a kindly smile on his face, for he was among the most genial and friendly of men, he would repeat that he was truly and honestly concerned about the CBC but that he had no right to suggest a course of action, and he wasn't going to do so.

"Ernie, that's your problem," Nowlan would say. "You're running the CBC; do what you like or whatever you think best. You have a board of directors; why don't you make them decide on the tough issues?"

"Look here Mr. Minister," Bush would reply, "I'm coming to you as man to man for some advice. I'm not asking for either your support or your intervention, but under the circumstances I've just outlined, what the hell would you do?"

"I don't know, and if I did I wouldn't tell you anyway," was Nowlan's stock answer. Then, there would be a few words of encouragement, the assurance that "right or wrong, I'll stand behind you," a slap on the back, and the interview was over.

The minister's high-principled rectitude, his determination to stay out of CBC affairs at all costs, made it certain that Bushnell never received any orders from the government, nor even an indication of what course he should take during all the fateful months that he was the corporation's acting president. Yet, while Bush knew this and had made public statements to this effect, he could not seem to convince people that the decision to cancel "Preview Commentary" was his own, "made on my own intuition and initiative". It should be apparent that Bushnell's warning that "heads will roll" was also made on the basis of "intuition" rather than knowledge.

He had heard that Nowlan had laid his job on the line because of the heated demands by his cabinet colleagues that he put a stop to the rot in the CBC, although Bush hastens to add that he hadn't got this information from the minister or his office. There were other sources: the CBC directors, all appointed by the Conservative government, had friends or contacts among cabinet ministers or members of Parliament who were not loath to tell them what they thought about the organization that they were supposed to be running. There was also Mrs. Meabry, with whom Bush was in constant contact; while she might not always be able to arrange for him to see the minister or talk to him on the telephone, she would pass on messages and was quite willing to tell him what she had heard in the way of criticism from on high. There was a rumour that Nowlan had told his colleagues that if they wanted him to tell the CBC what to do, "they could get themselves another boy". From what he knew of the minister's attitude, Bush figured that there must be some truth to this scuttlebut. He recalled one meeting he had had with Nowlan when the minister had been unusually frank in retailing the sort of denunciation of the CBC that he was getting from his cabinet colleagues; the situation was so serious that Nowlan broke one of his own principles by suggesting "the kind of action that might be taken to head off a political blow-up". Why couldn't the acting president get a few letters written praising the CBC and all that it stood for, and have them sent to the prime minister's office and to the offices of some of the cabinet ministers who were most virulent in their censure of the corporation?

Why not, Bushnell wondered. The idea of stirring up a counter-protest appealed to him, and he intended to do something about it when he went back to his office. However, "the one person I knew whose opinions were greatly respected by people in high places and who on more than one occasion had thundered 'Hands off the CBC' was, unfortunately, out of the country at the time". That was Donald Creighton, the historian and biographer of John A. Macdonald. Bush tried to reach him by telephone but, after several unsuccessful attempts, gave up and decided to get in touch with him immediately on his return. By then it was too late for, as Bush puts it, "the whirlwind had developed into a tornado and all hell had broken loose".

During this period, Bushnell began to hear disturbing reports about "Preview Commentary", "that two or three quite recent [programs] had been somewhat less than objective, and one of them had been almost an outright fabrication and a deliberate attempt to do a first-class hatchet job on the prime minister". There was evidence that certain reporters were using this program to vent their spleen on Mr. Diefenbaker, and Bush learned from what he called "personal and private sources" that "the prime minister was more than a little annoyed with the antics of the CBC". He discussed this with Bob Dunsmore, the chairman of the board, who said that he too had heard that Mr. Diefenbaker was angry. Their meeting, however, resulted in no decision.

In the meantime, Bushnell called for copies of several recent "Preview Commentary" scripts. He showed them to one of his associates at head office, D. C. McArthur who, as chief news editor, had been largely responsible for the creation of the CBC's superlative news service; Bush had the utmost confidence in him and describes him as "a person of great experience and integrity, and one whose judgment on such matters as to what was fair comment and what was not was respected and honoured by all who knew him". He asked McArthur to put in writing his evaluation of these "Preview Commentary" scripts.

Dan McArthur did so; he stated that they were biased, lacked objectivity and, in some cases, could be said to be disrespectful and rude. Dan said that, in his opinion, they should not have been allowed to have been broadcast in the form that they were written.

By any yardstick, "Preview Commentary" was not a great program; three and a half minutes long, it came at the end of the eight o'clock radio news. The commentary was rotated among a dozen or so members of the Parliamentary Press Gallery who were inclined to write it in haste, not because the fee of twenty-five dollars was so small, but because they had other things to do. The program received little attention or supervision and, as Blair Fraser said, "could be challenged on purely editorial grounds". There were a couple of scripts mentioned in newspaper and magazine accounts of the "Preview-Commentary" and "heads-will-roll" scandal. One was by Tom Gould, who was then the correspondent for the *Vancouver Sun;* the way that it was featured in the *Toronto Star* would seem to suggest that it was the broadcast that led to the cancellation of the program. Actually, it was a rather small-minded attack on Prime Minister Diefenbaker for accepting Harrington Lake Lodge, which the government had bought some years before, as an official summer residence, and contained this flourish:

> Even in Britain, there is no precedent. British prime ministers use Chequers, a country estate willed to the nation. France's President de Gaulle has his own summer home. And preliminary investigation indicates the summer White House was paid for by a group of Democrats. Previous Canadian prime ministers bought their own.

A "Preview Commentary" by Tim Creery, then with the *Montreal Star,* was quoted in the "Ottawa Letter" of *Saturday Night* magazine (July 18, 1959) written by Edwin Copps. This was broadcast on the day that Bushnell ordered the program off the air. It had to do with the case of John Pallett, a prominent Tory MP, who was cited in an Exchequer Court judgment for his involvement in a government land deal; Prime Minister

195

Diefenbaker had stoutly defended Pallett's integrity in the House of Commons and rejected the opposition's demand for a parliamentary inquiry. However, the PM had not impressed young Mr. Creery, who belittled his ringing speech by saying that it was "beside the point" and asserted that "the Commons should consider this a question of propriety". Although Creery's commentary was typical of the sort of disparaging and contemptuous attacks on the prime minister and the Conservative government, it was not one of those considered by Ernie Bushnell and Dan McArthur before the program was cancelled.

As a crown corporation, the CBC could not take political sides; it could not seem to be pro-Liberal or pro-Conservative or its very existence would be endangered. Yet there was no doubt that "Preview Commentary" was not providing a balanced political commentary during the period in question, and that in itself was justification enough for Bushnell to put a stop to it. The corporation's approach to such a sensitive subject was extraordinarily casual: the correspondent chosen to do the commentary merely read his script once, for timing, then went on the air. This was in sharp contrast to the care with which the BBC handled its political commentaries: the script would be carefully gone over with the producer, who made sure there was a balanced presentation of any controversial issue in the one broadcast. Bush recalls that his boss at the BBC in London, Tony Rendall, insisted on reading and passing on every commentary because he was ultimately responsible. The BBC as a corporation also accepted full responsibility for whatever was said on the air; the CBC tried to escape its responsibility through such disclaimers as, "The opinions expressed are solely those of the speaker", or " 'Preview Commentary' is a free expression of opinion." Bush did not believe that these disclaimers meant much, and the fact of the matter was that the corporation, like any publisher, was legally liable for any broadcast it put out, even a free-time political broadcast by one of the recognized parties.

The casual approach to political commentary was deliberate. The talks and public-affairs producers, who were almost all academics and liberal intellectuals, took a rather superior attitude toward politicians but actually were afraid of them and were inclined to see clandestine political influence between the lines of any directive from Ottawa. They were the self-appointed guardians of freedom of expression on the Canadian air waves. It may be arguable that, in a federation such as Canada, unlike the cohesive, unitary state of Britain, the CBC should not be responsible for every political commentary but should aim at a balanced presentation of views, but this position was never clearly stated or publicly approved. And the question was whether this wasn't the easy way out. The BBC producers had the right to insist on changes in the scripts; the CBC producers could only *suggest* changes, and seldom did because it was too much trouble and it wasn't expected of them—although it must be said that as long as a producer like Spencer Moore was around, "Preview Commentary" kept within bounds, but he was sent to Newfoundland during the critical period and was replaced temporarily by a newer and much less experienced producer. There was an abhorrence of the use of the blue pencil in the talks department at 354 Jarvis Street; the producers confused editing for fairness, objectivity and good manners with censorship.

Bushnell said that no one at head office in Ottawa knew what was being produced until he heard it or saw it on the air. What Bush wrote about the Montreal producers' strike applies equally well to the Toronto producers: "Any request for information was usually met with either suspicion or stony silence. Sticking our individual or collective noses into their business was regarded as an insult—or at least a reflection on their perspicacity, their well-informed judgment, their right to decide. . . . 'Keep your hands off us' was certainly implied if not always openly stated. There could have been many reasons for this glaringly apparent attitude but for my money the reason most often suggested was that we were all a lot of political harlots and were 'on call', as it were, most of the time."

Bushnell came to the decision to cancel "Preview Commentary" on June 11, 1959; he told his deputy, Charles Jennings, to see that the program was ended on Friday of the following week. It was to be replaced by a factual report on Parliament to be prepared by the Canadian Press. Jennings was, according to Bush's own account, "quite taken aback, thought I was wrong and said so". However, Charles's protests at this arbitrary action had no effect; the acting president said that he could see no point in any further consultation and that his decision was irrevocable. On June 15, Frank Peers, the supervisor of talks and public affairs, visited Ottawa on another matter but discussed the cancellation of the program with Jennings. Peers was upset and wanted to see Bushnell but, for various reasons, was unable to arrange for a formal interview, even though he didn't return to Ottawa until the following Wednesday. The supervisor then held a series of meetings with members of his staff, and on January 23, the day the parliamentary committee had chosen to visit the facilities of the CBC in Toronto, the producers walked out.

The telephone conversation that followed with Ouimet that evening Bush describes as being "brief but dramatic"; he implored the president "to support me and to pay scant heed to the rebellious, self-established monarchs of the Talks and Public-Affairs Department". He adds that he cannot recall receiving much encouragement or solace from Ouimet. It was during this conversation that Bushnell uttered the dire warning that "heads will roll", and later there was an attempt by certain Liberal politicians to suggest that he had been repeating a threat uttered by someone prominent in the Conservative government, if not Prime Minister Diefenbaker himself. This Bush denies. It was one of the impulsive Bushnellisms for which he had something of a reputation; in this case, it may have been motivated by his antipathy toward Ouimet and his bitterness and resentment that the president was not supporting him on the "Preview Commentary" issue.

Yet, there was confusion. Charles Jennings and Bud Walker bore conflicting testimony as to the content of Bush's conversation with Ouimet. Bushnell's explanation is that they had overheard only one side of it. "No one in my presence had ever said or implied that 'heads would roll'." But he adds that it was hardly an improper conclusion to be drawn from all that had happened in the preceding six black months. Bush anticipates the question, "Whose heads?" and answers: "Well, it seemed to me that mine might well be one of them. Although Mr. Ouimet had not been at work for months, maybe his too would fall into the basket. It also occurred to me at the time of the telephone call that Mr. Nowlan's challenge 'to get themselves a new boy' might be taken up by those who had a lot less political savvy and thinner hides than he had."

On June 24, the next day, the CBC Board of Directors met and reversed the decision to cancel "Preview Commentary". That was a heavy blow for Ernie Bushnell, and he angrily condemned the board for abandoning him, for "throwing him to the wolves", and said that its action could not be justified in any way. He charged that "one of the directors of the CBC spent two days closeted with several of the ring leaders of the mass resignees and heard only their side of the story". Then his former confidant, the man he had relied on when he was in trouble, turned against him. Davidson Dunton, president of Carleton University, according to a banner-line report in the *Ottawa Journal* issued the following statement: "If the board of directors of the CBC does not put 'Preview Commentary' back on the air, it is selling out the principle of national broadcasting." Bushnell felt betrayed. Furthermore, he was forced to leave the board meeting just as it was reaching its decision, and did not vote to reverse his cancellation of the program as he was reported to have done, although he had to announce the board's findings at a news conference. The acting president and two directors had had to leave the meeting to see a Manitoba minister who was pressing the CBC to install microwave facilities to some of the far northern towns in that province. Bush writes: "During my two hours enforced absence, the conscientious objectors were given the fullest opportunity to present their views—or so I was subsequently told."

The reversal of the decision to cancel "Preview Commentary" was hailed by the *Toronto Daily Star* as a victory for CBC freedom. In a lead editorial in the following day's paper (June 25), the *Star* blasted the acting president and virtually demanded that he be fired:

Mr. Bushnell, whose public statements on this dispute have comprised a tangle of contradiction and slithering evasion, has admitted that there were members of Parliament among the persons who complained about "Preview Commentary". He says they approached the CBC unofficially "but no one has commented to me in any official way whatsoever." This is a meaningless distinction if one is talking about influential political figures.

Although the CBC board has "reaffirmed" a policy of freedom of expression on public affairs programs, there is no real assurance yet that the management will resist political pressure in the future. That will require stronger men than the ones whose overriding determination appears to be to hang on to their jobs. . . .

However, the *Star's* reaction was one-sided and untypical. The *Globe and Mail* was even more forceful on the opposite side: the newspaper of Friday morning (June 26) had not only a lead editorial on the issue but next to it a Reidford cartoon of Bushnell watching a television screen on which was the "Canadian Producers Corporation", and beside him a copy of the *CPC TIMES*. The *Globe and Mail's* editorial was entitled "What Price Freedom?" and said there was no proof to the charge that "Preview Commentary" was suspended because of political pressure:

> Until it has been substantiated, we must assume that the CBC management took this unimportant program off the air for good and honest reasons of its own. What happened in consequence? The producers resigned, fanned up a storm of hysterical protest across the country and forced the CBC management to reverse itself.
>
> At sea this would be called mutiny—a successful mutiny at that, one which left the crew in full charge of the CBC. Where does that leave the public, or the people who are supposed to be running the CBC on the public's behalf? The producers are free—free to say what the CBC may or may not put on the air. The producers are independent—independent of the CBC's top officials. When the producers crack the

whip, even the CBC Board of Directors jumps through the hoop. Freedom is thus regained?

Only those papers that were completely committed to the Liberal party, such as the *Toronto Star*, sided with the producers; most of the others, the vast majority of the Canadian press, tended to stand behind Bushnell. It is wrong to assume that the acting president was alone and lacking support. The *Financial Post*, in its June 27, 1959, issue, charged the producers with sabotage:

> If they disagreed with the bosses on minor points, they should seek to resolve the differences by persuasion in private and not in public. If they disagree on major policy, they should resign. If they want to resign over trifles, that too is their privilege.
> But they do not have the right—any more than a government has—to sabotage the original concept of the CBC as a strong, non-partisan, thoroughly Canadian medium of communication. Mass resignations come close to being efforts at such sabotage.

It had been a midsummer nightmare, climaxing so many ghastly blunders, and press photographs taken of Bushnell at the time, especially the one of him presiding at the news conference where he announced the board's decision to reverse his cancellation of "Preview Commentary", show him to be drawn and grey and much older looking than his fifty-eight years. All the worries and tensions had driven him too often to the bottle and, by his own admission, the drinking had not helped. He looked deathly tired, and yet he would not admit to being tired, denying it when anyone commiserated with him. Arthur Blakely of the *Montreal Gazette* wrote of Bush at the time: "He looked like a man who enjoyed life when there was anything to enjoy. But there can have been few bright spots for him that day. Nor had there been for many days past. He seemed tired, worn, exhausted from carrying for too long the burden of too many responsibilities in circumstances that were too trying." Bushnell agreed so much with that description that he included it in his memoirs.

22 "Heads Will Roll" (the hearing)

A hush of expectancy settled on Parliament Hill the bright summer weekend it was announced that Frank Peers, the supervisor of talks and public affairs, and his assistants, Bernard Trotter and D. H. Gillis (the ring leaders of the rebels, or the freedom fighters, depending upon whether one read the *Globe and Mail* or the *Toronto Star*), were to appear before the parliamentary committee on broadcasting. It was all very intriguing: besides the possibility of a scandal that might rock the Diefenbaker government, there was a mystery about the whole affair, and especially about Ernie Bushnell's statement that "heads will roll". Who was responsible for that warning or threat? The political gossip in the capital took it for granted that there had been interference from on high. Reporters recalled the painful occasion, only a littly more than two years before, when former Prime Minister St. Laurent had been caught criticizing a CBC program; the excuse that he had given in Parliament was that he had written the letter to the corporation as a private citizen, an argument that convinced nobody and left St. Laurent looking a lot less like a statesman and leader.

The Special Committee on Broadcasting, as the parliamentary committee was called, was just another of an unending series of investigations of the CBC: there had been two royal commissions, the Massey commission and the Fowler commission, and the parliamentary committees which had met almost annually since the 1936 committee. Bush didn't suffer these inquiries gladly. The special committee had its organization

202

meeting on May 6 and held its first hearing on May 12; since then it had had met two and three times a week. The acting president of the CBC begrudged the time he wasted—waiting for a quorum, waiting to be called, and then answering questions which, in his view, were too often stupid, irrelevant or politically motivated. "How many of the committee members really want to find out what broadcasting is about?" he asked, and answered, "All they do is look at some program they don't like and complain." The 1959 committee had been more onerous than most since it had come when Bushnell was concentrating his every effort on trying to rescue the corporation from a quagmire of awful blunders; moreover, this committee had gone further than any other in demanding to know how much the CBC was paid by the sponsors of various programs and the cost of these programs. Such information, Bush says had been regarded as confidential because disclosure would likely help the corporation's competitors.

Although the committee took the precaution of having its hearing into the "Preview Commentary" affair in the Railway Committee Room, which was the biggest room it could get, there was such a crowd that many reporters had to stand. The high-ceilinged room, with its great framed copy of the Fathers of Confederation painting, was a vast echo chamber and the reporters, whether they were sitting at the press table or standing along the walls, had to strain to hear what was said. On several occasions committee members, who sat around long tables arranged in a squared horseshoe, had to ask for testimony to be repeated, and Ernie Halpenny, the business-like chairman of the committee, warned that everyone would have to speak loudly as "the acoustics in this room are about as bad as in any room in Canada".

Frank Peers was the first witness; he began his testimony by recounting the events which took place as he had witnessed them. During the course of this lengthy statement he quoted Bud Walker, who was his immediate superior, as saying that there was no possibility of changing the decision to cancel "Preview Commentary", that Mr. Bushnell had been placed in an impossible position, that he (Bushnell) had been given the alternatives of either taking the program off the air or endangering the corporate structure of the CBC, and that external pressures were involved. To which Chairman Halpenny remarked that this was hearsay. Peers went on to quote Walker as saying that the alternatives had been put to Mr. Bushnell by someone with a political connection.

Marcel Lambert, a Conservative MP for Edmonton who was to become Speaker of the House of Commons, began the questioning; an experienced counsel, he went right to the nub of the matter:

> Mr. LAMBERT: Regarding what you have told us that Mr. Walker had spoken to you about, have you any evidence to place before the committee of this so-called "clandestine political influence"?
>
> Mr. PEERS: I have not. I assume others in the corporation have. I think this statement will lead to those who have.
>
> Mr. LAMBERT: But you assume that?
>
> Mr. PEERS: I should explain, Mr. Lambert, when Mr. Walker told us that he could not reveal the identity of the person or persons who had been in touch with CBC management, I said, for my own part, that did not matter and, in fact, in some ways I would rather not know the identity of the person or persons. My stand was that it was a matter of what the CBC's action and procedure were after receiving complaints which may or may not have been legitimate. In other words, I was not concerned with anything other than the management's response to such influence.
>
> Mr. LAMBERT: You say there was this "political influence". What was your information as to who had wielded this influence? Did you have any names, or have you any names?
>
> Mr. PEERS: Mr. Lambert, I have not any names because I did not ask for names at any time and Mr. Walker explained each time the information was confidential and he could not divulge anything further than he already had.
>
> Mr. LAMBERT: Further, just on whom was this political influence wielded?
>
> Mr. PEERS: According to Mr. Walker, it was wielded on CBC

management, and he went further in our Monday morning meeting . . .

Mr. TROTTER: I would like to say . . .

Mr. LAMBERT: Go ahead Mr. Peers.

Mr. PEERS: . . . and reaffirmed or said again . . . there had been external pressures . . . and elaborated on the alternative put to the corporation. The alternative that was put to the corporation was—and I am trying to remember his words— "the removal of top management" . . .

Mr. LAMBERT: You said there had been pressure on management? Just on whom in management?

Mr. PEERS: I could not say that—"management"—by which I assume we mean "top management".

The CHAIRMAN: Do you wish to add to that, Mr. Trotter?

Mr. TROTTER: I want to remind Mr. Peers that Mr. Walker said—and it is in the statement—that Mr. Bushnell had been placed in an impossible position.

Mr. LAMBERT: Further, did you have any information as to when this had happened and under what circumstances?

Mr. PEERS: Only this, Mr. Lambert, that on Monday—that was the fifteenth—Mr. Jennings told me that he had received a call from Mr. Bushnell on Friday—I think it was in the afternoon—but Friday, at any rate, and what Mr. Bushnell had to say to him sent him—put him in a dreadful state of mind. He thought about it for an hour, and I think he said that he paced the floor and that he had, at the end of the hour, come up with this statement which he presented to me . . .

Mr. LAMBERT: Mr. Bushnell had been given two alternatives; by whom?

Mr. PEERS: Mr. Walker did not disclose that to us. But we questioned him in those general terms: "Was it someone outside the corporation?" "Yes." Then the other question was, "Was it someone with a political connection?" "Yes." . . .

Mr. LAMBERT: What did you do to check any information before you arrived at your conclusions?

Mr. PEERS: The attempts to check the information were:

my expressed desire to see Mr. Bushnell and discuss the matter with him . . . there was my discussion with the chief news editor [W. H. Hogg] in Toronto, whose department was being asked to replace the program, to see whether he had information that I did not have . . .

Mr. LAMBERT: This had nothing to do with information that there was political pressure or influence?

Mr. PEERS: Definite information that there was political influence did not come to me until Wednesday night. These very questions related to that.

Shortly after this exchange, Edmund Morris, a Halifax member, moved that "in view of the fact that the witness has testified that he has no information but only hearsay, that the witness be thanked for his appearance and be dismissed". However, since his own Conservative colleagues on the committee wanted to continue questioning Frank Peers, his motion was voted down. Although he was not a lawyer, Jack Pickersgill, the former Liberal cabinet minister, had acted as a sort of defence counsel with his objections to some of the Tory tactics and his interjections in support of the witness; his turn came and he had several questions to ask:

Mr. PICKERSGILL: The first question I would like to put to Mr. Peers is this: would he regard an opinion expressed to management by a politician about their programs, even a very unflattering and unfavourable opinion, as "political influence"?

Mr. PEERS: I would not regard it as political influence unless management seemed to give it undue and urgent consideration, to a degree they would not give such a representation from any other important person or person of substance.

Mr. PICKERSGILL: My second question is this: do you think that politicians, particularly ministers, should not express to management views on their programs?

Mr. PEERS: Mr. Chairman, I suppose I have to answer this?

The CHAIRMAN: Yes, that is a fair question.

Mr. PEERS: I think it is debatable. I think that opinions from members of Parliament certainly should be welcome and should be given careful thought, just as the opinions of any other responsible citizen. . . . The opinions of CBC—or rather of members of the cabinet—I think under the old system of financing programs with licences, that a member— this is pure opinion, as you can see . . .

Mr. FLYNN: Like the rest.

Mr. PICKERSGILL: Exactly.

Mr. PEERS: . . . think that an opinion of a cabinet minister is very much like that of the opinion of an MP. I am not certain I would say that it is now when the CBC has to go before Parliament for its grants on a basis which is not a statutory basis.

Mr. PICKERSGILL: The third question I want to put on this particular line is this: In your view, was the political inter- ference to which you understood Mr. Walker to make reference—was it accompanied by a threat of the consequences to the corporation if it was not followed?

Mr. PEERS: I am not sure it was accompanied by such a threat. I am at least sure that some in management thought there was a threat attached.

Mr. PICKERSGILL: Is it the apprehension or the suspicion of the threat that, in your view, constituted the pressure or the influence rather?

The CHAIRMAN: That is, in your view.

Mr. PEERS: In my view, it may have constituted an influence; but the important thing was the CBC action following upon the representation—whatever the representa- tion was, and however urgently it was dealt with.

H. G. "Bud" Walker, Frank Peers's immediate boss, was then called to the stand, and he read from "some informal notes" that he had written in a notebook so that he could recall the events better in "the last number of rather difficult days". When Walker quoted Jennings as saying that the specific heads that would roll were those of Mr. Bushnell and Mr. Nowlan, the reporters made such a commotion rushing for the door to get the news out that Pickersgill suggested there should be a recess for the press. However, when Dick Bell, the Conservative member for the Ottawa riding of Carleton and a lawyer, went to work on the CBC official, he reduced Walker's testimony to a quavering mass of hearsay.

Mr. BELL: Were there any names at any time mentioned of any political figure or person of political connection who was bringing the pressure to bear?

Mr. WALKER: Not in my presence.

Mr. BELL: At no time was there any name mentioned in any of the conversations at which you were present?

Mr. WALKER: Not in my honest recollection.

Mr. BELL: So that at all times you were operating on the basis of surmise and inference from what was said?

Mr. WALKER: I would choose to call it—you may be correct in identifying it that way—but I would choose to call it logic, by virtue of the fact that the corporation is in no position, obviously, to relieve Mr. Nowlan of his position; and if I may continue, nor as I understand it, is our president, who also presides over our board, nor the board itself in a position to relieve the vice-president of his duties.

Mr. BELL: What inference do you get from that statement?

Mr. WALKER: No inference at all. By logic I felt—and I imagine our other senior officers felt—that probably there must have been some kind of influence.

Mr. BELL: Did you ever ask Mr. Bushnell, Mr. Ouimet, or Mr. Jennings from whom this alleged pressure was coming?

Mr. WALKER: No sir.

Mr. BELL: Why not?

Mr. WALKER: I cannot answer. I do not know why. I did not feel there was any reason for my asking. I had been advised of what I chose to regard as a serious situation and, for reasons that I have recounted in my informal notes, I felt, in the interests of the corporation, I would pass it on to my senior officials. That was as far as I could go.

Mr. BELL: You are on the basis of intimacy with Mr. Jennings and Mr. Bushnell?

Mr. WALKER: Indeed so.

Mr. BELL: Therefore there would be no reason why you did

not ask a question of that sort, and, if you did so, it would not be considered as impertinent coming from you?

Mr. WALKER: Not at all.

Mr. BELL: Have you any further reason to advance why you did not ask the question directly to either as to who was the person involved?

Mr. WALKER: No sir, I had no reason to.

Charles Jennings, who was the next up the line from Walker, was then called. He read a statement in which he said that the explanation given to him for cancelling "Preview Commentary" was that, if it weren't cancelled, both the president and the acting president would lose their jobs and the position of the minister would be in jeopardy. However, Jennings waffled as much as Walker had under questioning by Douglas Fisher, the CCF member, which seemed to reveal an assumption on the part of CBC executives that an action such as the one taken by Bushnell must be a result of "clandestine" political interference or influence.

Mr. FISHER: Where did you get the information that Mr. Nowlan was involved with someone whose position was in jeopardy? Was that from Mr. Bushnell?

Mr. JENNINGS: I am sorry; I think I made that clear in my opening remarks. But I was instructed that the program "Preview Commentary" was to terminate, and so on. This was Mr. Bushnell and later the explanation was given to me by Mr. Bushnell and so on.

Mr. FISHER: Could I ask the same question that Mr. Bell was asking Mr. Walker. Did you question this at all and question the source of the pressure?

Mr. JENNINGS: At no time did Mr. Bushnell disclose or tell me the source which compelled him to take this action.

Mr. FISHER: Well, why did you not persist in trying to find out what the source of the pressure was?

Mr. JENNINGS: Again, I do not know that I can answer that, Mr. Fisher. I had been given the information. It was quite a shock to me and I think I went away and tried to prepare this formula of which I spoke.

Mr. FISHER: You did not at any time disbelieve the statement?

Mr. JENNINGS: I will say that I wondered if I was hearing my own ears at first.

Mr. LAMBERT: Was any name or names given to you?

Mr. JENNINGS: No.

Mr. LAMBERT: Did you ever ask for any names?

Mr. JENNINGS: No, I did not.

Mr. LAMBERT: Did you ask for an explanation of such a statement after you found it, as you say, rather strange?

Mr. JENNINGS: Not that I recall, Mr. Lambert. It was all rather a very strained time.

Mr. PICKERSGILL: Mr. Jennings, did you consider that to have asked a question as to the source of the information would be redundant?

Mr. JENNINGS: No, I did not think of that specifically; I am sorry, Mr. Pickersgill.

The last witness in the case was Ernie Bushnell. He too read a statement, only it was very brief; in it, he denied that any order or directive had been given to him or to Al Ouimet "by Honourable George Nowlan or by any member of Parliament or anyone else who could be said to wield political influence". He said that he included the president in his statement with his full knowledge and consent. In opening the questioning, Jack Pickersgill, who was asked to stand in order to be heard above the buzz of excitement in the reverberating Railway Committee Room, went straight for the the jugular:

Mr. PICKERSGILL: I would be very glad to stand. I would like to ask Mr. Bushnell whether the prime minister spoke to him about this program at any time, formally or informally?

Mr. BUSHNELL: No sir, never. I have not spoken to the prime minister—had the honour of speaking to him in two years.

Mr. PICKERSGILL: Might I ask Mr. Bushnell one other question? Did anyone purporting to speak on behalf of the prime minister speak to you about the program at any time?

The CHAIRMAN: What exactly do you mean by that, Mr. Pickersgill?

Mr. PICKERSGILL: Anyone who represented himself as speaking on behalf of the prime minister.

The CHAIRMAN: Who could that be?

Mr. PICKERSGILL: I prefer to ask my own questions if the Chair will permit.

The CHAIRMAN: And I would prefer that—you do not need to answer it, Mr. Bushnell, unless he gets down to cases—so we have an impasse on that. Would you like to change your question, Mr. Pickersgill?

Mr. PICKERSGILL: No, I will not change my question, Mr. Chairman.

The CHAIRMAN: Do you wish to answer it, Mr. Bushnell?

Mr. BUSHNELL: I think you will have to clarify for me what you mean by "purporting".

Mr. PICKERSGILL: I will be very happy to do that, and do it in the words I used the second time—anyone who represented himself to you as speaking on behalf of the prime minister?

Mr. BUSHNELL: No. Let me qualify that. As representing himself as speaking on behalf of the prime minister?

Mr. PICKERSGILL: Yes.

Mr. BUSHNELL: No.

Mr. PICKERSGILL: Did anyone representing himself as conveying views held by the prime minister speak to you about this program?

Mr. BUSHNELL: No, they did not.

Mr. FISHER: Mr. Bushnell, the question I think we are all very interested in knowing is, how Mr. Jennings got the impression which was passed on to Mr. Walker, which later got down to the three people who were called here today—that, in the slang phrase that Mr. Walker used,"heads will roll"?

Mr. BUSHNELL: Mr. Fisher, as Mr. Jennings said, he could not confirm that I actually used those terms. I did.

Mr. FISHER: You did use those terms?

Mr. BUSHNELL: Yes.

Mr. FISHER: Why?

Mr. BUSHNELL: This matter has rather a long association.

No heads were going to roll because of the cancellation of this program, but I think you will agree that it has been stated by the newspapers—I have heard it said that such a statement has been made, if you like, by members of political parties, and I felt convinced that this rather tragic series of unfortunate circumstances that we have had in the last six months, that if we did not pull up our socks, certainly somebody's head would roll, and quite properly.

Mr. FISHER: Do you mean that the atmosphere was such at this particular stage when, you made this decision that you felt your job and that of Mr. Ouimet were in jeopardy?

Mr. BUSHNELL: Rightly or wrongly, it could have been—and I think I felt that way.

Mr. FISHER: Mr. Walker reported on a telephone conversation that went from the Celebrity Club in which you spoke to Mr. Ouimet. Is it true that in that telephone conversation as reported in substance by Mr. Walker that you told Mr. Ouimet that if the program did not go, your job and his job were in jeopardy?

Mr. BUSHNELL: Inasmuch as there were two witnesses there, Mr. Jennings and Mr. Walker, I do not think I could categorically deny that. But what I did say or what I was trying to get at was this: that if, generally speaking, something was not done to correct some of the errors of our ways, that that could be a possibility.

Bushnell ended his testimony, which was over much more quickly than he expected, by asking to have the following undertaking put on the record: "So long as I hold my present position, I shall continue to uphold and apply the principles of free speech and responsible reporting of public issues." Although he had stepped forward almost jauntily when he was called as a witness, he felt tired and depressed now, despite the glowing tribute that Nowlan had paid him in Parliament the day before. Peter Dempson of the *Toronto Telegram* had reported in the restored "Preview Commentary" that morning that, judging from the minister's remarks, the government had the fullest confidence in Mr. Bushnell. Nowlan had said, "I've never seen any sign of weakness or incompetence on his part." The minister squelched rumours that the acting president was going to resign, but he seemed, as Dempson suggested, to leave the door open; Dempson quoted the minister as saying: "Mr. Bushnell is totally exhausted. He should be given a few weeks off to recover from the terrific strain of the past six months. Otherwise he may wind up in hospital."

It turned out that this was Ernie Bushnell's last appearance before a parliamentary committee; while he had never held a high opinion of these annual inquisitions and regarded them as being usually a waste of time, he was prepared to concede that they were a necessary democratic evil. However, the hearing on this affair had embittered him; he objected to being made a whipping boy, and it was in a mood of anger and anguish that he left the Railway Committee Room on adjournment that summer afternoon to take an extended leave.

At the committee's meeting on the following Thursday, July 2, the minister responsible, Honourable George Nowlan, was the only witness. He was asked by Douglas Fisher whether he had ever discussed programming with Bushnell, and it was then that Nowlan cited several instances of CBC producers defying the government and the corporation's management. There was the request to bring an "undesirable" alien from Europe (the Nazi desperado, Otto Skorzeny) to appear on a program. When a visa was refused, the producer had said that he would bring Skorzeny to New York and have the interview "piped" from there on to the CBC network. Nowlan heard of this and suggested that Bushnell give "very careful consideration" to the way this producer was "defying the government and involving the taxpayer in very unusual expenses in order to produce this program". As a result, the acting president cancelled the interview.

Then there was the "Algerian case": the French Ambassador in Ottawa had protested against the CBC's intention of interviewing "representatives of the Algerian so-called government", as the minister put it; the French prime minister had called in the Canadian ambassador in Paris and handed him an official note on this matter:

Mr. NOWLAN: I told him [Mr. Bushnell] of the representations which had been made to me. Mr. Bushnell said—and I remember there was no hesitation—if the representations are coming at that level the interview will not take place. It was only two days later that Radio Canada, Montreal, carried the same program but with a different individual. I again discussed this with Mr. Bushnell and said that I thought this was an example of loose management and defiance of management in the organization. Also, I discussed the Madame d'Youville case with him . . . and you may remember, I was asked about that matter in the House of Commons and I said disciplinary action would be taken. Afterwards, I was asked by M.. Bushnell what I meant by disciplinary action and, as I recall it, I said "I think the people responsible for it should be fired." He was quite shocked at that.

Mr. FISHER: Could you give us the date of that?

Mr. NOWLAN: I cannot remember. If you would look up Hansard you would find it. It was within twenty-four hours after I made the statement in Hansard. Mr. Bushnell said that he did not think that could be done. I remember asking him: "Has anyone ever been fired in this organization for disciplinary purposes?"—and he said he thought the last one was in 1942. I said that perhaps it was time somebody else was fired around here, to put some discipline in it.

(While Bushnell had appeared shocked at the minister's suggestion that some people should be fired, he later expressed regret that the CBC management didn't have the guts, as he put it, to wield the axe. He says that "half of those [Toronto producers] who resigned should have been fired long before", and adds that some of the Montreal producers should have been dismissed too. It was the inability of management to fire anyone that got the CBC into so much trouble. The only way around the security of tenure that went with employment in a government agency was to put some of the producers on contract rather than on staff; this was done, but it did not save the corporation from another crisis over the program "This Hour Has Seven Days".

Mr. FISHER: Mr. Chairman, did the minister make only one reference, in his conversation with Mr. Bushnell to firing?

Mr. NOWLAN: I think that is the only reference I made to firing. I remember once I told him, in dealing with some of these cases where I thought the thing was very loosely run, that the CBC reminded me of a cabbage patch, with a great lot of heads, and each one trying to get bigger than the other—and you know what happens when they get too big. They burst.

Mr. PICKERSGILL: Not roll?

Mr. NOWLAN: No, not roll.

Mr. FISHER: Could you give us an explanation as to why Mr. Bushnell used the expression, in connection with the withdrawal of "Preview Commentary", that "heads will roll"?

Mr. NOWLAN: I cannot give any explanation whatsoever of that.

Mr. FISHER: You have no idea how your name came to be included as one of the heads that would roll, either in communication with Mr. Jennings or Mr. Walker?

Mr. NOWLAN: I do not. I must say that I wondered if that was a threat or a promise because certainly there is nothing I would rather do frankly than be rid of the responsibility of reporting to Parliament for the CBC. I told Mr. Bushnell that on many occasions, and I told him I was going to try to get the prime minister to appoint someone else because I was sick and tired of these criticisms coming in from all over the country, from members of Parliament, from my colleagues and from the public generally.

Mr. FISHER: I will repeat the former question I asked. There is no way that you can see that Mr. Bushnell got the idea in his head, that his head, your head and that of Mr. Ouimet would roll if this program were not taken off at a definite time?

Mr. NOWLAN: As I said before, if he had the idea my head would roll vis-a-vis the CBC, then I hope he is correct. As far as any inference that his head or Mr. Ouimet's or anyone else's is concerned he did not get it from me. Going back over these other occasions, like the Algerian matter, the Mother d'Youville question, the case of the person being brought in from Europe and also the background of the strike, where I was told afterwards if they had exercised any control here the strike would not have happened, I probably told them, "You had better tighten up this organization or something will happen to somebody around here." I do not make any bones about having said something like that; but in respect of having made reference to it in connection with some particular program, I never did.

The hearing ended on a harmonious note with both Fisher and Pickersgill expressing their appreciation to the minister; Nowlan said that he was "very, very glad" to come to the committee and explain the situation as "somebody has made a mountain out of a molehill".

23 Down and Up Slater Street

The cottage on the wooded banks of the Gatineau River was one of the reasons Bushnell had given for moving to Ottawa and accepting the compensatory appointment of assistant general manager back in 1953—it was to this ideal Canadian retreat that he retired after the parliamentary committee hearing, to rest awhile and recover from the blows of what could only be called an outrageous fortune. He played golf on the rolling greensward of Larrimac's nine-hole course, which was only a short ride away, but mostly he pottered around the terraced garden of his cottage which was so beautifully located on a bend in the river. He would fish its languorous waters of an evening, not catching much and not expecting to catch much. During the whole of the months of July and August, he spent only a few days away from his beloved Gatineau River. He and Edna accepted a couple of invitations: Corey Thomson had rung up to say that his boat was "parked by the Chateau Laurier", and they went cruising with him down the Ottawa to Montreal; they also stayed with Clifford Sifton in his mansion on the St. Lawrence near Brockville, and saw the Thousand Islands from the deck of his yacht. Bush recalls that Clifford knew the narrow channels so well that he had developed a disconcerting—as far as his passengers were concerned—habit of navigating without looking.

As the letters came in, Bush realized that most people, including many of the so-called intellectuals, were on his side. He was particularly pleased with a letter from Ned Corbett, the honorary chairman of the Canadian Association for Adult Education and the grand panjandrum of mass learning, who wrote: "I don't expect you or want you to confirm what I am about to say but I am damn sure in my own mind that no other CBC senior manager ever had anything like the pressure upon him that you have had since last January. I don't mean only Ouimet's illness and the Montreal strike, God knows they were bad enough, but I also know and have known for some time about other pressures that it is difficult to talk about or define." Dr. J. R. Mutchmor, moderator of the United Church, said in a personal letter that the National Religious Advisory Council of the CBC, of which he was secretary, wanted it known that they supported him. "You have been on the firing line and given a good account of yourself," Dr. Mutchmor wrote. "We have every confidence in your leadership." Gladstone Murray sent him a "cheer-up" note, saying, "No doubt you are now sufficiently experienced to realize this whole thing soon will collapse and disappear. In my twenty years of radio I went through at least a dozen similar ordeals— the inevitable consequence of trying to do one's duty in a public service."

It was becoming increasingly clear to Bushnell that he had been a political scapegoat, that the charge that he had bowed to government pressure in cancelling "Preview Commentary" was the opening salvo of the anti-Diefenbaker campaign that the Liberals were mounting. In fact, they were insinuating, as Pickersgill had done in his questioning, that the threat of "heads will roll" came indirectly from the prime minister. Now the only ones doubting Bush's denial and implying that he had lied (he was not under oath at the committee hearing) were Liberal hacks and hatchet men. At any rate, his Irish dander was up, and there was no thought of quitting; the question of his retirement was dismissed as newspaper speculation. In fact, Bushnell recalled the satisfaction he had had in running the CBC—the frustrations and irritations were fading into the background while the sense of achievement came to the fore. He had enjoyed those last few months even though they may have been in some ways disastrous; he had enjoyed being on his own and not having Al Ouimet around. He did wonder what it would be like when the president returned; it was a sneaking thought to disturb his mind as he weeded the neat aprons of lawn around his Gatineau cottage. He told George Nowlan that he had "no intention of sitting around for another five years twiddling my thumbs", and he meant what he said.

One sweltering hot day, Bush was cleaning up and trimming some brush beside an old oak tree on his property; he mopped his brow as the sun beat down from the reflecting glass of the sky and decided to fetch himself a bottle of ice-cold beer. He had hardly reached the house and the door to the basement when there was an explosion as a lightning bolt struck the tree and shattered it. Bush was dazed. "So drink saved my life, he thought as he put out the small fires burning on the edges of the smashed tree. "There, if it hadn't been for me wanting a beer, I would have been killed." He hopped into his boat, rowed across the river and dug up some pine trees on the wild opposite bank and brought them back; he planted them around the base of the oak to hide its charred and broken trunk.

When he tells that story, Bush finishes it by saying that it occurred "during my drinking days"—they were numbered now and he must have been thinking about swearing off anything alcoholic when he went to fetch the bottle of beer on the day the lightning struck. There was no one incident that prompted him to take the pledge. "I just came to my senses," he says. "I finally realized that I was making a fool of myself, that, in my condition, I couldn't take any liquor." There had been occasions when, he admits, he had disgraced himself at public functions although he had had very little to drink; that summer, he had staggered and fallen at a diplomatic cocktail party in Ottawa. It was his diabetes that made drinking so hazardous for him. "Edna would say that there were times when a couple of drinks and I couldn't walk across the living room."

It was on September 17, 1959, that he gave up drinking. The night before he had had a spat with Edna, a family argument that happened to have nothing to do with alcohol; the next day, he went to the liquor store, bought a twenty-six-ounce bottle of rye, carried it back to his apartment at 38 Range Road, and sat down and drank it dry. Then he put the empty bottle on the shelf and said "That's the last", and it was. "No Alcoholics

Anonymous," Bush says. "Nothing like that—when I quit I just quit." He fell off the wagon once. That was in March 1960 when he was in Toronto for the BBG hearings for second television licence applications, and Bill Byles and some of his old cronies kept saying: "Come on, Bush, have a drink." He had one which led to another and many more. Edna heard of his fall from grace and went to Toronto to fetch him home. It never happened again.

Al Ouimet was back in his office when Ernie Bushnell returned to work at the beginning of September 1959, and the president was playing with his organization board, sticking in new pegs at the top. During his illness and convalescence at home, Ouimet had had a lot of time to ponder deeply the problems of the CBC and what should be done to make it less trouble-prone; he had come to the conclusion that there was nothing that a restructuring of top management would not cure. So he proposed to create five or six vice-presidents. However, Al was aware that Ernie would be unlikely to welcome his latest reorganization of the executive and might even consider that it was an attempt to water down his position; there was also the likelihood that the vice-president would argue against the approval of these appointments when he presented them to the board of directors, which was meeting early in the month in Halifax. Therefore, Ouimet directed Bushnell not to attend the board meeting.

The president's order was probably illegal, but what was the use of defying it and attending the meeting? Bush was furious. It seemed to him that Ouimet was planning to by-pass him with these five or six vice-presidents and leave him "twiddling his thumbs", which was what he had told the minister he would not do. From that day on, he began to think seriously about retiring.

Not long after, in October, Bushnell received a telephone call from N. A. "Nat" Taylor, president of Twentieth Century Theatres Limited, who said that he and Dave Griesdorf would be in Ottawa the next week and would like to talk to him about a business proposition. A lawyer who had become involved in show business, Nat was an old friend from their mutual interest in the Toronto Variety Club, and Bush had known Dave as the general manager of Odeon Theatres Limited. Thus, in a Chateau Laurier bedroom, BBA, Bushnell Broadcasting Associates, was conceived; it was to become the original and humble progenitor of the Bushnell Television Company, Bushnell Communications and the whole Bushnell empire.

Taylor and Griesdorf proposed to set up Bushnell as a consultant, primarily for their interests—a film distribution company and a production company, NTA (Telefilm) Canada Limited, as well as a theatre chain—but also for others. They wanted to get into television, but no one in the hotel bedroom had any clear idea of what could or should be done. Nat talked about selling his films to TV. At any rate, they offered Bushnell a much bigger salary than he was getting from the CBC (then sixteen thousand dollars a year), and a quarter share of BBA. Years later Bush said that he owed Taylor and Griesdorf a debt that he could never repay. "Generous to a fault," he wrote, " 'true blue' in every respect, their encouragement, their confidence and their money started me off on another career which could not have been a happier one if I had planned it myself."

Then, one day, a short time later, the balloon went up: "Why don't you apply for the television licence that is coming up for Ottawa?" Bush couldn't remember whether Nat or Dave asked the question.

But what with? There was a chance of losing forty or fifty thousand dollars on such a bid—Bush had got this figure from Frank Ryan, who was already working on his application for the Ottawa TV licence. However, the amount didn't seem to worry either of his sponsors. "So what?" was Nat Taylor's reply.

It was now up to Bushnell to resign, so he walked over to George Nowlan's office in the Parliament buildings and told the minister of his decision. That great hulk of a man (Bush's description) looked at him for a minute or two, then lifted his six-foot-five-inch frame off his chair and came around to the other side of the desk.

"Ernie," he said, "you don't have to quit. Tell those bastards who are hounding you over there to go to hell," and he pointed at the window of his office which looked out on Parliament Hill and the CBC head offices in the Victoria building. "You have a job to do and I don't want you to leave."

"Sorry, Mr. Minister," Bush replied, "but I can't take money under false pretences. My usefulness has ended. I have little or no responsibility. There are people working for me who in my judgment have been disloyal and others in whom I have no confidence and for whom I have no respect. I couldn't possibly continue to work in such a climate. I'm through as of December thirty-first."

Nowlan protested but, when he saw that he was not getting anywhere, he made friendly inquiries about the future. Bushnell said that he was going to apply for the Ottawa TV licence. The minister grunted.

"You know that Grattan O'Leary [later Senator O'Leary] of the *Ottawa Journal* is also applying," Nowlan said, "and he's an old friend. I'll tell you exactly how things stand. For what either is worth, Grattan will have my support and you will have my sympathy."

Bushnell looked the minister straight in the eye. "Sir," he said, "do you know what I think? Neither is worth a good goddamn."

"How right you are," Nowlan said between guffaws. "Now get the hell out of here," and he stuck out his big paw of a hand.

Bushnell returned to his office, advised Ouimet of his decision, and wrote out his letter of resignation; it was dated November 26, 1959.

Now that the dye was cast, he had mixed feelings. There was the relief he felt that he had made up his mind, and that he would no longer be "hauled" before royal commissions and parliamentary and government committees to explain the rightness or wrongness of this or that action. He would not be the target for any more abuse from politicians and the press. He hadn't minded being a public servant; in fact, he considered it an honour and would continue to be a public servant in the private sector, but he didn't feel that he had to be a public doormat. There was regret too: it was a wrench to leave the corporation which he had done so much to create and shape; the CBC had been his "baby"—he had nurtured it through its childhood and helped it grow to full adulthood. Furthermore, until recently, he had really enjoyed his work, and felt that he had made a significant contribution to broadcasting in general and national broadcasting in particular. Richard Lewis, the editor of the *Canadian Broadcaster,* had called him Mr. Television; he should have called him Mr. CBC, as his career had covered the whole span of broadcasting in Canada and he was more closely identified in the public's mind with the CBC than any other person.

His Irish emotions almost got the better of him as he accepted a "beautiful boat" and a forty-horsepower outboard engine as a farewell presentation from the staff of the CBC. It was a bittersweet occasion. The opening up of second television channels meant that there was "an opportunity to participate in an endeavour in which I had spent many happy years, an avocation and not just a vocation". So, at fifty-nine years of age, and with a light heart, Ernie Bushnell began a new career.

As there was not much time, Bush started to work on his application while he was still technically with the CBC, although he was careful to work in his home at night on the project. The faithful Georgie Appleby also resigned at the same time he did, and on January 2, 1960, they moved into new quarters above O. L. Derouin and Sons Ltd., Opticians, in a two-storey frame building at 130 Slater Street, long since torn down. Actually, Miss Appleby spent most of the month of January by herself, supervising the carpenters partitioning three offices in front. Bush was away looking after BBA's first two accounts. He acted as a consultant for two would-be television station owners: Pacific Television, which had been put together by a group of Vancouver millionaires; and Red River Television Associates of Winnipeg, which was his old friend, Clifford Sifton. He charged each of them three thousand dollars.

Neither was successful in its bid for a television licence, but Bushnell attended the hearings of the Board of Broadcast Governors in Vancouver and Winnipeg, and learned a lot that would stand him in good stead when he came to make his own application. He noted the way that a prominent lawyer appearing on behalf of one of the applicants for the Vancouver station attacked Art Jones, another applicant, like a prosecuting attorney in a B movie; he could see that the three older women on the board didn't like it at all, and swears he could almost hear them saying to themselves: "You're not going to get away with that kind of diatribe against such a fine upstanding young man who might be the spitting image of my grandson." Jones, an attractive young man who had his own small film company and had been a former president of the Vancouver Young Men's Board of Trade, had made an excellent plea, and Bush told his principals that they had lost to him largely because of their stupidly aggressive lawyer. He was going to see that his legal counsel would make a low-key defence of his application; he had no real need to worry, as G. E. "Ted" Beament, QC, was a suave, courtly, almost old-worldly figure, who had the board emotionally on his side.

The second floor of 130 Slater Street had a large room at the back, and it was there toward the end of February 1960 that the first meeting of Bushnell Television was held. The prospective shareholders—most were local businessmen but some had come up from Toronto—were ranged around the room on wooden chairs facing Bush and Ted Beament who sat at a table at one end. Bush started off the meeting by announcing that he had an original name for the company: it was going to be called the Bushnell Television Company. Actually, he had wanted the name "Inter-City [for Ottawa and Hull] Television" but found that it was already being used by another applicant, and it was Beament who suggested that he should give his own name to the company. Then, Bill Byles of the broadcasting representatives, Stovin Byles (Horace Stovin had been one of Bushnell's early associates in the CBC), gave a glowing account of the area's market potential.

Capitalization of Bushnell Television was set at one million dollars, with about a quarter of the money being put up by the main corporate shareholder, the Taylor group, which preferred to be listed as NTA (Telefilm) Canada Ltd., their production company, rather than Twentieth Century Theatres Ltd. (NTA was linked with National Television Associates in the United States and WNTA, New York, which meant that they could draw on the resources of the best American experience.) The rest of the capitalization had to be raised privately, and since the emphasis was on local ownership, most of it had to come from Ottawa citizens.

The founding meeting on the second floor of 130 Slater Street was really a pledging conference, and the men and women sitting on the hard chairs were asked to sign promissory notes as to how much of the stock they would take—they were offered a package of a dollar's worth of common to four dollars' worth of preferred shares: in other words, in order to obtain one hundred common shares at a dollar each, they had to buy four six-per-cent non-cumulative redeemable preferred shares of a par value of one hundred dollars each. All those at the first meeting on that cold winter afternoon were told that this was an unusual opportunity—they couldn't lose since the Taylor group and NTA were paying all the costs of the application. It was a gamble in which they didn't have to put up a cent, yet Bush had a difficult time finding enough Ottawa investors. He himself became the largest individual shareholder with twenty thousand common shares and eight hundred preferred; he raised the hundred thousand dollars needed by borrowing from the banks and from his principals and sponsors.

In preparing his submission, Bushnell had obtained the expert assistance of Ray Brining, a qualified chartered accountant, and "Sandy" Day, who was acknowledged to be the best technical consultant in the country. Ted Beament, who acted as secretary of the company, "played a major role and without his help we would never have succeeded in raising the necessary capital required to get into business should our application be successful."

On March 28, an old friend and former colleague, Stu Griffiths, turned up in Bushnell's office at 130 Slater Street. Stu had spent the last five years working as a program organizer and executive for Granada, part of the ITV network in Great Britain, but Bush had seen him recently during the BBG

225

hearings in Toronto for second station applications. Griffiths had been one of the applicants—he had put together a company known as Upper Canada Broadcasting Ltd., which included Peter Wright, a lawyer who was to become a judge, and such personalities as the conductor Sir Ernest MacMillan, actor and producer Mavor Moore, Wayne and Schuster and Tom Patterson, the impressario and founder of the Stratford Shakespeare Festival. It didn't require much insight to see that Upper Canada was being bankrolled by Granada. The time was eleven o'clock in the morning, and Griffiths was somewhat discouraged because he had learned that his application had failed. The twelve o'clock news carried the announcement that the BBG had awarded the Toronto TV licence to a company whose principals were John Bassett and Joel Aldred. Bush had a brainwave.

"Stu," he said, turning off the radio, "how would like to join with me—maybe we could team up again and try to do the kind of job we worked so hard to do when we put CBLT on the air?"

Griffiths was hesitant.

"I don't know, Bush," but he added, "I'll think it over."

He went to see Dr. Andrew Stewart, the chairman of the BBG, to thank him for the fair and courteous hearing that the board had given his group in Toronto; casually, he asked the chairman if he were to join Bushnell in his application for the Ottawa licence whether this would in any way lessen the chances of that application.

"Not at all—quite the contrary," was the answer, or so Bush was told. "Indeed, such a coalition might improve Mr. Bushnell's chances."

Griffiths then telephoned his principal, Sidney Bernstein (later Lord Bernstein), the proprietor of the Granada conglomerate in Great Britain. He expressed regret at their losing the Toronto bid but suggested that the door might be open for Granada to join Ernie Bushnell in his application for the Ottawa station; Stu explained that Bush was the most experienced broadcaster in Canada, had been his boss in the CBC, and was an old friend. Bernstein hardly knew Ottawa, but he was a man of action and didn't ask for any more details.

"Go to it if you think it's worth a try" he said. "I leave the decision entirely in your hands."

The next day, Griffiths returned to 130 Slater Street and, after a handshake and mutual congratulations, he, Bushnell and Miss Appleby got down to the urgent business of putting together a new application—the deadline for filing with the Department of Transport was March 31, just two days away. They pulled apart the old application, which was by then almost completed and ready for binding, inserted new ideas and, most important of all, they changed the financial structure of the company. Capitalization of Bushnell Television was increased from $1,000,000 to $1,200,000, with Granada putting up the extra $200,000 and acquiring 40,000 common shares and 160 preferred shares; the new arrangement would put the two corporate shareholders, Granada and NTA, on an equal footing. Bushnell had to get his principals' consent, but Nat Taylor had no objection and even saw an advantage in British capital being added to the American capital that his NTA represented. Ted Beament also agreed, although he was concerned that control of the company should be in local hands and that this should be made evident to the BBG.

So, a voting trust agreement was drawn up which all the individual shareholders from the Ottawa area were required to sign; the purpose of the agreement, as outlined in schedule twenty-four of the supplementary submission of Bushnell Television, was "to ensure that effective control of the company at all times rests with the shareholders of the company who are permanently resident in the said city of Ottawa and its environs to be served by the proposed television broadcasting station and to secure continuity in the management and policy of the company". The effect was to ensure that control (more than fifty per cent of the stock was represented by those who signed the agreement) remained in the hands of three trustees of whom E. L. Bushnell was one. Furthermore, the participants' agreement with the applicant spelled out that Bushnell should be employed by the company as its general manager, that his salary should be $25,000 per annum, and that his employment should be of "indefinite

227

hiring", termination of which would require six months notice on either side.

Bush, Stu and Georgie Appleby worked until four o'clock in the morning of March 31 at 130 Slater Street completing the revised brief. That afternoon, Miss Appleby received a telephone call from the Department of Transport inquiring politely if Mr. Bushnell intended to put in a submission, because if he did, there was only half an hour to go before the deadline of five o'clock. Miss Appleby found Bush at the stationers where they had had some trouble in mimeographing and binding, but there were enough copies completed (three were required) for him to rush them over to the department's office—he filed his application, together with a certified cheque for five hundred dollars, at quarter to five.

As a matter of courtesy, later that evening he took a copy of the brief to the home of Carlyle Allison, vice-chairman of the BBG. The next day Carlyle called Bush to say "You must have been in one godawful hurry to complete this thing because there are at least 40 pages duplicated." The Department of Transport was refreshingly unbureaucratic enough to permit Bush to make the necessary corrections the following Monday.

24 Resurrection in a Lumberyard

In schedule nineteen of the supplementary submission, Ernie Bushnell went into his philosophy of broadcasting; it had not changed in all the years and could have been a rewrite of a number of speeches he had made for the CBC that were filed in his black leather binder. Television, he wrote, "must inform, it must educate, it must make some people laugh and at other times must tug at the heartstrings of others; it must ENTERTAIN." At the beginning of this dissertation, Bush said that he had had a long experience in "show business"; he noted a tendency to denigrate "showmanship" with which he did not agree, for showmanship was an essential part of the entertainment business and TV was show business. His definition of showmanship was "the professional touch of someone who knows how to attract and hold the attention of the person or persons at which his or her performance is aimed".

Schedule nineteen also contained the "policy on French- and English-language broadcasting" and, while Bushnell was cautiously noncommittal about making any pledges "in terms of percentages" of time to be devoted to either language, in the next paragraph he said: "We do not anticipate any difficulty in providing a minimum of ten hours of French-language broadcasting each week." Actually, the "second" TV station in the Ottawa area (it was really the third as the CBC had a French-language station, CBOFT, as well as the English-language station, CBOT) was to be an English-language station, and Bush knew from experience that a bilingual station was totally impractical. Ouimet had said, at the time of the bilingual commission's first hearings in the capital, that broadcasting in both languages, which had been tried at the beginning of CBOT, was a failure and served only to irritate both the French- and English-speaking groups. However, one of the applicants, Inter-City Broadcasting, was putting forward a plan for "simultaneous bilingual television"—there would be simultaneous interpreting of programs, similar to the simultaneous interpreting newly introduced into the House of Commons, which would be heard on a separate FM receiver. Although the feasibility of SBT, as Inter-City called it, was open to question, the plan had the effect of escalating the language stakes. Such was the state of Canadian politics, even in those days before the "Bi-and-Bi" report, that an applicant had to promise so much French-language programming even though he knew that it would be difficult to deliver, if he expected to get the licence.

It must be said that Bushnell Television did try to honour its pledge: the early schedules included a daily half-hour French program for pre-school school children entitled "Voici Babou", and the Créditistes bought time to spread their Social Credit gospel in French, but the reception of French-language broadcasts was most discouraging. There would be telephone calls protesting whenever French was used, and often the switchboard operator, who was usually a French Canadian girl, would be reduced to tears. If anything the protests became more virulent with the passage of time and the promotion of bilingualism in the civil service, as if the ordinary English-speaking Ottawans were giving vent to pent-up emotions—some of them said they were afraid that the station would be turned into a bilingual station. "Even a few words of French in a program, and the switchboard would light up," Bush says; furthermore, aside from the Créditistes, no one was prepared to sponsor a French-language program—not a Hull businessman, nor even a government department—and Bushnell pointed out, in a service-club speech, that his was a commercial enterprise that received no subsidies whatsoever.

The supplementary submission paid a good deal of attention to news reporting, and Bush recognized that this would be the second station's most important function, especially a second station in the national capital. However, there was some confusion as to whether the news should be presented by a news reader (an announcer) or by a newscaster (a newsman). In the part of schedule nineteen where he dealt with his philosophy of broadcasting, Bush seemed to take it for granted that the news would be prepared by editors from the available news services and read by announcers; he warned that news readers would become personalities and that the bulletins which they read "should be tailored to suit their particular style of reading". The news readers, he went on to say, would be expected to "convey to the viewers a feeling of friendliness without seeming to appear or sound either smug or 'chummy' ".

Yet, in the same schedule nineteen in a special section on News Reporting and Commentary, Bush quoted with evident approval from an article on "Television News Reporting" published by the McGraw-Hill Company Limited which outlined the qualities of a newscaster:

> He must be more than an ordinary reporter. In effect, he is a master reporter. The reasons why he is sitting there facing the camera are many but perhaps the main reason is his high integrity based upon his total experience as a newsman. It is his prerogative to change the script a writer has prepared for him, to write it over again, to edit it as he thinks best. When he speaks on the air, he speaks with the authority of a man who has looked deeply and intelligently into the news.

The section went on to say that such a newscaster should be used in "reporting local news as well as national and international news". But what about the news readers and their personalities, which were discussed a few pages before the paragraph on the qualities of the newscaster? Were there to be both?

The confusion in the supplementary submission was due to the fact that TV as a news medium was so recent that it was still in the process of being developed, and Bushnell merely reflected the schizophrenic attitude that the CBC had on this subject. Since the CRBC and the earliest days of radio, it had been a tenet of public broadcasting that the news should be read by an announcer; Dan McArthur, the architect of the CBC news, believed that this would assure a corporate and objective presentation and would avoid the sort of personalized and subjective treatment of such American newscasters as Gabriel Heater, Raymond Gram Swing, Lowell Thomas, and even Edward R. Murrow. McArthur's model was the BBC news: it was perhaps too cold and impersonal for North American tastes but he felt that it could be adapted by a little brighter writing and a little more warmth in the reading. The only trouble was that the Canadian public had been corrupted by American broadcasting and could not differentiate between a news reader and a newscaster; in fact, the public could draw no distinction at all and considered the news reader to be a newsman and reporter. Thus, the announcer, through no fault of his own, got an entirely false reputation and, in some cases, exploited it to the extent of delivering lectures on the news and news events.

With the advent of television, the situation became even worse: it drove one announcer/news reader to pose as a foreign correspondent. He would go abroad on his holidays and return to address public meetings on the Middle Eastern situation or the future of Communist Europe; sometimes he would dress up in a national costume to lend authenticity to his lecture and, since he was a celebrity as a news reader, he was able to command high fees. By the time the CBC decided to change to newscasters, the system had been institutionalized and a union representing the announcers had a vested interest in reading the news. As a result, when Stanley Burke, a bona fide newsman and foreign correspondent, became the first CBC newscaster, the union rules were such that he found he was reduced to being a news reader who was not allowed to alter a word of the copy that had been written for him; he was assured time and again that this anomaly would be cleared up but it wasn't, and in the end he quit.

Bushnell's supplementary submission was otherwise a well-prepared application that loses nothing in retrospect; it dealt not only with programming but with every aspect of a private television station, including market data, and was one of the reasons why Bushnell was awarded the Ottawa licence.

At the end of May, the supplementary submission was filed with the BBG. It had been an exhausting three months. Even before Stu Griffiths had joined in the enterprise, Bush had been working night and day on the application; then there had been the revision made necessary by the enlargement of the company to include Granada, and finally the supplementary submission, the most important summation of all his arguments.

He needed a holiday before the hearing, which was due to begin on June 23. It so happened that the Canadian War Correspondents' Association, to which he belonged, was planning to mark the fifteenth anniversary of the end of the war with a visit to London; Charles Lynch, president of the CWCA, and Rod McInnes, the public relations director of Air Canada, combined forces to produce the last of the great junkets. The war correspondents, every member of the association which included public relations officers who had served overseas (McInnes himself was an RCAF PR and a member of the CWCA) would be taken on the inaugural flight of the trans-Atlantic jet service. Bush joined about seventy members of the association plus top Air Canada officials, including Gordon McGregor, the president, on a sweltering hot night at the end of May in Uplands Airport. A barbershop quartet from London, Ontario, which was said to have won the world championship of barbershop-quartet singing, was brought along on the inaugural junket in order to entertain Prince Philip, who was to be the honoured guest at a dinner the CWCA was giving at the Café Royal in London. The quartet also entertained the war correspondents in flight, and the captain of a west-bound airliner who contacted the east-bound Air Canada jet inquired what was the noise that he heard in the background, the sound of revelry all night. Bush complained that he couldn't sleep because of the partying: it was a severe test for him, and he figured that if he could survive the war correspondents without a drink, which he did, he would never fall off the wagon again.

The BBG hearing was held in the Diocesan Hall of the Charities Establishment on Parent Street in Ottawa's By Ward market area. Bushnell's application was the last to come before the board, largely because it was the last to be filed with the Department of Transport, but it was not a bad position to be in: Bush had a chance to size up his rivals and to note what effect they were having on the fifteen men and women of the Board of Broadcast Governors. The other applicants were Lawrence Freiman, the department store magnate, who relied for his presentation on a film made by one of his associates, Crawley Films Ltd.; Grattan O'Leary, who had the resources of the *Ottawa Journal* behind him and who was a gifted orator and a formidable spokesman for any cause; Roger N. Seguin and the Inter-City group, who had the gimmick of SBT, "simultaneous bilingual television"; and Frank Ryan, who owned and operated a successful Ottawa radio station, CFRA, and was a popular local showman.

Full advantage of the provision for rebuttal was taken and then the order was reversed. Bushnell led off, and Ted Beament was lucid and smooth as silk as he dissected the corporate structures of the various applicants: he suggested that effective control of the Freiman group lay with the Southam Company, that Grattan O'Leary was a front for the Sifton interests which controlled FP Publications, the owners of the *Ottawa Journal*, and that these facts should be carefully considered by the board. Mr. Beament made the most of the voting trust agreement which, he said, meant that the control of the Bushnell Television Company would remain in the hands of the thirty individual Ottawa shareholders. Finally, he compared the paucity of experience of those selected as station managers by the other applicants with that of Ernie Bushnell, who was under contract to run the stations that his company proposed.

On July 5, the BBG announced that it had approved Bushnell's application for a second television station, but it was not till August 19, which Bush points out was his thirty-fourth wedding anniversary, that the licence was issued.

Immediately, there were charges that the Bushnell award was "fixed", just as there had been angry assertions that Bassett had had the Toronto television station in his pocket—why, hadn't he said so? It was all a political payoff. Much of the calumny and innuendo were being spread by disappointed applicants, some of whom were Liberals, but Bush was sufficiently concerned to write this reply:

This might be as good a spot as any to lay low some of the canards that floated around and about regarding the political pay-offs that were made by the Board of Broadcast Governors at the instigation of the Diefenbaker government. During January and February of 1960 I had acted as a consultant for two applicants—one in Vancouver and another in Winnipeg. I don't deny that attempts were made by several applicants to use political pull but I cannot and will not believe that the BBG's decisions were influenced one iota, one jot or tittle by the direct or indirect intervention of any politician.

If such were the case why wasn't Mr. Grattan O'Leary given the nod? And what about my client, Pacific Television, which was loaded with big-shot Tories? They didn't get the licence— Art Jones did, and God knows what his politics were. It was suggested that the Conservative government owed me something. For what? For getting them into one juicy mess while I was vice-president of the CBC? Maybe Mr. Bassett was somewhat indiscreet when he intimated that the then prime minister had more or less assured him that the application in which he was involved would receive sympathetic consideration. Undoubtedly it did but not because of the fact that John Bassett was a Tory. I attended the public sessions in Toronto. I heard Joel Aldred make the finest presentation of all the applicants and after he had finished I came away with the feeling that if he wasn't successful, there was something more going on than that which met the eye—or struck the ear.

Now, Bushnell had to produce. It was one thing, as he himself said, to get the licence, but quite another thing to put together a competent staff, to purchase vast quantities of equipment and build adequate modern studios and offices. However, he had one great advantage in that he had Stu Griffiths as his assistant and strong right arm; Stu had decided to leave Granada and return to Canada to put into operation the television station that he had helped to found. For him, and for Bush too, this was really a re-run of getting CBLT, the CBC's Toronto station, on the air seven years before, only there was less time now, greater urgency, more limited expenses, and there were all the disciplines that a private enterprise imposed. Bushnell would have liked the call letters CHOB (H for Hull, O for Ottawa and B for Bushnell) but they were already taken, so he settled for CJOH.

First priority was temporary studio space; the second floor of 130 Slater Street was overcrowded, with new employees taking turns at desks, and there was no space left for a studio. All that was available was a small one-storey office building in the Kemp Edwards lumberyard, and Bush seized on this gratefully although it was no bigger than an average suburban home. CJOH erected a tower and a "dish" on the roof after a struggle with Mayor Charlotte Whitton and the Ottawa City Council, so that they could direct the signal to the already built, six hundred-foot transmitter at Hazeldean. The studio in the Kemp Edwards building was downstairs in the basement, and it was like doing television from a small recreation room. There was so little space that Bushnell did not have an office at the temporary studio—he continued to work at 130 Slater Street.

Meanwhile, the construction of the permanent studios was underway. Bushnell had an option on four acres of land at City View, but a soil test showed that this was bog which would have meant thirty thousand dollars extra in piling to build there; after some litigation, Bush got four acres on the other side of the road. Later, when the company was set on an expansion course, another adjoining six acres were acquired. Crossing the road (Merivale Road) proved to be a wise move, for when the company came to build, they struck granite. Captain Tom Fuller, a leading Ottawa contractor and one of the original shareholders, put up Television House quickly and at a remarkably low cost considering the fact that special insulation was required because the site was on the edge of the flight path to Uplands Airport. The board of directors had put a limit of $708,000 on the construction of a two-storey building that was to include three studios, two of them larger than any in Ottawa, and the usual offices. Nat Taylor had had some experience in building movie theatres; he shook his head and said that it couldn't be done, but Captain Fuller did it for $702,000.

After the inevitable last-minute scramble, CJOH-TV got on the air on Sunday, March 12; it was less than six months after Bushnell received the licence, compared to the three years that the CBC took to get the first Toronto and Montreal stations operating. It was a tribute to Stu Griffiths's abounding energy and drive; he seemed to be everywhere at once, which wasn't really so difficult in the confined quarters in the lumberyard. CJOH began with eight hours a day of broadcasting and, while the producers and technicians performed miracles in the single basement studio, it was not possible to increase that output until the company moved to the spacious new quarters at 1500 Merivale Road in Spetember of that year; then they were on the air for twelve hours a day. A plaque in the old lobby of Television House, which eventually trebled in size, says that it was officially opened by Dr. Andrew Stewart, chairman of the BBG, for "service to the viewing public, the arts and commerce".

It was logical that the second stations should be hooked up in a second television network, and Spence Caldwell had won the right to organize that network from the Board of Broadcast Governors. This was actually a consolation prize since Caldwell, an eager beaver of a broadcasting executive, had been one of the unsuccessful applicants for the Toronto licence. He was so anxious to get a piece of the new television action that he was ready to accept the network, even though he knew from American experience that a network didn't make as much money as a single station, if it made any money at all. At any rate, Spence Caldwell and his CTV network had been licensed by the BBG, and he went around hat in hand to the second stations asking them to sign up as affiliates and invest in his company. It couldn't have come at a worse time for Bushnell. CJOH had only just started; there had been little revenue and a vast amount of expense. However, Spence was an old colleague and friend and Bush knew that CJOH would have to join, even though, as he puts it, they were "up to their hips in debt". Rather reluctantly, the company signed up and became one of the eight founding stations of the CTV network. The tab was $57,800, and they wangled an agreement to subscribe to this over a period of five years.

On balance, as Bushnell says, "the network proved to be an asset, although it had its problems and created problems" for the stations that they could ill afford in their early years. Caldwell, in his eagerness to get into television, had not really fully considered the question of whether a network without the financial backing of a single station was a viable enterprise—the only comparison he could make was with the American networks, all of which owned more than one station. With the CTV teetering on the edge of bankruptcy, Spence realized his mistake and together with other financial interests sought to rectify the situation by acquiring a station or stations; early in 1966, he made an offer to take over Bushnell Television but his bid was warded off. It was too late. In the end, the CTV network had to be dissolved as a private company; it was restructured as a co-operative owned by the affiliated stations which supported it on the basis of revenue. Thus Bushnell and CJOH, which was one of the better-off stations, ended with about fifteen per cent of the liabilities and assets of the network.

Less than two years after Bushnell Television began operating, it was broadcasting on two channels instead of one—the original Channel 13 in Ottawa and Channel 8 in Cornwall. Before the end of 1962, the Board of Broadcast Governors had approved the purchase of Cornwall's CJSS-TV and its conversion into a satellite of CJOH-TV. This was an early expansion that had really been forced on Bushnell. The fact was that the seaway city was not large enough to afford the luxury of its own television station, and CJSS had lost half a million dollars in three years—the only way to save it was to turn it into a satellite. However, for a station to operate as a satellite of another station, it had to be owned outright, according to the BBG rules, by the master station. It was a complicated deal since the corporate shareholders of Bushnell Television, but not the company itself, owned half of Cornwall Broadcasting Limited, the other half being in the hands of the

Canadian Marconi Company which had the pioneer radio station, CFCF, and had been awarded the second English-language television station in Montreal. A plan was drawn up whereby Bushnell Televsion acquired all the shares of Cornwall Broadcasting. The purchase included not only CJSS-TV but CJSS-AM and CJSS-FM, but the latter were split off and sold to a local family. Once again, payments were spread over a number of years.

The acquisition of Channel 8 meant that CJOH programs would be seen not only in Cornwall and along much of the St. Lawrence Seaway, including the American side, but in the western suburbs of Montreal. This would mean a substantial increase in audience and revenue; a satisfied Bushnell informed his shareholders that the advertising rate cards could be increased by thirty per cent. He believed that it was "one of the wisest moves we could have made although the purchase of this modern plant meant a further delay in the repayment of capital", or the declaration of a dividend.

It might have been a thrill for the shareholders to read the claim that Bushnell TV now had a potential audience of three million, but they were beginning to grumble about receiving no return on their investment. As they told Bush, they had thought that a private television station was a licence to print money—hadn't Roy Thomson said that?

Bush cursed Lord Thomson under his breath; he knew that Roy regretted that remark which had now come to haunt him. With the knowledge he had, Bush could refine Thomson's sally to the following terms: "Dollar for dollar, give me a licence to operate a radio station located in a metropolitan market and I'll guarantee any investor a much larger financial return a lot faster than on his investment in a TV station." Actually, CJOH was showing an operating profit within a few months of beginning broadcasting; it was the extraordinary capital expenses involved in becoming an affiliate of CTV, and especially the acquisition of Channel 8 in Cornwall, which delayed any payoff for the shareholders.

Altogether, Bushnell was enjoying his new career; he was much closer to the people running a television station like CJOH than when he had been with the CBC, and he enjoyed "a relationship with my colleagues and the community the like of which was previously unknown to me". It was deeply satisfying for his private enterpriser's spirit that he should have his own company, that CJOH should be producing more programs than CBOT, the CBC's English-language station, and have a greater audience. The physical conditions of his work were not so different: his office in Television House was smaller than his CBC office, but that was as it should be; there was the picture of his father's prize-winning horse on the wall and Miss Appleby had the office next door, within easy shouting distance. Much of his contentment in those days was, as he himself says, due to the untiring efforts of Stu Griffiths. At the end of November 1962, after they had acquired Channel 8, he rewarded Stu by having him made vice-president and general manager; E. L. Bushnell became president and chairman of the board; G. E. Beament, QC, continued as secretary, and Miss G. Appleby as assistant secretary.

Pleasing the public (and that was what a private television station had to do if it expected to stay in business) was no easy task, and Bush often wondered what the public really expected and wanted. "I suggest that no one knows—not even Mr. Fowler [Robert Fowler of the Fowler reports on broadcasting]. The best one can do is to try to gauge public needs and public tastes and to try to be a step or two ahead of both." That required a degree of omniscience no one could attain, at least not all the time; Bush himself had abuse and praise heaped on him in about equal proportions, so that he figured his batting average was a consistent 0.5.

Perhaps his greatest shock was to find how much a creature of habit the public was, how greatly change was resented, and how callously indifferent people could be to the most tragic event. On the day that President Kennedy was assassinated, CJOH adjusted its program schedule to conform with what was suitable at a time of international grief and mourning; the situation comedies, the variety shows, the shoot-em-ups were dropped, and the station plugged into the network coverage of the events following the assassination and the funeral. Hundreds of telephone calls were received that night, mostly from irate viewers who complained bitterly about their favourite programs not being on the air. Some of them used the foulest language; they wanted to know what the hell CJOH thought it was doing, and why a blankety-blank Canadian station should pay all this attention to the death of an American president. Bushnell was confounded; he saw the telephone operator, who wasn't able to cope with the calls, break into tears. It was such a shocking situation that he and Stu Griffiths took over the telephones and, Bush says, "I'm afraid requested several callers to take their carcasses to a warmer climate."

One of the station's most popular programs was a simple discothèque show called "Saturday Date", emceed in the beginning by Peter Jennings—teen-agers were invited to come to dance to records in one of CJOH's larger studios. This was in the days before the Beatles, and long hair was not in style; the boys and girls who lined up for an hour or more to take part in the program were neat and tidy and looked respectable enough. However, the Twist was the rage, and while the weird gyrations of the young people fascinated many older viewers, they apparently horrified some others. Bushnell remembers that two principals of Ottawa high schools called "to accuse us of encouraging a not-too-subtle form of immorality"; he got a dressing down from these pedagogues but after some argument, he suggested that "maybe these youngsters were doing nothing worse than having a good time". Bush wasn't sure whether he had convinced the principals but, he says, the same kind of young people came back year after year to "Saturday Date" and "we haven't noticed any mass character deterioration".

25 The Pivotal Mid-Sixties

The mid-sixties were really a turning point for Ernie Bushnell and his company. From the time he named Stu Griffiths executive vice-president and general manager, Bush began to relinquish more and more of the company's control to his protegé, and he got rid of most of his shares. Even before Caldwell came up with his take-over bid,* Bushnell had disposed of his holdings to Stu, senior members of the staff and to his original sponsors, the Taylor group. The pivotal period for Bushnell Television was spread over a longer time: while the CTV take-over attempt and the move into CATV or cablevision later in 1965 were important, the crucial occurrence, as far as the company was concerned, was Stu Griffiths's recognition of the fact that he was not going to become president of the Canadian Broadcasting Corporation. Then, as Bush said, all his

---

* Although the first bid to take-over Bushnell Television was thwarted easily enough, it was remarkable because it established a price for the common shares—which represents a noteworthy development in the affairs of any private company, as far as its shareholders are concerned. The take-over bid was an attempt by the newspaper and magazine publishers to get hold of the medium that was cutting so deeply into their revenues. Spence Caldwell had put together a consortium that included not only his founding CTV network company but the Maclean-Hunter Company, the biggest periodical publisher in the country, and Castleton Developments Ltd., an offshoot of All Canada Radio and Television Ltd. which was an amalgam of Southam and Sifton broadcasting interests.

On January 27, 1965, an offer was made to purchase "not less than fifty per cent of the preference and common shares of Bushnell TV Co. Ltd." in units of one $100 preference share and 25 common shares for $600 a unit, which worked out at $20 a common share. There had been rumblings of such a bid for some weeks, and Bushnell management had

dynamic energy was released and he was determined to make the company, if not bigger than the CBC, certainly "the biggest little broadcasting company in the world". But that didn't happen till 1967, the centennial year.

On November 19, 1964, Bushnell was sixty-four years old; he had been long enough in the CBC and the public service to know that sixty-five was the time for mandatory retirement, but aside from that instinctive bureaucratic reaction, there was an overwhelming reason for his wanting to sell out. Edna had had a serious operation. Her illness weighed heavily on Bush, who was not well himself, and he felt that he should clean up his estate while he had the time. There were the bank loans of two hundred thousand dollars with which he had bought his original shares; he was not used to such a debt and, in his present frame of mind, he was only too anxious to pay it off. At the time Stu Griffiths had joined forces with him to apply for the Ottawa licence, Bush had promised to divide half his holdings between him and other members of the staff—Stu had no equity in the company when it was founded. This Bush did, and the other half he divided among Nat Taylor, Dave Griesdorf and the others who had helped him to get started in business.

Although the going price at the time was twenty dollars a share—it was only shortly afterward that the CTV offered that amount in its take-over bid—Bushnell sold his holdings at fifteen dollars a share. In a notice dated January 26, 1965, shareholders

---

taken defensive measures; they had circularized the shareholders to find out who wanted to sell and buy at that price and found that, while "20,525 common shares and 821 preference shares were offered for sale, requests to purchase amounted to 32,250 common shares and 1,290 preference." Within ten days of the formal offer, a meeting was held at which the shares were allocated to purchasers on a pro rata basis in a $500,000 transaction that left Caldwell nothing else to do but to withdraw his bid.

Spence, who had attended the meeting, expressed his disappointment to Bush. He might have expected to have done better, considering the moguls of publishing he had lined up in his consortium, but the bid was not big enough. It was just another case of Canadian businessmen not having the guts, not having a broad enough vision, and not being willing to gamble or to take a real risk. No wonder the Americans were taking over! Shortly afterward, Caldwell's CTV network company, as such, collapsed, and was turned into a co-operative owned by the affiliated stations.

were informed that E. L. Bushnell had transferred 6,250 common shares to Stuart W. Griffiths. After that, the company records showed that the founder of Bushnell Television had only two hundred common shares to his name while his wife had eight hundred—he was to acquire more shares during the company's expansionary period, but he didn't borrow money to do so. He paid off his bank loans, and "I haven't owed a cent since." Bush maintains that, contrary to public opinion, he is not a rich man.

"My entire estate," he says, "is worth less than two hundred thousand dollars—that should shatter some illusions."

He had never had any desire to be wealthy. The reason probably was that his father had been a miser, and he remembers that family rows had always been over money; after such a row, his father might sulk for days. The only cash his mother had was what she made selling chickens and eggs. His father bought the clothes for the family and, while he insisted on the best quality, the storekeepers would always put the prices up by ten dollars or so when they saw him coming because they knew that Jim Bushnell would beat them down. When Ernie was fourteen years old and the family had moved into the village of Omemee, his father suddenly got over his miserliness and went to the opposite extreme; where before, he had refused to give his mother any cash, he now turned his bank accounts over to her.

"I've sworn never to let money come between me and happiness," Bush says.

It was as a result of the Taylor group's close association with Famous Players that Bushnell Television got into CATV (community antenna television) or cablevision as early as 1965. Famous Players had been something of a pioneer in the new system of wired TV, at least in Canada, seeing in it an extension of the theatre into the home, and had put up a pilot "pay-television" project in the Toronto suburb of Etobicoke some years before. The idea was that a subscriber could have the latest film on his TV set simply by putting so much money into a slot machine connected to the set. However, pay television was a flop—it may have been tried too soon, while people were still revelling in all the free entertainment on TV—and Famous Players lost a fortune, but the big American-owned theatre corporation was not deterred by this financial fiasco from investing in cable. Nat Taylor and Dave Griesdorf were good friends of J. J. Fitzgibbons and Reuben Bolstad of Famous Players; they were in the same theatre business and, in the end, Famous Players acquired part of the United Century Theatres' holdings in Bushnell Television and thus became one of the Bushnell TV company's larger shareholders.

By 1965, Famous Players was making an all-out bid for cable anywhere and everywhere in Canada. While acquiring a large CATV system in Montreal, Reuben Bolstad heard that the owners of the Inter-Provincial Cable Company of Ottawa were ready to sell out as they were looking for a quick capital gain. He suggested that Bushnell should join Famous Players in buying this company. Although Inter-Provincial had a relatively small cable system, it was the only one of any size in the capital area. Despite its name, its operations were confined to Hull in Quebec, but this was due to the fact that Ottawa City Council had not granted permission to any company to establish a CATV system in the city. Certainly, Bolstad saw Inter-Provincial as a means of wiring Ottawa and he was not alone; Bush recalls bumping into George Nelms, a former mayor, on the street one day and asking him if he would like "to join us as a partner in forming a cablevision company for Ottawa". George paused for a moment and said that it was a funny thing, but Hy Soloway, a prominent local lawyer and businessman, had already asked him to do that; George had given his word that he would.

So there was competition. Ernie found that Soloway had been in touch with Inter-Provincial Cable and obviously intended to use the company as a stepping stone to Ottawa in the same way that they did. Bushnell urged Stu Griffiths and the Famous Players' people to redouble their efforts to conclude an arrangement with Inter-Provincial, which they did. "Now," as Bush said on the phone to Hy Soloway, "You're dealing with us."

Although Bushnell Television and Famous Players had been

partners in acquiring Inter-Provincial, with fifty-one per cent control in Bushnell's hands, and would have much preferred to continue this arrangement in applying for Ottawa Cablevision, it was felt that a number of prominent local businessmen should be associated with them if they expected to succeed. Ottawa City Council had at last adopted a by-law authorizing the establishment of a CATV system, and there was a suspicion that the city would favour a company whose shareholders were taxpayers. CJOH was located in Nepean Township, so Bushnell Television did not pay taxes to Ottawa, but most of its shareholders did, and a letter dated October 14, 1965, asked them to give an approximate "round" figure on the amount of city taxes they paid. The letter said that Laurentian Cablevision, the name of the proposed new company, was applying for the whole city, but pointed out that the capital might be split into two segments, an eastern and a western segment, with Bank Street as the dividing line. This was what happened, and Bushnell Television and associates were awarded the eastern half, while another group calling itself Ottawa Cablevision, which had already a small CATV system at Bells Corners, got the western half.

As the same company, Laurentian, had been used to acquire both the Hull and Ottawa Cablevision interests, and since Bushnell had only a minority (thirty per cent) interest in the company awarded the eastern half of Ottawa, but a controlling (fifty-one per cent) interest in Inter-Provincial Cable, there had to be a corporate split. So a company called Skyline Cablevision was established for the area east of Bank Street, while the name Laurentian was retained for the CATV on the Quebec side. At the time Bushnell acquired these cablevision interests, there were no regulations governing CATV except those imposed by the cities, which were only interested in dividing up the spoils and getting their share of five per cent of the gross revenue.

The 1965 election had been a distinct disappointment for Prime Minister Pearson: instead of the majority that he had been promised by Walter Gordon, and fully expected, the Liberals had emerged with two more seats than they had had in the last minority government, while the Progressive Conservatives under John Diefenbaker, who were supposed to have been wiped out, also ended up with two more seats. A cabinet shakeup was inevitable, especially as Gordon had resigned, blaming himself for the election failure, and the ministerial changes were made on December 18, 1965. As everyone expected, Judy LaMarsh was involved in the shuffle: she was moved from the Department of National Health and Welfare to the Secretary of State's office, which had the responsibility for cultural affairs. Judy said that she picked this portfolio from the meagre choice that had been presented to her because it included the Centennial Commission and broadcasting; she was interested in "the new Broadcasting Act and the whole scope of broadcasting, and not in the CBC and its internal problems".

However, it was the internal problems of the CBC with which she was first concerned. Once again, the producers were in revolt against top management, and this time the issue was the Sunday night TV show, "This Hour Has Seven Days", a public-affairs program which was said to be second only to hockey in popularity. This remarkable rating was achieved by presenting challenging issues spiced with sex and sensation. Confrontation was the subtitle of the show. Interviews with politicians were often edited so that they seemed to be condemning themselves out of their own mouths. The producers showed a fine disregard for journalistic ethics or ethics of any kind, which would have been reprehensible on any program, but was even more so on a government-sponsored program.

One of the co-hosts, Laurier Lapierre, was an emotional young academic, a sentimental socialist and a Quebec nationalist who verged on being a separatist; he had a contemptuous disdain for the opinions of others. In an interview with Réal Caouette, he pressed the Créditiste leader on a point, then, not getting the reply that he wanted, threw up his hands and said, "Oh, my God", implying that Caouette was either a fool or a liar. There was the celebrated occasion when he wept on air; actually, he wiped away a tear after watching an interview with Mrs. Dan Truscott, mother of Steven Truscott. Judy LaMarsh recalled an interview with him in which he became increasingly abusive and ended by shouting that she should resign because she had not been able to get the pension legislation through Parliament. In her book of memoirs, she wrote of Lapierre:

> As the program attracted more viewers, his opinions and slant dominated the program. He seemed unable to understand that he was not, as host, there to promote his own views exclusively.

At long last, the CBC management acted—but Ottawa headquarters was much further removed from the Toronto production centre than the distance between the two cities, and the order it issued to fire Lapierre or to drop his contract and suspend the program was harsh and designed to infuriate the producers. The "Seven Days" crew, whom Al Ouimet, the president, charged with building "a little empire within the CBC, an organization within an organization," decided to do battle. Patrick Watson, the other co-host, and Douglas Leiterman, the producer, were as scornful as Lapierre of authority and also fearful of its interference with their freedom of expression. A command post was set up in the Four Seasons Hotel opposite the CBC studios at 354 Jarvis Street, and the "Seven Days" crew went to work soliciting support by thousands of telegrams and telephone calls (including a number to the minister herself). A "Save the 'Seven Days' Committee" was formed in Toronto. There was a threat of a network-wide producers' strike which Prime Minister Pearson averted by appointing Stu Keate, the publisher of the *Vancouver Sun,* as an informal mediator in the dispute.

However, this move didn't prevent the "Seven Days" issue from coming before a parliamentary committee; it was a case of history repeating itself, for the "Preview Commentary" issue had come before a special committee of the House of Commons, almost seven years before to the day, and some of the actors were the same. Patrick Watson had been among the Toronto producers who walked out in 1959, and now he was a ring leader of this revolt. (The rebel leaders of seven years before, Frank Peers, Bernard Trotter and D. H. Gillis, had all left the CBC, just as the new triumvirate of Watson, Laurier

Lapierre, and Doug Leiterman were to go—which might indicate that management was a lot tougher and more durable than it appeared.) Ernest Bushnell, who had been the central figure of the "preview Commentary" storm, now felt like a "sidewalk superintendent", looking on from outside at the "Seven Days" row, in fascination and horror.

What was a parliamentary committee doing, Bushnell wanted to know, spending hours and days of its time, examining publicly what was an internal problem of the CBC, an honest difference of opinion between management and a few of its employees. "Really, really," he wrote, "how stupid, how inane, how preposterous can we get!" Most of the members of the committee were, as he described them, "politicians, first and last". Some of them had personal axes to grind: others had close ties with labour or artists' unions, and the odd one was an out-and-out free enterpriser. But knowledgable and objective they were not. Bush quotes from a letter to the editor in the *Ottawa Citizen* which said that the general conduct of the 1966 committee was a "sorry reflection on the parliamentary system":

> It was my understanding that this committee was originally established for the purpose of examining the estimates of those public services for which the Secretary of State reports to Parliament and therefore, by necessary implication, is required to inquire into the operation of the various services in so far as they may feel this is necessary. By definition, the function of inquiring requires an unbiased and unjudged investigation. It is obvious that certain members of the committee are completely biased in their views and they have been permitted to dominate the conduct of the inquiry. Perhaps the most unfortunate aspect of this whole matter is the fact that they have been permitted so to dominate in a rude and insulting manner, often being permitted to badger witnesses, ask questions and make remarks in sneering and otherwise offensive manner, many of which would be ruled argumentative or out of order in any court of law, and most of which would bring a sharp rebuke from any judge.

At the committee hearings, there were allegations that the "Seven Days" principals had fallen foul of management because of their involvement in the second Fowler report on broadcasting, which came out in 1956. Those allegations were denied by H. G. "Bud" Walker, now vice-president and general manager of the English-language networks. Roy Faibish had prepared a study for the commission while on leave of absence from "Seven Days", and Patrick Watson, as president of the CBC producers' association, had made a submission, although his name was not in the acknowledgments. The report began with a ringing declaration that became a slogan for any disaffected producer: "The only thing that really matters in broadcasting is program content; all the rest is housekeeping"—the report was highly critical of CBC's top management.

While Ernie Bushnell would have agreed with the commission's declaration about the importance of programming, he was too recently a management man to take this criticism kindly, even though it meant that he was lining up with Al Ouimet. In fact, he accused Robert Fowler of being more responsible than anyone else for the "Seven Days" imbroglio. (Besides Fowler, the other members of the commission had been Marc Lalonde and G. G. E. "Ernie" Steele who was to become Judy LaMarsh's deputy minister.) Bush says that the report "contributed more to the unrest and to the explosion that took place over "Seven Days" than anything else, big or little, large or small"; that it gave a blanket approval to the producers to do and say what they liked.

The real issue in the "Seven Days" uproar, just as it was in the "Preview Commentary" scandal, was the question of freedom of expression. Ouimet recognized this when he said, in testimony before the committee, "The present public-affairs malaise . . . arises from a conflict of opinion over how much freedom public-affairs producers should have to determine the over-all character and future course of development of CBC programming". The "Seven Days" crew wanted unlimited freedom, even to the extent of showing a girl in bed with two young men; that sequence was part of a documentary on youth and was the sort of thing that the CBC president characterized as "sleazy". In Bushnell's opinion, such freedom was nothing but licence, and he quoted from a Paris newspaper article that "total freedom constitutes aggression the minute TV or radio is used to force a single point of view upon all listeners or viewers." The article dealt with the case of Max-Pol Fouchet, whose political commentaries on the RTF had been cancelled; it went on to say—and this was quoted by Bush too—"When the unseen TV public is addressed, there is at least one frontier that should not be violated, that of other people's opinions. The fact that no rebuttal is possible calls for a minimum of tolerance and in this case [the case of Fouchet] such tolerance is identified with intellectual fair play."

However, Bush's main concern was the parliamentary committee itself, and he wrote that "from the vantage point of a sidewalk superintendent", he was convinced that the committee on broadcasting should not deal with such a dispute as the "Seven Days" affair but should bend every effort to provide a set of principles or guidelines so that the CBC management would have a better idea of what it was supposed to do.

For Judy LaMarsh, the "Seven Days" hearing was the last shock of a series of tremors that brought the building crashing down; she lost what little confidence she had had in Ouimet and the CBC management. At a Young Liberal Conference session in Ottawa, she blurted out that the sort of estrangement of programmers from management which the "Seven Days" issue represented was, in her view, "only the tip of an iceberg"; she considered what she had said innocuous enough and was surprised at the sensation it caused. So was Prime Minister Pearson, who decided that he would have to take a hand in settling this matter—he was able to stifle the revolt with the delaying action of the Keate examination and informal mediation, a masterly stroke and worthy of a great diplomat. Meanwhile his loquacious Secretary of State had, as she herself admitted, "put the cat among the canaries" by sounding off about the "rotten management" in the CBC during a television interview. Bushnell was furious. Once again, he found himself in the ironic position of defending Ouimet; he felt that the charge of "rotten management" was a "scurvy trick" that no minister

251

of the Crown should have ever made. He never had a very high regard for Judy LaMarsh, and he grew to like her even less when she came to look on Stu Griffiths as her answer to "rotten management" and talked to him about the possibility of becoming president of the CBC.

In her memoirs, Miss LaMarsh makes no mention of Griffiths by name, but does volunteer this revealing confession: "Had I had the confidence of the prime minister, Alphonse Ouimet would by then [the winter of 1966] have been long gone from office, and one already familiar with the CBC, who could have sliced away the deadwood without having to go through a two-year indoctrination course, would have been ensconced in the president's office." From this, it was obvious that she was referring to Stu and comparing his qualifications with those of George Davidson, the mandarin civil servant whom Mr. Pearson chose for the CBC's top job. However, Judy did mention Patrick Watson by name; she said that he was "an enormously talented young man", and that she "had in mind that Watson, despite his youth, might soon become a senior officer of the corporation" . . . the precise job she had in mind was vice-president and general manager of the CBC's English-language network, to which "Bud" Walker had been promoted.

This was fully understood by Stu Griffiths, who had the same high regard for Watson as the minister—in fact, there was a rare meeting of minds between the pudgy general manager of Bushnell Television and Miss LaMarsh—and Patrick attended some of the discussions that Stu had with Judy, although not all of them. There was the odd dinner party, including one in the minister's apartment, when Judy prepared the meal and showed herself to be an accomplished cook.

At Miss LaMarsh's suggestion, Griffiths sought the good will and co-operation of Radio Canada in Montreal; he was particularly anxious to talk to Raymond David, head of the French-language networks and noted for his independence. Roy Faibish, who had joined Bushnell Television as executive assistant to the general manager in June of 1965, arranged for Griffiths to meet André Paquette, a former CBC correspondent in Paris and a confidant of David's, at a dinner party in the Café

Martin in Montreal. Watson also attended the dinner, at which Paquette agreed to act as a go-between. Some weeks later, an appointment was arranged and Stu, accompanied by Roy, had a private meeting with David in his Radio Canada office which lasted for several hours. Griffiths spoke at length about his philosophy of broadcasting and assured David that if he (Griffiths) were appointed president that he would want David to continue as vice-president and general manager of the French-language networks, only he would like him to come to Ottawa. So far, David had refused to leave Montreal, and there was some discussion about the conditions under which he would move to the capital. The interview had been cordial, and Stu and Roy emerged believing that they had his support, although they hadn't moved him from his opposition to coming to Ottawa. Stu, with Judy's encouragement, had let David know that he was in line for the statutory number two job of vice-president of the CBC.

There was another disappointment when Griffiths found that Marc Lalonde would not consider the position of vice-president. Patrick Watson was at the dinner party which Griffiths gave Lalonde when the subject was discussed at length. Of course, the appointment would have to be made by Prime Minister Pearson but Judy had said that he was on Mr. Pearson's short list—only Lalonde was not interested. It is possible, as Patrick surmised, that Lalonde knew then that he was to become the prime minister's advisor and the government's éminence grise.

Altogether, the minister's discussions with Stu Griffiths went on for three to four months in the winter of 1966-1967. Ernie Bushnell took a dim view of them; he had every selfish reason to resent this attempt to lure his chief executive away. However, he said to Stu that if it was what he wanted, "Well then, God bless you, and go to it." He did add that he thought Griffiths would be stupid to accept such an appointment, that the CBC was in such a mess that there was no way of coping with it. Bush also knew Griffiths's weakness, his reluctance to delegate authority, which was matched in a way by his enormous energy. Bush said to him on one occasion:

"Look, if you do get this job and you find a chair out of

place on the fifth floor [the executive floor at CBC head-quarters], call someone to move it, won't you—don't move it yourself."

In the spring of 1967, the talks with the minister came to an end; there was really no more to discuss. Judy LaMarsh had made her recommendation. "The next voice you'll hear," she said, "will be that of the prime minister, but then you may not."

26 The Rise and Fall of the Bushnell Empire

It was 1967, the centennial year and, as Secretary of State and Keeper of the Great Seal, Judy LaMarsh was the hostess and official greeter of the nation. With the opening of Expo in Montreal and the arrival of the first state guests, she was here and there and everywhere in Canada, giving a full-blown welcome to all and sundry, from foreign presidents to the sweat-stained, dirty voyageurs who had paddled across the continent in one of the pageants that her people had organized. Judy in a picture hat, Judy at the controls of the Centennial Train, Judy doing a curtsey to Queen Elizabeth II and Prince Philip. What time she had left from this hectic social round was devoted to the new Broadcasting Act and its propulsion through the various legislative stages, the cabinet committee, the cabinet and Parliament. All that remained for Stu Griffiths during that spring and summer was to wait for a telephone call that he never really expected. Meanwhile Bushnell Television marked the centennial year by going public and preparing itself for the expansion that both Bushnell and Griffiths expected as a result of the new act, particularly the clause that limited foreign ownership to twenty per cent. They knew that in the new cablevision field, foreign ownership was closer to one hundred per cent, largely because Canadian capital was afraid of anything new. Little did they know that the expansion would turn into an explosion.

A notice to shareholders, dated September 15, 1967, announced a re-organization of the company: the memorandum pointed out that the present capital structure had a "limiting effect" with no unissued shares; furthermore, the number of shareholders in a private company, such as Bushnell, could not exceed fifty. The plan, on which the board of directors had laboured long and not fully agreed, was to create a new class of non-voting shares which could be traded freely on the market without contravening any of the rules and regulations and restrictions governing a broadcasting licence. The last sale of common shares the company had negotiated had been at the rate of twenty-five dollars a share, and the notice said: "the reorganization is based on an assumed market value of twenty-five dollars per share and for the preference share of one hundred dollars per share, this being the par value of the existing preference shares." Thus, the common shares were to be subdivided five to one, with four of the new shares being the non-voting "Class A" shares, while the fifth remained the controlling common shares, and the preference shares, of which there were only 4,700 left as more than half had been redeemed, were to be subdivided twenty to one, all into Class A shares.

Supplementary letters patent had been applied for which would increase the capitalization of Bushnell Television Ltd. to 1,600,000 non-voting Class A shares, and 250,000 voting common shares. This would mean that there would be more than 500,000 extra Class A shares in the treasury and these, as the notice to the shareholders said, "will be available to finance future programs and meet future needs"; any increase in the capitalization of the company required an increase in the number of common shares but an assurance was given shareholders that if the 10,000 extra common shares were ever sold, they would be offered to the existing shareholders on a pro rata basis so that they could maintain their equities.

During 1967, CJOH switched to colour, and became the first station in Canada to have nothing but colour cameras; it sold its black-and-white cameras to the ETV division of the Ottawa Board of Education. Meanwhile Judy LaMarsh, when she could take time off from glad-handing everyone, found that the new broadcasting legislation was making miserably slow progress; she had made up her mind that the centennial year was to be her last political fling but she was determined to get the Broadcasting Act passed before she would resign—it was as if this were to be her legislative memorial. Ernie Bushnell and Stu Griffiths acquired a copy of the bill as soon as it was printed, and Bush, with his knowledge of the parliamentary process, foresaw that there would be few if any changes in the measure during its slow movement through the parliamentary mill. He and Stu paid particular attention to the proposed regulations that there could only be twenty per cent foreign ownership of any broadcasting enterprise, including a CATV or cablevision undertaking, and they decided to put their own house in order before they tried to acquire other foreign properties. They found that it was a long and thankless task to persuade their British and American corporate shareholders to divest themselves of a proportion of their shares, or at least to make arrangements that would meet the law. On November 15, the shareholders were circularized to find out how many, if any, would sell their common or Class A holdings for seven dollars a share, an indication that this was now the assumed price. At the end of 1967, Bushnell Television paid its first quarterly dividend of five cents a share.

On February 7, 1968, the new broadcasting legislation was given third reading in the House of Commons and passed; a month later, royal assent made it law. Bushnell Television had been reorganized and was ready to take full advantage of the new act: the company was now a public company, with Class A shares being traded over the counter and being quoted on the "unlisted" market, and there were more than 500,000 shares in the treasury should more capital be required. However, the first expansionary move was really unfinished business, the attempt to acquire control of Skyline Cablevision. The Thomson-Davies deal, which seemed such a daring venture as it would have turned the Bushnell company into an instant "mini-network" covering the whole of Eastern Ontario, had its origin in a begging letter which Ernie Bushnell sent Lord Thomson. At the time, Bush was a member of a fund-raising committee for the Ottawa Children's Hospital and he wrote a "Dear Roy" letter, asking for a donation of fifty thousand dollars. Very firmly, but very politely, Lord Thomson turned down the request, but wrote in a PS:

> I hear your company is going public. We have been thinking along the same lines. Maybe you would consider a merger. Let me hear from you.

To which Bushnell replied, in his rather exaggerated style of bonhomie, that he had no intention of merging with such an infamous and parsimonious character as Lord Thomson. However, he added, "if you're ever again in this country and you wish to dispose of those down-at-heel radio and TV stations of yours, give me a call." Three weeks later, a Thomson executive in Toronto, Sid Chapman, phoned to say that Lord Thomson would be in Canada in a couple of weeks time and would like to see him.

"How interesting," Bush said. "Well, tell him I'll be delighted to see him in Ottawa but warn him that I'll be expecting him to bring along that fifty thousand bucks."

"I'm sorry," Chapman said, "but Lord Thomson will only be in Toronto for a couple of days. Do you think it would be possible for you or one of your colleagues to meet with him while he is here?"

If Thomson were serious about getting out of the broadcasting business, and Sid Chapman said that it was his impression that he was, then Bushnell would be prepared to go to Toronto. An appointment was made, and Bush took with him Stu Griffiths and Ray Brining, the vice-president in charge of finance. As soon as the introductions were over, they got down to business; according to Bush's account,

> Roy, as usual, started off by telling us how valuable his broadcasting properties were but went on to say that he was fed up with so much regulatory interference. To which I replied that I didn't blame him for that but he had better get out before his licences were either cancelled or not renewed. He avowed that he could use the money more advantageously, said that he wanted twenty times earnings, and agreed to show us the annual statements of each and all of his stations

(including those belonging to the Davies family of Kingston which he ran). Then two hours of haggling began. He stuck to his guns—twenty times earnings or no deal, but ended up by saying: "Ernie, take it or leave it—that's the price, but for old times' sake, and the fact that you started me in broadcasting, I'd rather sell to you than anyone else."

The preliminary discussions ended with handshakes all around. Bush left Stu and others to carry on the negotiations, which were complex and time consuming. The Thomson-Davies holdings included three television stations, CKWS-TV Kingston, CHEX-TV Peterborough and CFCH-TV North Bay; six AM radio stations, CKGB Timmins, CKWS Kingston, CHEX Peterborough, CKJL Kirkland Lake, CJTT New Liskeard and CFCH North Bay, which was the original Thomson station that Bushnell had helped to set up, as well as three FM stations, CKGB-FM, CKWS-FM and CHEX-FM. Altogether there were seven different companies with different groups of shareholders, mostly members of the Thomson clan, as Bushnell puts it, and separate documents had to be signed by each and every one of the shareholders; as a result, the legal and accounting work was tremendous and costly, and the deal was not closed till the early autumn of 1968.

One effect of these negotiations was to revive Stu Griffiths's flagging spirits. Bushnell understood his deep disappointment at not being named president of the CBC—aside from the prestige, it would have been a vindication of the shabby treatment he had received while in the International Service and opening the first television station. Stu talked about quitting, of taking off in the yacht that he had built in a shed behind the CJOH building (which became known as the "marine studio") and sailing around the world, or returning to Britain and Granada; he wasn't interested in running a single station. Then the Thomson-Davies deal came along, and he saw possibilities of expansion, especially with cablevision. Griffiths noted that the one company Thomson did not want to sell was Cablevue (Belleville) Ltd., which was a CATV undertaking serving Belleville and Trenton; Griffiths insisted that it was part of the package and in the end Thomson reluctantly agreed.

At the same time, Bushnell Television was engaged in a determined effort to acquire control of Skyline Cablevision, which served the eastern half of Ottawa. Between them, Bushnell and Famous Players had just under forty-nine per cent; slightly more than fifty-one per cent was in the hands of what became known as the Ottawa Group, which included such prominent citizens as Hy Soloway, former mayor George Nelms, Kathleen Ryan, widow of Frank Ryan of CFRA fame, Robert Campeau, the contractor, and David Loeb who was later to become owner of the Ottawa Rough Riders football club. In order to ensure that neither of the corporate shareholders, Bushnell and Famous Players, would get control of Skyline by buying shares on an individual and separate basis, the "group" had taken a leaf out of Ted Beament's book and put all their shares under a "voting trust agreement". It was a case of being hoist on their own petard as far as Bushnell was concerned.

Some of the group wanted to sell and realize a substantial capital gain; others would have gone along, but two or three held out. On three separate occasions, Bush recalled, agreement was reached, hands shaken, and the negotiations seemed to have come to a mutually satisfactory conclusion. Not so. One or another of the members of the voting trust agreement refused to sign with the result that a fresh start had to be made. Bushnell described it as a "most disappointing and frustrating experience if there ever was one". He said that if there hadn't been such a delay caused by so many "yes-and-no decisions", it was "entirely conceivable that our application for control of Skyline would have been heard and approved by the CRTC at least a year prior" to the hearings in June of 1970.

During the spring of 1968, there was fairly active trading in Bushnell shares on the unlisted market, with the Class A selling at $11.50 to $12.50. Not much change in price occurred till the fall, when news of the company's activities became known. In November, several thousand Class A shares were offered the staff at $13; by the beginning of December, they were being quoted at $17.50 bid, $18 asked. In a letter to the shareholders prior to the annual meeting in November 1968, Bushnell wrote:

Your company is expansionary minded and we believe that cablevision is essential in a broadcasting company's future. Our investment in cablevision systems has yet to return a profit but both Laurentian and Skyline Cablevision have each made substantial gains in the past eleven months of our fiscal year. We have made applications to participate in other cablevision systems and would hope to receive the decision of the CRTC in the early part of 1969 . . .

A rather pious hope, as Bush commented, in the light of what actually happened. By Christmas, the Class A shares were over twenty-five dollars; in a little more than a month, they had almost doubled in value.

A special shareholders' meeting in April 1969 was told that Bushnell was spreading its cablevision net wide in eastern Ontario and beyond; beside Skyline and Laurentian and a small system at Rockland, just outside Ottawa, mention was made of CATV undertakings in Arnprior, Carleton Place, Renfrew, Smith Falls, Perth, Pembroke, Sudbury, Kingston, Belleville and Trenton, and the company was even reaching out to British Columbia for cablevision in North and West Vancouver, Nanaimo, Nelson, Trail and other places. Between twenty and thirty million dollars would be needed and, in the event of an underwriting, the present shareholders were assured that they would be given preferential treatment. Negotiations had begun to acquire the broadcasting interests of the Canadian Marconi Company which included not only CFCF-TV, the second largest private television station in the country, but also the pioneer radio station, CFCF, as well as FM and short-wave outlets. At the April meeting, Bushnell announced he was stepping down; Griffiths had been running the business for some time now and he was named president and general manager, while Bush continued as chairman of the board. Since the company was to become an integrated broadcasting enterprise with the expected acquisition of radio and cablevision, its name was changed to Bushnell Communications Ltd. The shares reached a peak of $30.00 bid to $30.25 asked on the unlisted market in May.

Stu Griffiths had become obsessed with the prospects of

cablevision. He saw in it the future of broadcasting. "Technical capability presently exists," he said, "to provide twenty video channels on cablevision systems, which could make available to Canadian viewers a much wider choice of programming." But he talked about forty or more channels, when the viewer, by pressing buttons, could have whatever he wanted in the way of entertainment or information or education; if he wanted the local news, he would push one button, another for national and international news, and there would probably be several buttons for sports events, and many for plays or films; the housewife could get the latest information on supermarket specials and a complete run-down on classified advertisements simply by pushing buttons; the student could get his courses in the same way. This was the concept of the "wired city" and Griffiths was one of its earliest advocates. His enthusiasm for cablevision affected Bushnell, who realized too that CATV was essential as far as a broadcasting company was concerned since the choice that it offered, even the present meagre choice of half a dozen more channels including two American stations, meant that the CJOH audience was being fragmented. Bush also saw it providing another source of income, and Griffiths spoke of people paying two hundred dollars a year for the full "push-button electronic media service" which was four times the existing cablevision tariff.

The fact that Bushnell Television was in Ottawa meant that it was physically closer to the Canadian Radio Television Commission than other broadcasters, but there was a spiritual closeness too. Ernie Bushnell and Stu Griffiths, Pierre Juneau and Harry Boyle all had the same outlook—they believed that broadcasting was a public service. They talked the same language and they came from the same background. Harry Boyle had come to the CRTC as vice-chairman from the CBC where he had worked for Bush just as Stu had done. It was no wonder that press and public believed that Bushnell Television had the "inside track" as far as the commission was concerned.

At first, the commissioners were enthralled by Griffiths's visionary ideas and plans which he discussed with them on several occasions—as Bush says, Stu was a particularly good salesman when he was selling his own schemes. The CRTC had always had a high regard for CJOH and considered its programming to be a model for a private television station. However, after a while both Juneau and Boyle began to wonder whether Griffiths wasn't going "hog wild", as one of them put it, over expansion; they were being told by their financial advisors that he was paying too much for some of the cablevision systems. "He was so obsessed with the idea of cablevision, of the wired city," a CRTC official said, "that when you asked him how he was going to pay for all the properties he was acquiring, he would brush aside the question and say that money was the least of his worries." Griffiths's answer to such criticism was that he was paying the going rate but, unfortunately, the market was reaching its peak when he was buying and was to fall steeply before the CRTC hearing on the Bushnell applications.

Everyone concerned agreed, that the hiring of Patrick Watson and Laurier Lapierre turned out to be a mistake. Watson had been taken on as Bushnell Communications' vice-president in charge of programming in the summer of 1969, and Lapierre as a program director. The return of the "Seven Days" co-hosts to TV—and they co-hosted the CJOH news program—was hailed by the newspapers as a broadcasting "coup", but they were never meant to be newscasters and it turned out to be a disastrous stint which lasted less than six months. Watson and Lapierre resigned on January 31, 1970, the day that the second phase of Television House, the more-than-doubling of the CJOH facilities to take care of the expected expansion, was officially opened by Pierre Juneau. The press theory was that Watson and Lapierre had been taken on to impress the CRTC, but the commissioners were not impressed; in fact, they complained that the "Seven Days" stars had not improved the station's service, but made it worse.

In 1969, the negotiations to acquire communications properties became more and more hectic; Bush recalls that the air was charged with "wheeling and dealing". At each meeting, the board of directors considered new recommendations for further acquisitions from the indefatigable president and "the parcel began to get bigger and bigger". On almost all occasions, the board supported Stu Griffiths, and most of the directors shared in his belief that a broadcasting company had to be big and diversified, particularly in cablevision, in order to produce the programs and provide the public service that was required by the government's regulatory agency. However, there was one director who became uneasy at this rush to acquire properties at almost any price, and it was over the negotiations with the Canadian Marconi Company that Ted Beament broke with the board and resigned.

Some years before, there had been a report that Granada, one of Bushnell's largest shareholders, was considering buying out the Canadian Marconi Company, not just its broadcasting interest but the manufacturing side as well. After Bushnell acquired the Marconi interest in CJSS-TV in Cornwall, the thought did occur "that some day we might consider purchasing CFCF-TV in Montreal". However, it was not till the new Broadcasting Act was passed that an approach was made. At the time, there were accusations that Bushnell Communications was bent on setting up a third TV network which would consist of CFCF in Montreal, CJOH in Ottawa and CHCH, the independent Hamilton station which covered the Toronto area, but Bush denies this. He says the reason for buying the Marconi broadcasting interests was a very simple one: "By amalgamating the two systems, the Bushnell company would then have a wider and greater opportunity to produce bigger and better Canadian-made programs." They had the studios and technical facilities to do so, but it was in the area of news that the greatest benefit should occur. "It seemed to us," Bush went on, "that living and operating in the nation's capital, someone had a responsibility of more frequently and more accurately reflecting what was going on in our sister province." The news departments of the two stations would be integrated and connected by telex and telephone, and the original intention was for Patrick Watson and Laurier Lapierre to co-host a two-city newscast. Another reason for acquiring the Marconi interests was that Bushnell wanted to add CFCF, the pioneer Montreal station, to a small radio network that it was putting together which included not only the Thomson-Davies stations but CKPM in Ottawa.

The first offer that Bushnell made for the Canadian Marconi Company's broadcasting interests was for eighteen million dollars, and there was a report to this effect in the *Ottawa Citizen* of April 18, 1969. However, according to Bush, this bid was not taken seriously. "They laughed at Stu," he says. The English Electric, the owners of the Canadian Marconi Company, had a reputation for being hard bargainers. Griffiths then consulted Professor O. J. Firestone, an economist who was a member of the Bushnell board; he saw him in his University of Ottawa office and there worked out a valuation of $22,700,000 for the Marconi interests, based on Dr. Firestone's calculations. The board of directors had relied on the professor's advice on the purchase price of the properties they were acquiring—Dr. Firestone was regarded as the leading financial analyst in the broadcasting field, and had written a book entitled *Broadcast Advertising in Canada: Past and Future Growth* which had been published by the University of Ottawa in 1966; he was an expansionist and encouraged Griffiths in the acquisition of more and more properties. The board had approved the original bid of eighteen million dollars but Stu Griffiths went ahead and made a formal offer of $22,700,000 without bringing it before the board; there was a question of timing, and Stu took it for granted that the directors who had shown such faith in Dr. Firestone would go along with this offer. However, when the board met, Ted Beament said that the offer had been made without the knowledge of the board, that he would have no part of it, and he resigned.

It was a bad blow for Bush: he had lost his old friend and legal advisor, one of the founders of the company and the architect of the voting trust agreement. Yet, while he was dismayed at this turn of events, he realized that Ted might have been looking for a way out as he had sold most of his shares and was more or less retired and spending most of his time in England; then, Bushnell was a broadcaster while Beament was a businessman and corporation lawyer. Ernie saw eye to eye with Stu that this was "a golden opportunity materially and significantly to assist in the gradual development and creation of worthwhile Canadian-made programs". Both were aware of the financial risks involved but were prepared to accept such risks if there were a chance of "making a substantial contribution toward repatriating Canadian broadcasting". The price of $22,700,000 might have been justified at the time, although it was said that no one else put in a bid as high as the original offer of eighteen million, which showed what hard bargainers the English Electric people were, but it was out of line when the CRTC finally held its hearing on the Bushnell applications.

Bush complained of the commission's dilatory ways, and says that "the CRTC has, in my opinion, never earned high marks for promptness in its decision making". The commission was supposed to have decided on the company's first applications "some time in the early part of 1969", according to the letter to shareholders prior to the annual meeting of November 1968. At that time, the Class A shares were around twenty-five dollars and reached a peak of thirty dollars on the unlisted market in May. However, the hearing was put off till the fall of 1969, then to February of 1970, and was finally held in June of 1970, by which time the stock had fallen to twelve dollars a share and was continuing to drop. Such procrastination on the part of a government agency would have been scandalous, but the commission maintained that Bushnell Communications were at fault in that they did not have their applications ready; according to Faibish, Griffiths had agreed with the CRTC not to put the Bushnell applications in piecemeal but as a "package" so that it could not be said that he was trying to fool the commissioners as to his real intentions with regard to the expansion of the company.

Whoever was responsible, the delays cost Bushnell dearly on the financial market. He says that "the one thing that may well have been given too little consideration was the threatened, and, in some instances, all too apparent decline in the over-all economy of the North American continent". However, by the time the storm broke, several agreements had been negotiated and signed; while "aware of the distress signals, there was nothing left to do but plough straight ahead". Their only hope was that the members of the CRTC would understand what was happening and how far they were committed.

It was to meet these commitments that, in the spring of 1969, 400,000 Class A shares from the treasury were sold to institutional purchasers at $21 a share which, at the time was three or four dollars below the latest quotation on the "unlisted" market but was regarded as a good price considering the size of the transaction. With more than eight million dollars accruing from that sale, the company was able to pay for the construction of the second phase of Television House and the equipping of the biggest studios in Canada, as well as the downpayment of one million dollars on the Thomson-Davies purchases and the two million-dollar deposit on the Marconi deal, and still have some money in reserve. In preparation for expansion, the voting trust agreement was rescinded as there was no need for this guarantee of local control with the company on a broader national basis; the difference between the common and Class A shares was eliminated, making them all common shares; and supplementary letters patent were sought to increase the number of common shares to three million and to create two million twenty-five-dollar preference shares.

On June 16, 1970, the CRTC hearing on the Bushnell applications opened before an assemblage of some three hundred people, mostly broadcasters, in the International Ballroom of Ottawa's Skyline Hotel. In his statement, Stu Griffiths referred jocularly to the way that he had been "buying up the country, as the press so picturesquely put it"—and the full extent of the Bushnell "empire" was disclosed for the first time: it stretched from Montreal, where there were the "anchor" stations of the Canadian Marconi Company in both television and radio, through the original motherlode of CJOH in Ottawa and CJSS in Cornwall, and the array of Thomson-Davies transmitters, along strands of cablevision to Toronto where the VTR studios had been already acquired and Metro Cable TV Limited provided distribution in the richest market in Canada; then, with a gap to avoid the prairies, to beautiful British Columbia where the CATV system known as Community Video led through Nelson and Trail to the suburbs of

North and West Vancouver. Altogether, the empire included six television stations, eight AM radio stations and four FM stations, covering much of eastern Canada, and a score of CATV systems. The expansion that Bushnell was seeking would cost a total of eighty million dollars, which was divided roughly between cablevision and the television and radio outlets, and would be paid for with bank loans and a fifty million dollar underwriting.

Griffiths argued the need for large integrated broadcasting units. He quoted with approval the chairman of the CRTC, Pierre Juneau, as saying: "It seems to me that we need some groups in Canada that will be large enough to be able to compete in the entertainment, the cultural, the informational and the educational fields with the enormous entities that are being created in other parts of the world and particularly by our neighbours". He warned that the economic survival of small stations was already in jeopardy because of increased programming costs and the demand for colour and added that there were pressures on larger stations to merge. The nub of Griffiths's argument was contained in these two paragraphs:

> Briefly stated, our position is that, given the fact of cablevision in Canada and the greatly increased choice that is being asked for by a large segment of the Canadian viewing public, and the statement of broadcasting policy for Canada set forth in the Broadcasting Act, the private elements of the Canadian broadcasting system as it now exists will have to muster much larger amounts of money and human resources to provide programs of variety and quality to earn the willing acceptance of Canadian viewers. Bushnell's plan is to provide some of what is required.
>
> We believe that if there are to be large broadcasting units in Canada, such units should take the form of public companies whose securities are widely held by Canadians, thus offering the maximum participation to Canadians in their broadcasting systems and enabling companies to have ready access to the Canadian money markets for the funds they require to develop their activities. We further believe that such units

should be integrated, combining where possible television, radio and cable.

At the end of this statement, Griffiths said that he preferred the term "agglomerate" rather than "conglomerate" to describe the integrated broadcasting enterprise that he sought. He quoted the vice-president of the Canadian Pacific Railway, who defined a conglomerate as a composite rock of rounded and water-worn fragments of other rocks united by a cement often called "pudding stone"; an agglomerate was a mass of volcanic or eruptive fragments united by heat. He went on:

> Mr. Chairman, I have been involved in broadcasting for some thirty years. I can testify that one of the conditions that has been a continuous factor is heat and volcanic action. I cannot imagine that it will change very much in the future. Our request is therefore that from this crucible, you send forth an "agglomerate", something new for Canadian broadcasting and, we believe, helpful in its development.

Ernie Bushnell, who with other directors attended the CRTC hearing, had nothing but praise for Stu Griffiths's presentation. Afterwards he wrote that, in all his experience of royal commissions and parliamentary committees, he had "never heard a more logical, practical, feasible and impressive presentation of facts and forecasts than that put forward by Stuart Griffiths". He went on to say that Griffiths's statement was a combination of the present situation with "a well-considered, well-thought-out realistic future course of action which, in my opinion, had it been accepted by the commission, would have largely resolved many of its problems". He contended that Griffiths had dealt with basic principles through which it might be possible for what Bush called "the competing media of television and cable" to live together and provide the kind of service to which the Canadian viewing public was entitled.

Sitting there in a front row seat, Bushnell kept a close watch on the faces of the commissioners as they listened to Griffiths's presentation. It seemed to him that they were impressed and that, if he were any gauge of reactions, they had come "to understand and for the most part to accept the validity of the proposals put forth by Mr. Griffiths". Obviously his assessment was wrong, because "the verdict of the jury announced some weeks later was not a total negation of the 'package' idea, but instead contained only the arms and legs of the corporate body and forgot about any of those organs upon which it must depend if it is to survive in a highly competitive and somewhat unforeseeable technological era that may well include the use of satellites, laser beams, multi-channels and God-knows-what-else still on the drawing board". Later, he wrote:

> What was the main element apparently either not favourably regarded or thought to be unimportant by the commission? Simple 'Cash Flow'. Cablevision systems have the advantage of providing their owners with money on a regular monthly basis. This, in itself, would have provided the company with a highly desirable financial foundation upon which it could meet all its obligations not only to pay for its acquisitions but to devise, create, and produce Canadian-made programs which in the final analysis was really the sole purpose and object of getting involved in such a large and costly undertaking.
>
> The second reason clearly indicated in the commission's refusal to approve all of the 'package' applications was its apparent fear of bigness. There is no denying that the acceptance of such a principle might have created some sort of precedent. But if the regulators, with the authority of a Broadcasting Act giving them such wide and sweeping powers, including the cancellation of licences, feel competent to invoke such powers . . . then why in heaven's name should they be so afraid of bigness? It seems to me that a dozen or more reasonably large, financially responsible Canadian-owned communications systems operating potentially on a non-renewable licence basis would be much easier to cope with and to regulate than a proliferation of anywhere from one thousand to fifteen hundred little systems spread all over the country.

On July 6, 1970, the CRTC handed down its decisions: the

commission approved the acquisition of the Canadian Marconi broadcasting interests and the Thomson-Davies stations, but it rejected all seventeen applications for CATV systems, including even Bushnell's attempts to gain control of Skyline Cablevision of Ottawa in which it already had thirty per cent interest. As Bush said, the CRTC decisions left the company in a "much less advantageous position than envisaged". To raise thirty million dollars to pay for the television and radio outlets in the uncertain financial climate of the time was a "formidable task". The company did not attempt to do so until "a thorough review of projected earnings over a five-year period [was made and] indicated clearly that it was still financially feasible to proceed" with the purchases.

All of which took time; then came the real hard slogging of trying to raise the money while the economy was sinking—it reached the lowest point in November of 1970 according to no less an authority than Finance Minister Benson. Even the indefatigable Stu Griffiths was exhausted. Many large investment houses and several Canadian companies seeking diversification were approached but, while almost every one of them expressed interest and confidence in the future of Bushnell Communications Ltd., "they were completely disenchanted with and frightened to death of the dangers lurking around the corners for any business directly under the control of such a powerful regulatory body as the CRTC". One after another turned down the opportunity of participating, Bush says, "at least until the ground rules were more clearly defined". More time was needed and an extension of the closing date for the transactions from the end of October 1970 to February 26, 1971, was negotiated, but at a cost of another two million dollars added to the two million-dollar deposit on the Marconi properties. Then, the staff had to be cut back; the number of employees had multiplied to such an extent that there were almost twice as many as were needed for a single-station operation.

On November 19, 1970, there was a party held in one of the empty rooms in the new section of television House—a room that was occasionally used for rehearsals, very occasionally—to celebrate Ernie Bushnell's seventieth birthday. It was more like a wake. Some of the first lay-off notices had been sent out, and Ernie, who was as soft as a marshmallow beneath his tough exterior, didn't like it at all.

"This is not my happiest birthday," he said but, ever the optimist, added, "There'll be better ones."

Early in January 1971, it became apparent that Bushnell Communications could not raise the full amount of thirty million dollars, and the board decided that it would have to drop the Thomson-Davies stations and forfeit the $825,000 deposit (reduced from the original million-dollar deposit because the CRTC had turned down the Belleville-Trenton cablevision company). Bush wrote to Lord Thomson to say he was sorry that they could not complete the deal. They were going to concentrate on the Marconi purchase, but could they raise the eighteen million still needed? It was a last desperate gamble, according to the newspaper headlines:

CJOH OWNER HAS ALL HIS CHIPS IN ONE LAST POT
A DREAM BECOMES A NIGHTMARE

It was too much to expect in the slough of a major recession, and when Bushnell announced that it had written off the four million that it had put down for the Marconi broadcasting interests and was abandoning all its expansion plans, the papers cried out:

END OF A DREAM
BUSHNELL DROPS $4 MILLION ON TV BID
BUSHNELL THE UN-EMPIRE

Afterwards, Bush wrote, "We came very close but as the old bromide goes: 'For want of a nail, the shoe was lost; for want of a shoe, the horse was lost; for want of a horse, the battle was lost.' We may have lost the battle but we have no intention of losing the war." There was no doubt that the company's idealism and aspirations, as well as its determination "to rise again" had impressed several large investors, and once the uncertainties in the role of the communications industry were resolved, Bush was sure that they would be prepared to "put

272

their dollars where their mouths are". And, he adds, "We believe them."

27 Other Flowers Will Bloom

There was every expectation that the annual meeting of Bushnell Communications Ltd., which was held on February 26, 1971, the closing date for the "aborted acquisitions" as Lord Bernstein called them, would be a tense and traumatic experience. The *Ottawa Citizen,* which had been carrying on a vendetta against CJOH ever since the station's newscaster, Peter Reilly, attacked the paper for its handling of an employees' strike, proclaimed: GRIFFITHS FACES MUSIC (OF STOCK-HOLDERS' BAND). Ernie Bushnell was in a black mood; he was furious at the way that Lord Bernstein had criticized the board's actions in a series of telegrams, and he talked about resigning and having his name removed from the company's. However, Ernie's bark was often worse than his bite, and he and Stu Griffiths went to the hotel to meet his lordship on the evening before the meeting; they spent a couple of hours arguing with him that he should not air his complaints in public, but without success. Stu stayed on to have a sombre dinner with his erstwhile employer, but Bush refused. "To hell with him," he said and went home.

By the time the meeting opened in a large unused room in the new part of Television House, Bush was still seething, and some of his friends among the shareholders warned that "Ernie's going to blow his stack". However, he kept his temper and when Lord Bernstein got up to speak, he left the lectern to gaze morosely out the window at the mounds of snow left by Ottawa's worst winter. There was really no confrontation since his lordship, who was in a front-row seat, chose to address the shareholders and turned his back on the company's officers. The British financier prefaced his remarks by saying that he was one of the original founders of Bushnell and that he held twenty per cent of the stock either through the Granada group of companies or through his family; he had not sold any shares as others had done to realize a capital gain, and this had cost him dearly.

"If I criticize the board," Lord Bernstein said, "I could be accused of rocking the boat, although God knows, the boat has been pretty shaky during the past two years. But if we don't comment, this indicates unqualified support for the board's actions, and we're not prepared to give that."

"We want more information than is given here," he went on, holding up the company's annual report, and then listed a series of questions: Was it necessary to forfeit four million dollars to the Canadian Marconi Company? Was it necessary to pay $825,000 to the Thomson-Davies group when that purchase plan collapsed? Why had the Bushnell shares slumped on the market even before the Canadian Radio Television Commission ruled against acquisitions of seventeen cablevision systems? What date had the company learned from its underwriters that a proposed stock issue to finance the Marconi and Thomson-Davies acquisitions would be too costly? What pilot programs does the company have under way and what is the sales potential?

There were other questions that Lord Bernstein read from notes he had made; he complained again of the lack of information and said that he had got all his news from the press and not from the company. The British magnate caused some confusion when he asserted:

"I should be very surprised if you still have the confidence of the city."

At which, Bushnell quit his window perch in high dudgeon and asserted that the station had served the city well for a long time and had the people's confidence and trust. Lord Bernstein looked baffled and there was an uneasy shuffling pause until Stu Griffiths explained that "city" was an Anglicism meaning the financial community.

The Granada chairman concluded his remarks by moving a resolution calling on the directors, within sixty days, to provide shareholders with "a fuller report of the past, particularly in regard to the aborted acquisitions, and also a report on the future plans of the company and the financial implications and profit and progress for the first six months of the current fiscal year [which began September 1, 1970]",

Bushnell was obviously annoyed at Lord Bernstein's motion; he labelled it "a sweeping condemnation of actions taken by a board on which you have had a representative since the beginning". Although he did not name him, he was referring to Dr. O. J. Firestone, who was absent from the annual shareholders' meeting. Later, Stu Griffiths asserted that the "Granada representative" on the board had supported every action taken until recent weeks, and he argued that if his lordship had a communications problem it was with his own representative on the board, and not with the company.

Some of the questions posed by Lord Bernstein were answered at the meeting. Griffiths explained once again that the CRTC ruling against the acquisition of seventeen cablevision systems had upset the whole financial plan of the company. The banks reduced the amount of money they were prepared to lend to fourteen million dollars or just half of what they had been ready to put up on the original deal. Furthermore, they made this loan conditional on the company raising another fourteen million in a way that would not require any additional payments of interest or principal—in other words, through common shares. However, the recession and tight money conditions, as well as a sharp drop in the value of Bushnell shares, made such a move unrealistic; Griffiths said that there were discussions with six major companies, two of them with short-term bank deposits in excess of fourteen million dollars but, after due consideration, they would not countenance such a deal as long as there were uncertainties about the commission's rules and regulations.

At any rate, Bushnell decided it could not buy both the Thomson-Davies group at $7,750,000 and the Marconi interests, and informed the former that it would not be proceeding with the purchase. Charles O'Connor, the company's lawyer, told the shareholders that the $825,000 deposit was forfeited because there was some uncertainty about Bushnell's right to its return and because the directors feared that a lawsuit would hinder any chance of raising funds needed for the purchase of the Marconi stations. As to the latter, O'Connor maintained that the company had had to double its deposit to four million dollars to eliminate the possibility of any other future liability if the proposed sale were not concluded. Under the original terms of agreement, Bushnell was liable for the difference between its $22,700,000 offer and whatever Marconi was able to get from another buyer, and, in O'Connor's view, this would have rendered the company liable to another three million dollars in losses—an indication that the CFCF television and radio stations would not fetch much more than fifteen million dollars now.

"I cannot be grateful," Lord Bernstein said, drily, "but at least I can try to be gracious."

Once the Thomson-Davies project was dropped, the banks reduced the amount of the loans they were prepared to make again but agreed to allow the company to issue some convertible shares. As a result, a new and final offer was made to Canadian Marconi; this consisted of the deposit, another thirteen million in cash, and a note for the balance of the original $22,700,000 purchase price which would be interest free over a period of seven or eight years. The Marconi company, after discounting the interest free loan, estimated the Bushnell offer to be worth $18,500,000, and rejected it.

Griffiths insisted that in the future there would be a smaller number of large companies in the Canadian broadcasting system, and that Bushnell had just been ahead of its time; he was sure that the CRTC would change its position and would permit the growth of these large companies which would be able to produce the type of Canadian programming that could compete with that coming from Britain and the United States. Stu had said much the same thing to a staff meeting the week before when it became known that Marconi had turned down Bushnell's final offer. He said that advertising income was drying up, and that the only other source of revenue was the money people paid for cablevision which was not going into broadcasting; he asserted that cable was growing faster in Canada than anywhere else, and that already twenty-five per cent of the people were watching television on cable. As a result, there was a dilution of the station's audience. "The point of our proposals", Griffiths told the employees who sat in the bank of audience seats in the studio where the "Galloping Gourmet" shows were made, "was to introduce money from the cable into programming". But the CRTC has not understood them, and this was apparent from their action—they had approved all the applications for traditional broadcasting outlets and disapproved all the cable.

At first, Bushnell and Griffiths opposed Lord Bernstein's resolution, and Bush grumbled that they should not be asked to provide the information that was requested because it would be of value to their competitors. When a vote was called, it was defeated by twenty-nine to eighteen in a show of hands, but the Granada chairman insisted that the shareholders be polled, although he had repeatedly said that it was in the power of management to defeat his move. It was after the ballot papers were being collected that Ernie Bushnell announced that he and Mr. Griffiths had "a surprise" for shareholders; they would vote the 769,861 shares they held in proxy in favour of the resolution, and Bush banged the lectern and glowering at the reporters present and Lord Bernstein in his front-row seat cried out:

"Let no man or woman or reporter say or attempt to say that any officer of this company is trying to hide anything—or I'll call him a damn liar."

Thus, the resolution called for more information was accepted, but another proposal by the British financier that the board of directors be elected for a temporary three-month period was rejected; Lord Bernstein was told that the company by-laws required a one-year term. All the directors were re-elected, and the meeting ended with a ringing declaration from the Honourable Alvin Hamilton, the former agriculture minister and himself a shareholder, who said to the cheers of his fellow shareholders:

"Frankly, I'm proud to be associated with a company that has the courage to dream and the guts to attempt to make that dream a reality, even if it ends in failure."

Afterwards, Bushnell breathed a sigh of relief. He was glad the meeting was over and yet, in a way, he was glad that it had taken place; if nothing else, the meeting had served to clear the air. There was no doubt that they had gambled and lost, and some of the criticism at the meeting was justified—he was willing to grant that, although he says in his down-to-earth way that "hindsight was better than foresight by a damn sight". Some of Lord Bernstein's remarks, especially that caustic crack about the need for the directors to show "a little more modesty and a little more humility" were, he felt, "unwarranted and uncalled for", and he was still smarting from them. However, Bush was pleased with the reports in the press. There had been columns and columns on the front pages and the financial pages of Saturday's papers. Never had an annual shareholders' meeting been so well covered, but he felt that the treatment, while it had been full and perhaps too detailed, was fair. The *Ottawa Citizen,* which had no love for CJOH, said: "All's well in the Bushnell Communications home now that the family argument has blown over."

Sitting at home in his big armchair, brooding over the annual meeting, Ernie Bushnell thought of his place in the Gatineau, and especially the terraced garden: he would have gone to his riverside cottage which he had always found to be a balm in times of stress but it was buried under piles of snow. Still, his mind dwelt on the peaceful pleasures of the garden and the pottering around that he would do there in the spring. He comforted himself by drawing an analogy between the company's plans and the flowers that bloomed, became full blown, then withered and died; there would be other blossoms to succeed them, if not immediately, then the following year. If that could happen in the garden, why not in business? There would be other plans for development and expansion—that would be certain with Stu Griffiths still running things. The company would be rebuilt and would grow again, and Bush sat up with a grin, having got over his fit of depression; he was looking forward to the future with a jaunty expectation.

The collapse of the Bushnell empire was a blow for Pierre Juneau, the chairman of the Canadian Radio Television Commission, and Harry Boyle, the vice-chairman, as they had had a certain responsibility for its rise and fall. In fact, when the Bushnell expansion plans seemed to be foundering, it was Juneau himself who made it known that the board looked with favour on these plans. That was ironic since the reasons investors gave for not putting up the money were their fear of government control and the uncertainties caused by the vagaries of the CRTC policy statements. Both Juneau and Boyle had the highest regard for Bushnell as a broadcasting company, and were counting on it to provide some of the increasing amount of Canadian programming they insisted on. If there was a particular company in Juneau's mind when he spoke of the need for "some groups in Canada that will be large enough to be able to compete in the entertainment, the cultural, the informational and the educational fields with the enormous entities that are being created in other parts of the world and particularly by our neighbours," it was Bushnell.

Yet the CRTC had destroyed its own chosen instrument by refusing to provide it, as Bush said, with "any of those organs upon which it must depend to survive"—he was talking about cablevision systems. The commissioners had heard Griffiths argue that there was only one other source of revenue for private broadcasting companies—the monthly rental (usually five dollars) which people paid for their CATV plug—that revenue was not going into programming, and it was all the more important now that advertising was decreasing. Stu had told the Senate commission on the mass media in the spring of 1970, before the CRTC hearing, that broadcasters would have to expand into cable if they were to stay in business. The fact of the matter was that Juneau and Boyle didn't believe this and didn't really understand that private broadcasting was a business, perhaps not like any other business, but nevertheless one that had to make profits. "Neither of them has ever had to meet a payroll"—that was the constant complaint of harassed station operators. The reason the commissioners gave for refusing Bushnell's application for seventeen CATV systems was that this "would create excessive concentration of ownership in the communications media", but they could have avoided such a monopoly situation and salved their conscience by doing precisely the reverse of what they did, by approving the cablevision applications and rejecting the acquisition of the Marconi and Thomson-Davies stations. That would have been a wiser judgment and would have indicated that they appreciated the economic impact of the cable; it might have restored confidence in the future of broadcasting and communications.

As it was, Ernie Bushnell was to assert, some time after the annual meeting, that he had "never seen so much confusion in broadcasting" and that he had never known a commission that was "so uncertain and confused". He wondered whether this "chaotic situation" was a result of the Broadcasting Act or the inexperience of the people who were appointed to implement it, and he was inclined to believe that it was a combination of both. "Whatever the reasons may be, it seems to me they just don't know what the hell they're doing", he said. At the same time, Bush was critical of the private sector of broadcasting.

"There's no real leadership," he grumbled. "The CAB [Canadian Association of Broadcasters] as the defender of the private sector of broadcasting has been conspicuously ineffective. For forty years government, its regulating bodies and royal commissions have for the most part looked down their noses at private broadcasters as if they were trespassers or burglars—or both. True, some broadcasters have accumulated a fair chunk of this world's goods. But so have thousands of those who laboured in other vineyards, those who started from scratch, worked hard, and made a useful contribution to society. Should a broadcaster be damned because he made a reasonably good living? I think not."

The worst fault of government, or any arm of government, like the CRTC, was, Bush feels, its dilatoriness, the length of time it took to do anything. He gives as an example the case of a very small CATV system in Rockland, a community some twenty miles east of Ottawa which the company had acquired. It took the CRTC well over eighteen months to give its approval; meanwhile the former owners, who were local businessmen, almost went broke because they couldn't touch the money which was lying in a bank awaiting the official sanction. Bush wrote:

> The wheels of government and its offspring grind slowly, and in the light of the bitter experience of Bushnell Communications, with much more uncertainty than would seem to be necessary. At no time in my memory has the communications industry been in such a bloody mess. It is true that never since the days of earphones has the structure of broadcasting been so complicated and so entangled in the web of technological advancement. How it will be resolved is a conundrum wrapped in a mystery . . . One thing is sure and it is this: The CRTC had better make up its mind, and that damn soon, which way it proposes to direct the traffic before we end up in such a snarl that the highways and biways of our communications system will be blocked for years to come, and chaos not order will be the result. Should that happen, who will suffer most? The public, John Q. Public, who pays his money but unfortunately finds it difficult if not impossible to make his wishes known . . . .
> Is it too much to hope that the communications industry will be told precisely what its role in society is to be, and not be given just guidelines that are about as unclear as tombstones in a cemetery on a dark night?

It was typical of Bushnell that he would not countenance what he considered to be unfair criticism of the CBC by some of his private broadcasting pals. He remained just as strong a supporter of the corporation as he had been when he was vice-president or director general of programming and was Mr. CBC to most people. In fact, he found himself in the rather invidious position of defending Al Ouimet during the "Seven Days" crisis and against the "rotten management" accusations of Judy LaMarsh. Although he was born and bred a private enterpriser and, as he himself said, had been more or less "shanghaied" into the public service, he had come to accept the need for a government agency such as the Canadian Broadcasting

282

Corporation to counter the cultural invasion of Canada's air waves by the rich and powerful American networks. Even a dozen years after he had quit as vice-president, he still spoke of the CBC as "my second-best love (in broadcasting)". He feels that the corporation was much maligned and didn't deserve so much criticism and so little praise.

As Bush puts it, "The roots of the CBC are dug deep in the soil of this country" and "it will take a lot of hacking and chipping to kill this tree". However, he had foreseen the management of the corporation being constantly pilloried by politicians and members of Parliament, especially after the government changed, and he considers it likely that "heads will roll" again. That does not mean to say that, in his view, the CBC is sacrosanct. There are things that are wrong with it, but "nothing much that a bit of housecleaning couldn't improve". Then, there had been the problem of the unions which, Bush wrote, "had the CBC by the throat":

> I daresay that about as much time is devoted to ironing out petty grievances and trade-union agreements as is spent on program planning. Part of the trouble may well be the fault of CBC management but I would hazard an educated guess (based on some considerable experience) that the high percentage of unionized staff feels completely secure and confident that no government, be it Grit, Tory or socialist, will ever permit bargaining to reach the point where a strike becomes more than a serious threat. As one Department of Labour official said to me one time, "What are you worrying about one per cent or one and a half per cent?—you know damn well the government will find the money you need . . . ."
>
> One thing I do criticize the CBC for is its commercial rate structure and especially its policies with respect to local advertising . . . . The Massey report strongly recommended that the CBC should not seek local retail advertising. To this the CBC has thumbed its nose and is more active now soliciting the almighty dollar from the local merchants than ever before in its history. The CBC is known to be the "worst

rate cutter" in the business. Private commercially operated stations in the large urban areas where the CBC has its own radio and TV stations have bitterly complained about this unfair competition, to which the national system has paid little or no attention. This, I believe, is one area where the CRTC might order the CBC to change its policy.

Otherwise, there was nothing wrong with competition from the CBC. As an advocate of free enterprise, Bushnell believes in competition, "good, healthy competition", and says that in the long run this will benefit listeners and viewers. He feels the country needs two television networks—the survival of the CBC was obviously assured by the government, but he does not think that the CRTC is sufficiently concerned about the survival of the privately owned CTV network, which depend entirely on commercial revenues and cannot call on government subsidies. He warns that the days of a privately owned and operated network might be numbered, and that possibility "has many frightening aspects for a great many Canadian viewers who for one good reason or another just like the idea of being entertained".

Bush always emphasized the primary role of entertainment in broadcasting; he does not deny the educational side, especially in television, but he contends that without entertainment there would be no one to educate. He draws attention to the French-language TV network of Radio Canada which has "outranked its bigger brother and for years had the reputation of being the best French-language network in the world". Nevertheless, CBFT in Montreal is easily outdrawn, day-in-and-day-out, by the private French-language station, CFTM; and CBOFT in Ottawa, where there is no competing French-language station, has only fifteen per cent of the audience whereas the area is forty per cent French speaking. Furthermore, many of the top-rated programs in the Montreal area are American films and situation comedies that have been dubbed into French.

Ever since the twenties and the appointment of the first Aird commission on broadcasting, the government, or more particularly, the Canadian establishment, has been worried by the effect of American programming on Canadian identity. Successive commissions and committees have dealt with this menace, and if the government could have, it would have prevented American broadcasts from crossing the border and sullying the Canadian character. But there was no way of doing that, and it has been faced with ever-increasing penetration of the Canadian air waves by satellite transmission. No legislation, Bushnell says, will ever change the listening or viewing habits, or the likes and dislikes of Canadians, and he adds:

> After forty years of trying to find an answer to the problem of preserving our Canadian identity by legislative action pointed directly at the heads of both public and private broadcasters, I can come to only one conclusion: such action may be a partial remedy of a very small dimension but, sure as the Good Lord made green apples, it is not the cure.

There is, he points out, the awful example of Victoria, which none of the establishment ever mentions; Victoria is below the forty-ninth parallel and not too well served by Canadian television. Most Victorians watch the American TV stations which can be received perfectly without benefit of cable—and, as Bush remarks drily, no one can accuse Victorians of becoming Americanized.

Looking back on half a century in what he calls "the entertainment business", more than forty years of which has been spent in broadcasting, Ernie Bushnell admits that he has had his "ups and downs". But mostly they were ups and, in retrospect, knowing now the mistakes he has made, he probably would do just the same if he had to do it again. Certainly, he wouldn't have wanted any other career. "I know of nothing," he says, "more fascinating, more challenging, more gratifying than a lifetime spent in that complex, mixed-up bag called broadcasting."

Postscript

It was Bushnell's memoirs that prompted me to write this biography. I knew that Ernie had been in broadcasting from the beginning, and, back in 1964, I had taped an hour long interview with him for a CBC program on the early days of radio (others whom I interviewed at the time included J. Alphonse Ouimet and Charles Jennings), but I didn't realise the richness of his experiences until I was given this thick wadge of typewritten manuscripts. The memoirs were not in a publishable form, and Bush realised this, saying that he was no writer, but they contained the raw material of a book, and I have used them, and quoted from them, extensively.

Also, I have had the advantage of hours of conversation with the subject of this biography, and have discussed with him the work as it progressed. I have had access to his papers and the CBC files that he kept which included not only the reports he made but the minutes of many administrative and program meetings and other memoranda. I was able to find the record of the 1936 Parliamentary Committee hearings (on the Mr. Sage broadcasts) and obtained the verbatim report of the House of Commons Special Committee on Broadcasting, 1959, which dealt with the "Preview Commentary" issue.

Mr. Bushnell's papers included the relevant BBG and CRTC announcements and statements. Then, there were the Bushnell TV Limited, later Bushnell Communications, files, the letters to shareholders and annual reports. Such periodicals as *Saturday Night,* the *Queen's Quarterly,* the *Canadian Forum, Liberty* and

Maclean's magazine, had articles dating back to the early forties dealing directly or indirectly with Mr. Bushnell.

As broadcasting in Canada was so closely related to politics, the history books of the period all have a bearing; I paid particular attention to *The Struggle for Canadian Broadcasting* by E. A. Weir, and *The Politics of Canadian Broadcasting* by Frank Peers, as well as Judy LaMarsh's Memoirs, and *The Haunting of Cashen's Gap* (about the talking mongoose) whose co-author, R. S. Lambert, became one of Bush's collaborators in the CBC.

I am grateful to A. E. Powley for allowing me to quote from the manuscript of his forthcoming book, *The War Voices,* and I wish to thank Graham Spry, Neil Morrison, Andrew Cowan, Harry Boyle, James Gilmore, Stu Griffiths, Roy Faibish, Patrick Watson, Miss Georgina Appleby, and others, for the help they gave me.

Index